Wakefield

JACK'S DAUGHTER

Christine Ellis is a strategic communications consultant. She has lived in Adelaide since 2002 but maintains strong links to her hometown of Broken Hill. Christine is a director of Foundation Broken Hill, a not-for-profit organisation supporting the Silver City's transition to a diversified economy independent of its rapidly declining mining industry.

Jack's Daughter is Christine's second book and follows *Silver Lies, Golden Truths* published in 2015. Both narrative non-fiction works link the colourful history of Broken Hill to her family.

Jack's Daughter

Growing up German in World War II Broken Hill

CHRISTINE ELLIS

Wakefield
Press

Wakefield Press
16 Rose Street
Mile End
South Australia 5031
wakefieldpress.com.au

First published 2017

Edited by Margot Lloyd, Wakefield Press
Typeset by Michael Deves, Wakefield Press

ISBN 978 1 74305 509 0

 A catalogue record for this
book is available from the
National Library of Australia

CORIOLE
McLAREN VALE

For Cameron, Ryley Jae and Griffin –
the Gran you adored lives on in you

Contents

Preface

Narrative non-fiction can be a tricky genre to negotiate – both for readers and writers. Readers are sometimes distracted wondering how much they should believe and writers often struggle with the urge to embellish facts for a more compelling story. I had no such struggle in writing this book. It's a simple tale and unfolds of its own accord. My passions are family, Broken Hill and storytelling, and *Jack's Daughter* is about all three. There was no need to invent or sculpt and very little need to 'reimagine'. So I hope that removes a distraction for you. Believe it all.

The genesis for this book lies in an oral history project I undertook to celebrate my mother's 70th birthday. As the tapes rolled and she valiantly gave herself to my intimate probing, the story of her father – Reinhold (Jack) Schuster – demanded to be told. So I wrote it first. But, always, this second book was in my mind.

So, even as the pages of the manuscript for *Silver Lies, Golden Truths* stacked ever higher on my desk, my mother and I continued our conversations exploring her life and her father's everlasting impact on it. In quiet hours alone, she wrote notes for me – pages and pages in her beautiful script as she relived specific events, with only an occasional one or two words crossed out or a clarification added later to correct chronology.

I started the manuscript for this second book before her death, but then left it idle while I busied myself in grief. When I returned to it years later, I found there were only one or two questions I wished I'd asked. So I asked them of others – her cousin and friend, her bridesmaid, a neighbour, an employer who had guided her, and the current generation of my father's family. The picture my mother and I had painted together of her life was confirmed and the tiny holes filled. Her selflessness, or selfishness, is laid bare for your interpretation.

And what of Broken Hill's starring role in this book? Just as my mother's story is not a literary biography, neither is this an academic and all encompassing record of this remarkable city. You will need to find its industrial history elsewhere. What is presented here are slices of the Silver City's colourful story, the parts that impacted on my mother or her family. They give a better understanding of the setting for her life. My mother's spirit is likely linked as much to this setting as to her heritage – but for those who grew to love Jack Schuster in *Silver Lies*, he's still very much here too.

So, dear reader, don't be distracted seeking to distinguish fact from fiction. Accept this work for what it is – non-fiction delivered in a narrative voice. There's been no need for tinkering. I hope you enjoy the tale.

Stepping back in time can be a glorious journey but, if it wasn't *your* time, you may find the occasional trip hazard. For those born to metric measures and decimal coins, I offer the following (with the help of the Australian Government National Measurement Institute):

5 miles	*is approximately*	8 kilometres
1 foot	*is approximately*	30 centimetres
1 inch	*is approximately*	2.5 centimetres
2 pounds	*is approximately*	1 kilogram
1 ounce	*is approximately*	28 grams
10 fluid ounces	*is approximately*	285 millilitres
1 pint	*is approximately*	450 millilitres
1 gallon	*is approximately*	4.5 litres

£1 = one pound

There were 20 shillings in a pound and 12 pence in a shilling.

The Reserve Bank of Australia estimates a representative 'basket of goods and services' costing £10 in 1940 would cost $811.12 in 2016, and an item costing 1 shilling in 1940 would cost $4.06 in 2016.

Chapter 1
Abandoned
August 1940

Maisie stood alone at the foot of the grave, her stillness remarkable given how long she had been there. She was incapable of motion, even to rub at her little bare legs stung by the dust. Her brown ringlets occasionally lifted on the wind or whipped out long and taut in stronger gusts, but they soon remembered their place. Even her dark eyes were fixed firmly in front – dry, unseeing.

Sounds intruded. Sometimes it was a burst of male laughter from the miners telling a story of her father's practical jokes underground. More often it was renewed sobs from a group of women as one recounted a kindness 'the gentle German' had extended. Intermittently, she heard her mother's voice calling her. But she didn't move.

Her father was dead. He was here, buried with his first wife Lillian and his first child, the baby Reinhold. They were now a little composite family in the ground and she was left above it, unprotected. The peculiarity of the burial arrangement pierced her numbness as nothing else had done. Rose had been so possessive of her husband. That she had lain their first child with the bones of another woman had surprised Maisie when she learned of it, but to see her now allow Jack there too was bewildering. It was another senseless act in what had become a senseless world without him – and she felt senseless in it. If even her mother could not be relied upon to behave as expected, what did that mean for every part of every day she was now expected to live?

This thought caused her to look toward Rose standing among a group of women under the pepper trees. It was the first eye contact between the two for hours and it so heartened the grieving widow that she immediately began to move toward her.

Up went Maisie's chin and the defiant look she threw was enough for Rose to smoothly detour toward another group of mourners. There was no time to savour the victory before a gentle hand came down to rest on Maisie's shoulder. This caused the chin to tremble and the tears to finally flow, because the touch was so like her father's.

'Dulcie, what do I do now? What do *we* do now? How do we live without him?'

Dulcie was Jack's step-daughter, the youngest child of Rose's first marriage. At 20, she was 10 years older than Maisie and age wasn't the only difference. Dulcie was tall, pale and slightly freckled with beautiful auburn hair, whereas Maisie had inherited their mother's darker tones. Yet, of the hundreds of people at the funeral, Maisie felt only Dulcie loved Jack as she did. Young Jackie and Maxie adored their father too, but they also had their mother's love, whereas the two girls believed that was withheld from them. Their relationship with each other and with Jack therefore had had a specialness they felt belonged only to the trio. Dulcie was his *Tochter* and Maisie his *kleine Tochter*, with the German words for daughter and little daughter their special code of endearment. It was only Dulcie's hand that could finally lead Maisie away from the grave to the waiting car. It was the turning away, the walking off, she couldn't manage on her own. Somehow leaving her father there in the ground made him more dead.

The Fred J Potter & Son funeral car gave her a measure of protection from the crowd. The windows were coated in red dust and she felt safe enough sitting beside Dulcie to finally look out at the people who had been looking so intently at her throughout the day. She supposed the looks had been kindly – but she still felt bitter toward some among the crowd.

'How many of them do you think remember being mean to Dad?'

When this drew no response, she went on. 'Do you see the two policemen at the end of the path? Are they the ones that took our stuff? Do you think they're here to say goodbye to Dad or just to see which German people are here and whether they're talking to each other? Maybe they think we'd use his funeral to pass on secrets!'

Dulcie indulged Maisie with a scowl for the young constables. Police had seized the radio she'd bought for Jack's birthday when they'd raided the Schuster house just one week into the war. Dulcie hadn't seen it happen, but she'd seen the aftermath. Three terrified children, Rose raging against the absurdity of it as she tried to right the shambles of their home, and Jack, quiet and still, shamed that he hadn't been able to protect them from it.

'I think they're here because they grew to respect Dad when he went to the police station to report each week,' she whispered, not just to mollify Maisie, but because she believed it. 'If it hadn't been for them, the petition to save Dad from the internment camp wouldn't have worked y'know. They had to endorse it.'

Dulcie was right. The inspector of police sent to Broken Hill to oversee registrations and internments of so-called enemy aliens had recommended Reinhold John (Jack) Schuster be imprisoned as 'a Nazi sympathiser'. Thousands of Broken Hill residents had signed a petition rejecting this and calling on the Aliens' Tribunal to exempt him, citing his good work in the community. But it would have had little effect without the consensus of the local police.

Still, Dulcie noticed the two policemen *were* keeping a close eye on the German men at the funeral – and these friends were being careful not to be seen 'fraternising' with each other. The *Aliens Registration Act 1939* and *National Security (Aliens Control) Regulations 1939* forbade it. The men looked decidedly uncomfortable and shuffled their feet in the dirt whenever one of the constables looked their way. No jocularity here among Jack's countrymen as there was among the miners – although each of them would no doubt also have had a good yarn to tell about Jack's sense of fun.

'Look. There's Horrie and the others who used to come when Dad was sick and tell you stories about him underground. Do you remember? You loved it,' Dulcie offered as a distraction.

Maisie did remember. It made her smile for a moment to recollect the stories of her father's strength and his caring for his co-workers (including the huge Percheron horses used to haul the ore trucks to the surface). But right next to Horrie and his mates were Godfather Peter Petersen and his wife Caroline. They'd been her father's best friends from the time he'd arrived in Broken Hill with Lillian, seeking temporary adventure in early 1914. The German men with their Australian wives had become closer during the subsequent ostracism of foreigners during the Great War, and Peter and Caroline had helped Jack during Lillian's long illness, comforting him when her death broke his heart soon after the war ended. Now it was a new war and they were the heartbroken ones. Their visible grief brought Maisie's bubbling back to her throat and she looked away. It was difficult to breathe.

A little distance from them a group of women from the Broken Hill Housewives' Progressive Association stood with hats in place and handbags held uniformly over bent elbows.

'They're *her* friends, not his!' Maisie hissed.

'But they grew to admire him too, Maisie. Even the ones who wouldn't have anything to do with anything remotely German would have a chat with Dad. Do you remember him teaching Mrs Fraser-Paterson to eat a tomato off the bush like an apple, with a shake of salt between bites?'

Both girls smiled at the memory of tomato juice on the proper Mrs Fraser-Paterson's chin.

'Besides, Mum really needs their support now.'

Maisie softened a little. Conflict between mother and child always simmered near the surface, but she loved Rose – and though she was not yet ten years old, she could understand her mother's sternness was seated in a hard life. Rose had lost her own father very young, been rejected by her mother, given birth to 11 children, lost three and raised eight. Now she'd lost her second husband, a wonderfully kind and loving man, who'd been well-loved in return.

Family portrait. From left: Maisie, Rose, Jackie, Jack and Maxie, 1937.

Yes, Maisie had some sympathy for her mother, but this was no match for the scalpel of anger that cut through her compassion. Rose had stopped her from being with her father during his last days – the ultimate victory in an ongoing battle between the two for possession of Jack.

For more than six years, the children had watched Jack's struggle with pneumoconiosis (known as 'minerstitis' or 'dust on the lungs'), but his final days were in isolation from them. No chances were taken with underground miners showing the same symptoms as highly contagious tuberculosis patients, so all lung diseases were cramped together in a weatherboard building at the rear of the old hospital grounds. The children had been forced to wait on a stool outside while Rose went alone to visit her husband. Maisie reasoned it was Rose who had kept father and daughter apart. Now they were to be apart forever.

She so wanted to talk to Pastor Zweck. It wasn't that she didn't like the new Reverend Miller, but Pastor Zweck had led the local Lutheran congregation since she was just three months old. She'd grown up knowing and trusting him, despite also being a little intimidated by him. Pastor Zweck had a pious approach to leading his flock that sometimes had him at odds with the local townsfolk, mostly because he refused to give communion if they remained a member of one of the many Lodges in Broken Hill. The pastor thought the Lodges were Satan's work. Although they may have been *meant* to be benevolent or temperance societies, he maintained their rituals made them religions – and those religions were false. His Lutheran congregation, he insisted, should know no one other than Christ. He wrote to the synod:

> I had a man here the other night, a really fine fellow, Norwegian. But he was a member of the freemasons. He advised me to not be so strict about the Lodge, but what is the good of numbers if we sacrifice a vital scripture principle and be indifferent about a body that clearly swears false oaths?

Maisie had stood wide-eyed and watched Pastor Zweck in many a stern argument (sometimes even with her father, because he chose most often to find his God in gently tending plants and animals and children rather than formal services), but she had personally little reason to be chastised by the pastor. She was diligent in practicing the list of all the books of the Bible (and their authors) and being able to recite the Ten Commandments (and describe their meanings) before she fronted for Sunday school each week.

Now she needed Pastor Zweck's piousness and his determination for absolute truth no matter the consequences. She wanted to know what was happening to her father.

'He'll be eaten by worms,' the boys up the road had told her the day before the funeral.

'Nonsense,' said Dulcie. 'Dad's up in heaven now and he's watching over us. He'll take care of us.'

Maisie had refused to entertain a vision of the worms for long (though she considered for a moment that her father may be happy at that, if only the worms had then gone on to enrich the soil so beautiful things could grow). Dulcie's version had generated an image of a five pointed star up in the sky, with her father sitting on one of the horizontal cross points and holding on to the apex, smiling down at her past his dangling garden boots. Even to a ten-year-old that seemed ludicrous. She needed Pastor Zweck to tell her the truth. But he was gone too.

Pastor Zweck's absence from the funeral bothered Maisie beyond her quest for truth in what was happening to her father's body. She thought it was he who should have led her father's soul to heaven. She had no doubt such a beautiful soul would make it independent of help, but Pastor Zweck knew her father so well Maisie thought he was the one best placed to make an appropriate introduction to God. But it was more than that. It was the cloud that hung over the pastor's departure from Broken Hill. Some among his shocked congregation felt he had been run out of town by bigotry, while others maintained it was a flight from justice. Either way it was unfair.

Elmore Zweck was the first resident Lutheran pastor in Broken Hill, straight from graduation at Concordia Seminary in Adelaide. His first service was delivered on 1 February 1931 in a small room at the back of the Druid's Hall in Argent Lane – to a congregation of five. During the next nine years, he built the congregation to more than 200, doggedly going door to door in blistering heat (on foot and bicycle in the early years) competing with the Methodists, Presbyterians, Baptists, Congregationalists, Adventists, Salvation Army, Church of England and Church of Christ for the non-Catholic souls in the mostly heathen outback-tough town.

His hard work was rewarded with the purchase of a Manse at 471 Chapple Street for £950, which he promptly extended to accommodate his two new sons, Ian and Graham. By May 1933, he and his congregation had built St Paul's Lutheran Church at 41 Iodide Street. It was built on the site of the town's former German Club, which had been destroyed on New Year's Day 1915. A violent mob set it ablaze in a misguided retaliation for a 'Turk' attack on a picnic train carting families between Broken Hill and Silverton. Two cameleers – an Afghan Afridi and an Indian Hindu, flying a Turkish flag – had ambushed the train, killing four people and wounding many others. The incident is recorded in the National Record as the only enemy attack to take place on Australian soil during World War I and, despite the nationality of the perpetrators, the townsfolk were determined it was 'the Germans'. They were no more forgiving 17 years later when Pastor Zweck and his working bees were busy building their church on the site. Abuse was constant from passers-by, but the dutiful pastor chose to ignore them, encouraging his congregation to do the same, and continued to fulfil his calling.

He added a hall for Bright Hour meetings for women, a basketball court for girls and a volleyball court for boys. He taught confirmation classes in homes on Saturdays and led young people fortnightly in Bible study by establishing a Luther Society. His dedication was so fierce, he personally drove an old car around town to collect reluctant adults for church services and children for Sunday school – and, when destitute parents said their children could not attend Sunday school because they had nothing to wear, he bought those children shoes and purchased long rolls of flannel which willing members of his congregation made into dresses, trousers and shirts. It seemed no obstacle was too great to block Pastor Zweck from swelling his flock and delivering the doctrines of reformist Dr Martin Luther.

Just three days into the war, on the night of 6 September 1939, a fire destroyed a hangar at the Broken Hill aerodrome, along with three planes belonging to members of the Aero Club (two Gypsy Moths and a Tiger Moth) and a Fox Moth used by the Flying

Doctor. Sabotage was obvious. To gain access, the arsonists broke a padlock in a back door and tore away a sheet of iron from a front door. Telephone wires were cut some distance from the aerodrome so the fire brigade couldn't be summoned in time to minimise the damage. The townsfolk were incensed and the local newspapers began to reprise the horrors of the 'Turk' attack. 'The Huns' were at it again! Much was made of the fact one of the planes had been used by the Flying Doctor and that this showed 'the callousness of Britain's enemies'.

Inspector Homann from the Central Police Station led the initial investigation into the fire, but was forced to defer next day to a team from Sydney led by Detective Sergeant T. Wilson, Chief CIB Arson Squad Officer. Detective Sergeant Wilson headed straight from the train to the Lutheran church.

Pastor Zweck was offended there was so much distrust of Lutherans despite repeated public protestations that the congregation was at odds with the Nazi regime and loyal to Australia and Britain. He wrote to the synod the following week:

> In spite of the fact that we Lutherans are most loyal citizens, and that, next to God, we owe our undivided loyalty to our King and Empire, our poor Church is grossly misunderstood and misrepresented.
>
> Yesterday I received a complete surprise and shock when Detectives from Sydney came to visit me and questioned me about the functions and ideals of our church, its position in regard to our country and so forth. In a sense I was glad to have the opportunity of confessing our sincere and wholehearted loyalty to our King and His Empire, and our deep-rooted thanks to God for the religious liberty which we enjoyed under the British flag. On the other hand it made me depressed, that since we are loyal from the bottom of our hearts, that our loyalty should even be questioned. However, through ignorance of what we are and for what we stand, we are often misjudged.

The main street of Broken Hill, Argent Street, 1940s.

Despite being Australian-born of Australian-born parents, the pastor was pronounced an enemy alien during the interview. He resented having to provide the names of his children and details about his car licence as well as profess his innocence of the crime. The detectives returned ten days later and demanded Pastor Zweck show proof that he and his congregation were loyal to the King and had no interest in sabotaging Broken Hill's air capabilities. During their investigations they had been told the pastor was rigid in his control of his flock and could persuade them to his bidding (since some women had relinquished membership of the Women's Guild of the Grand United Order of Oddfellows to receive communion from him). The pastor duly provided church newsletters where loyalty to Britain was proclaimed as second only to the Lutheran Church's loyalty to God and Christ.

The Inquest into the aerodrome fire concluded on 10 October 1939. Coroner A.B. Collins found the fire had been 'wickedly and maliciously set', but with not enough evidence to identify the perpetrators. The Broken Hill people didn't need any evidence. They were convinced it was the local Germans and, more specifically, the Lutheran Church, led by Pastor Zweck.

Within two months of the hangar fire, Pastor Zweck accepted a calling to the rich wheat-growing and sheep-grazing region of Nhill in western Victoria. His supporters felt the accusations about the arson and the subsequent persecution from Broken Hill agitators had driven him out of town, while others claimed his departure proved the truth of the accusations. The pastor's diaries reveal he had simply had enough:

> After nine years in what has been a most difficult and isolated field, I feel that the strain is beginning to tell and it seems that the Lord wishes to head me to another field of activity.
>
> My work here has been solely mission in character and I look forward to a more solid congregation in Nhill, which is an established field.
>
> Broken Hill is really overrun with Lodges and the number of women and children connected to them is astounding. I have had many difficulties to overcome. Broken Hill people are a very sporty crowd. Drinking, gambling, dancing and Lodgeism are predominant here and the devil is very busy against the doctrines.

At the time of Pastor Zweck's disillusionment and departure from Broken Hill, Maisie had felt only relief from the difficulties of learning her catechism, but Jack was a little sad for him, so then she was sad too. As the weeks went on, she took her father's lead and was happy for the pastor – that he was somewhere green and pretty with people who wanted to go to church and children who had shoes to wear to Sunday school. Now, though, with Jack's death, she was angry at Pastor Zweck. She needed him. She needed his unflinching dedication to truth. Every unbearable minute of her day was filled with her father's absence and she had no idea where his presence was. Had he achieved salvation despite his infrequent attendance at church? Was he really in heaven watching over her?

She resolved that, just to be sure, she would every night tell him she loved him and say, 'Goodnight, Dad'. And that she did – for the rest of her life.

Chapter 2
Home-grown enemies
August–September 1940

Life would never be the same for any of the three Schuster children – or the Vales. The five surviving children from Rose's first marriage to Tom Vale now ranged in age from Dulcie's 20 to Evelyn's 32, but Jack's loss was nonetheless keenly felt. He'd been a wonderful step-parent – and the only father Dulcie could remember.

Eve's family in South Australia tugged her away again soon after the funeral, but Topsy, Tommy, Jimmy and Dulcie spent extra time at 25 South Street to comfort Rose and provide some distraction for their young siblings.

Rose, Topsy and Dulcie drank tea in the kitchen, their maunderings slipping under the door to the side veranda where the lovable larrikins Tommy and Jimmy (now married and in their twenties) entertained their young half-brothers. They recounted tales of youthful escapades Rose would have preferred her 'good boy' Jackie (11) and rascally Maxie (almost eight) didn't hear.

At any other time, Maisie would have been in there among the four boys. She adored her big brothers and delighted in their visits, but now she was wooden. She ate the meals Rose prepared or someone else delivered. She did chores obediently and uncomplainingly (which heightened Rose's concern). Each morning she docilely washed, and dressed in her school uniform as her mother instructed – but then sat stolid and refused to leave the house. There was only a week until the spring school holiday break, so an exasperated Rose relented and all three children were allowed to stay home to await the resumption of school in September.

The timing of the school holidays was kind to the Schuster

children in another way. On the night of 24 August 1940, just ten days after Jack's death, the first German bombs fell on London and, on 7 September, 'the Blitz' (shortened from the German *Blitzkrieg*, 'lightning war') began in earnest. The continuous bombing would last for eight months, targeting 16 cities and killing more than 40,000 civilians (half of these in London), but never was the hostility toward anything German more intense in Broken Hill than in the first days of the barrage. Headlines screamed of Hitler 'raining death on thousands of women and babies'. The community that had so supported Jack twelve months earlier to save him from internment and turned out in droves for his funeral now forgot his gentleness and remembered only his German-ness.

The Schuster children had had a year-long reprieve from jeers and taunts and fisticuffs rolling in the dust during Broken Hill's quest to save their father. Now any kindness to them was over. Just as the local children had been earlier influenced by their parents' support of the Schusters, now they absorbed the recharged hatred for all 'Huns' (whether they were murderers overseas or murderous hearts living in the local community). The school holidays at least gave Jackie, Maisie and Maxie almost a month to grieve for their father in peace.

Space to grieve was more short-lived for Rose. With Jack's death, the question of her nationality arose.

Early in the war, Canberra had made clear its position regarding women married to men labelled 'enemy aliens'. Wives of British subjects were British and wives of enemy aliens were enemy aliens – and, in some circumstances, these women were also required to register with police. Rose would have none of it. She was British by way of her birth in Wilcannia 123 miles north-east of Broken Hill and she was incensed enough that Jack was forced to register (with all the restrictions that triggered) – she was adamant she would not join him. [*Author's aside: Prior to 1949, Australians were British subjects. It was not until 26 January 1949 that the status of Australian citizen was created through the* Nationality and Citizenship Act 1948.]

Rose was no more impressed when the government acknowledged the alien registration approach for married women might be a little unfair and proudly announced a way around the issue.

The Canberra Times 29 September 1939

MARRIED TO ALIENS

Women May Regain Nationality

Hardship imposed upon British born women married to enemy aliens has been removed by powers conferred upon the Government under the National Security Act.

This authority enables women who have lost their British status, to re-gain it by applying for naturalisation certificates.

Under the Nationality Act of 1937 British women marrying foreigners are not deprived of British nationality if they apply for retention of this status within 12 months of marriage. A number of women married during the last 12 months, are taking advantage of this provision but there are others who are prevented from resuming British nationality by the time limit as they were married to enemy aliens before September, 1938.

The National Security Regulations enable women debarred by the time limit clause to apply to the Minister to resume British nationality.

During Jack's illness, Rose had steadfastly refused to entertain the concept of registering as an alien – or applying for a naturalisation certificate – in the country of her birth. She had simply ignored both proclamations. Jack had continued to report weekly to the police station as required and Rose had continued to live her life. She had done nothing to keep a low profile and her name and address were often published in the local newspapers for hosting meetings and social gatherings of the Housewives' Association. When she had given it any thought at all, it had been to assume the issue would simply disappear when Jack finally succumbed to his lung disease. She was wrong.

Two weeks after Jack's death, the officer in charge of alien registration at the Central Police Station knocked on Rose's door. Constable Munro was leading a review of enemy aliens resident in Broken Hill. The initial local registration process had been completed in January and Constable Munro was now intent on confirming all aliens were abiding by the requirement to notify any change of address. Notices had been sent to registered addresses demanding an impromptu attendance at the police station on 20 August. Jack had not attended the snap audit and Constable Munro claimed he had come to investigate.

Rose's temper overcame her common sense.

'My husband is dead. You bastards can't bloody hound him anymore. Now get off my bloody property!'

Had she not been fogged by grief, Rose may have been a little more circumspect. Enemy aliens were not permitted to own property.

'Reinhold Schuster may be dead, madam, but he's a dead German. If he was your husband, then you are German. And you're not registered. If you're not registered, then this property can't have been registered with the Government Trustee. And that's against the law.'

Constable Munro took his work seriously. He already had four prosecutions under his belt for local men who had failed to notify their change of address within the required time – and these men were now on their way to the Gladstone Gaol in the Southern Flinders Ranges of South Australia. He had also notified other police stations across the country of enemy aliens in their jurisdictions who hadn't been given permission to leave Broken Hill.

It didn't pay to be 'out of place'. Giocomo and Maddalena Morellini had lived in Broken Hill for 26 years, but when Italy entered the war on 10 June 1940, they were found to have a son Egidio working in the northern goldfields of Western Australia.

This led to the discovery Egidio had served 18 months across 1933 and 1934 with the Italian Alpini (an elite mountain military unit charged with protecting Italy's northern boundaries with France and Austria). It was all too suspicious and Egidio was arrested, spending the next three months in an internment camp on Rottnest Island and another three months in a camp east of the Western Australian town of Harvey, before being released on parole on 18 December.

Constable Munro had actually known of Jack's death before he'd gone to the house – his target was Rose. Jack's investigation dossier and internment orders remained at the police station and when Constable Munro went to mark his file as deceased he read the report of the September 1939 raid on the Schuster home – a report which had not been kind to the Schusters.

Although Schuster denies that he is sympathetic towards the Nazi regime he is known to have definite Nazi sympathies and is a frequenter of German meetings which are held in this district. A search was made of Schuster's house and a large quantity of German literature including a very complete map of Australia which was printed in German was taken possession of.

During the interview with Schuster his wife ne Rosina Mary Seward age 49 years native of Willicannia [sic] New South Wales expressed herself as being sympathetic towards Nazism. The children are as follows Jack 10 years Maisie 8 years and Max 6 years.

From our observations we are of the opinion that Schuster is definitely not of the neutral type of alien.

The 'German meetings' mentioned in the report were of the Lutheran Church and the confiscated German literature included postcards and letters from Jack's family, his apprenticeship papers, poetry books, song books, photographs with captions and the family Bible. Added to the impounded property were a leather briefcase,

Jack's leather overcoat, a pair of binoculars Jack and Maisie used to watch kangaroos and the wireless radio Dulcie had given Jack for entertainment as he lay gasping for breath on the side veranda. Rose's 'expression of sympathy toward Nazism' was instead a string of expletives toward the police and their actions – far worse than those directed now at Constable Munro!

As an adult, any reference to the night the police ransacked the house in their long black overcoats would wash Maisie in the fear she'd felt as a child, but the feeling was always accompanied by the awe in which she held her mother for refusing to be intimidated by them.

Now, however, Rose was beaten. She could stand her ground again and not register as an enemy alien, but further conversation with Constable Munro confirmed she would be prosecuted if she did. She feared for her children if that prosecution ended in internment. This was entirely likely, for there were many Australian-born people with German connections already locked in the camps. There was also the matter of the property at 25 South Street. It was in her name (as was common practice in Broken Hill where miners risked their lives daily and wives were protected by having ownership of the family home), but if she was indeed German, she couldn't actually own any property. It could be held in trust for the family by the government, but not until she became part of the enemy alien registration process.

On 6 September 1940, Rose fronted at the Central Police Station and stood before Constable R.R. Munro. She had a frightened Maisie in tow, ostensibly to encourage the police to see her as a mother rather than a threat. Maisie thought it was because her mother needed an audience in order to be brave.

At five foot three and a half inches tall, Rose was dwarfed by the tall policeman. Over the next few hours she was measured, fingerprinted, examined for notable marks and photographed. She gave clear but terse responses to Constable Munro's questions about her background and occupation, but as the process lengthened her voice became quieter, so that on several occasions she was asked to repeat her response. Maisie's alarm at being in the police station amplified in inverse proportion to her mother's voice. If her mother was unnerved, there had to be very good reason for it.

Constable Munro typed directly onto the form as the questioning progressed so that each answer was followed by a period of silence save the clatter of the old typewriter. At one point he looked at Rose for quite some time without asking anything, before typing 'brown eyes, dark brown hair, medium build'. The length of time he had taken for this observation was more about intimidation than deliberation. He recorded her birthplace as Wilcannia, New South Wales, but her nationality as German. It was impossible to complete other sections of the registration certificate. For example, 'Date of entry to the Commonwealth' was marked 'Not applicable' and at the bottom of the document an explanation was offered, 'Australian born, married to German subject (now deceased)'.

Rosina Mary Schuster's Alien Registration Certificate (number 16815) was issued in triplicate with her photograph attached to each copy. Rose often appeared dour in photographs; she was 50 and a tough life had been etching for some time upon what had begun as a handsome face. But this photograph is different. The bush-tough Rose is gone and instead a sad, defeated woman shows a slackened mouth and empty eyes that don't see the camera, but focus on some other point in distance or time. The alien registration process was degrading for her. The best way to cope was to remove herself from it.

Eventually she was instructed to report to the police station weekly and was read a long list of items she was prohibited from owning which, apart from firearms and ammunition, included things such as a camera, binoculars, homing pigeons or more than three gallons (collectively) of any type of fuel including petrol, kerosene and methylated spirits. Maisie knew there was already more than this stored in the back shed and thought fleetingly of reminding her mother about it.

Then Constable Munro pronounced Rose was now 'on parole', which forbade her to attend places of public amusement such as hotels (which was fine by Rose) or cinemas (which was *not* fine by Rose).

'I will *not* bloody well sign this,' she told Constable Munro through gritted teeth.

It was just the one act of defiance she needed to restore her self-respect (and Maisie's confidence). Rose had no opposition to the requirements on the parole form that required her to 'promise and undertake that I will neither directly nor indirectly take any action in any way prejudicial to the safety of the British Empire during the present war' and could easily commit to 'not leave Australia during the present war without the permission of the Minister for Defence' and 'not be absent from the registered address for more than 24 hours without police permission', for she had neither the means nor the inclination to do so. She felt humiliated that she was being asked to make such a formal commitment in writing, but was prepared to do it until she had come to the final section on the form.

AMUSEMENTS CURTAILED.

Alien enemy subjects will find their amusements curtailed, for they are not permitted to frequent hotels or other licensed premises, nor any place of public amusement. Withdrawal of parole will follow in cases where this order is disobeyed.

This brought forth her familiar fire.

'I have submitted to this stinking process and registered myself as German even though I don't believe it, because I have three children who *do* have German blood in their veins and I'm proud of it.'

She pushed Maisie forward, who was heartened enough by her mother's restored demeanour to glare at the big policeman.

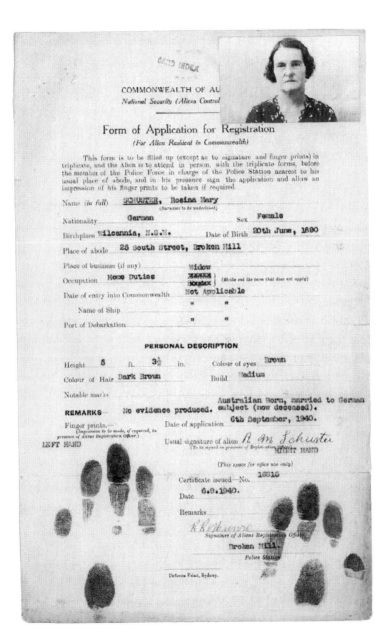

The first page of Rose's six-page alien registration application.

'There's many an Australian born of British ancestors who would do bloody well to have some of Jack Schuster's blood pumping through their heart.' Rose continued. 'There'd be far less bullying in the world, the like of which I've endured here today, I can bloody well tell you that.'

Maisie nodded her head to give emphasis to her mother's words.

'So I will fill out your bloody ridiculous registration form and sign my bloody signature at the bloody bottom next to my bloody fingerprints worn down from bloody hard work ... but I will *not* sign a form that says I am on parole like a criminal. I will *not* say I accept that I cannot take my children to the Metropole. Do with me as you will, Constable Munro.'

Constable Munro wasn't quite sure what to do with Rose.

'Take the form with you and bring it back when you've signed it. It'll give you time to read it properly,' he said as he pushed the form toward her and left the counter before she had time to push it back.

In due course, Constable Munro would win this little battle, but Rose wasn't to know it yet and the mini-rebellion had been enough. She felt less broken. Maisie felt a little less vulnerable in a world without her dad.

Ultimately the restrictions would bring additional issues for Rose and the children in a number of ways, but – for all of them – life then had to focus on learning to live without Jack.

Maisie began to use her skipping rope again, kick a football with her brothers and even go bush with Jimmy looking for mushrooms. She had yet to pick up all the pieces of her life, but ever so slowly she was finding them here and there. There was no warmth about her, or for her. Jack had been her sun. It surprised everyone that she took no further interest in her father's vegetable gardens or fruit trees even though she had obstinately fought the drought to keep them alive while he was.

She was taken to sleep in her mother's bed. Regardless of whether this was intended as comfort for Maisie, comfort for Rose, or simply because she was becoming too grown to share a room with her brothers, Maisie was decidedly unhappy with the arrangement. She lay awake at night listening to her mother repeatedly get up to dribble into the bedroom pot and longed for summer, simply so she could escape to her own bed again in the sleep-out.

She woke each morning to a few moments of peace before the pain of her father's death thumped her chest. Then she despaired at the thought of filling the empty hours between sunrise and sunset without him.

Some of those hours weren't as empty as she would have liked. In the school playground Jackie, Maisie and Maxie would group together with the Schipanski children, so that by virtue of numbers they had some protection from cruel bullying. The worst to be endured during school hours was therefore some jostling and name calling or, if a satchel was left unattended, returning to find its contents scattered and mettwurst sandwiches wrapped in their cooling grapevine leaves stomped and squashed into the ground.

The walk home, however, was different. The Schuster children needed to walk east of Alma Primary, while the Schipanskis walked south. On more than one occasion Jackie, Maisie and Maxie found themselves surrounded by a circle of children who alternately threw rocks and punches.

For Maisie, though, there was an outcome to these incidents the other children didn't intend. A volcano erupted. The anger she felt at the injustice of her new world found its way to bunched little fists. More often than not, it was she who roused her brothers to retaliate. Then the three of them flew at their tormentors with such ferocity they quickly dispersed a mob much larger in numbers, but unable to match the passion of their targets.

Resistance wasn't the only reason the violence subsided. Children had been influenced by parents exposed to inflammatory anti-German horror stories from a government determined to strengthen the war resolve. Newspapers had willingly delivered appropriate propaganda. Once emotion had been suitably provoked, articles became less rabble-rousing. (The true horrors were yet to come.) The town settled a little, the children followed their parents' lead and the Schusters began to fit in again. Jackie continued to excel at any sport he chose and Maxie continued to use his dimpled charm on teachers and students alike. Maisie moved through a cycle of well-behaved student at school and defiant daughter at home, but her grief enveloped it all.

People tried to help. Peter Petersen slipped fully into his role as the children's godfather and talked to each of them individually about how to cope with grief and about how their father was no longer suffering. The children had loved Peter dearly all their short lives, but somehow his presence only highlighted their father's absence. Maisie was particularly resistant. She felt detached from everything and everyone. Every attempt to engage her or divert her only annoyed her. She didn't *want* to feel any happiness. Rose took her aside one day to explain she was hurting Peter's feelings.

'You can keep trying if you want, Godfather,' Maisie said quietly the next time he visited. 'I know my Dad asked you to, because Mum told me. But I don't think anything you can say will make me feel any better. My dad made the world better. Not just for me, but for everyone else. The only person who would know what to say to make me feel better about Dad being dead is Dad.'

Peter didn't give up – and neither did Rose – but each of the children had to find their own way in this new and different life.

Chapter 3
Visit with an angel
October 1940

Maisie very quickly decided her life without Jack would no longer include school. She enjoyed learning, but had enjoyed it more for the praise from her father when she came home with a school report or good test results. Without him, there seemed no point. Rose thought schooling a waste of time for girls. Even for her boys, education was only about marking time before the prize of a job on the mines.

In the weeks since Jack's death, Maisie had taken to sitting alone on the white-washed rocks surrounding the fruit trees in the backyard as she had with him. Now the trees were withering and so was she. She held her own hand or sat awkwardly with one hand up on her shoulder to try to feel him there. And it was here in her solitude she hatched her plan. She would become a nurse.

She knew she would make a good nurse, because she had the experience of tending to her father during his long years of illness and, on the one occasion she had peered in the window of Jack's hospital ward as he lay dying, she knew the current nurses were not good at placing a cool hand on a hot brow or telling stories to amuse their patients or sitting quietly and simply holding a hand when eyes were closed.

About two months after Jack's death, Maisie dressed in her Sunday best and slipped her house-dress over the top. She took the shopping list from Rose more eagerly than usual and set off on the boys' bike to 'do the messages'. Instead of stopping off in Patton Street, Maisie rode straight past the string of shops and headed down toward Bonanza Street, which she knew would take her up and over the spine of toxic skimp dumps that ran through the city.

She hesitated when she saw South Hill. The boys' bike was still a little big for her and, while she managed quite well once mounted, standing on the pedals (needed for going up-hill) usually resulted in bruising to her private parts because of the cross-bar. Then she remembered the little dirt track adjacent to the road that her father had used when dinking her to see Godfather Petersen. This was flat for the length of the hill, with a very steep lift at the end which was impossible to ride up, but could be negotiated by getting off and pushing the bike to the summit. She managed this, although the effort left her perspiring with tendrils of hair plastered to her cheeks and forehead. The rest of the ride to the hospital was without incident, but she was concerned about the length of time she had been away from home already, with still much business to conduct.

When she reached Thomas Street, however, time stopped. She stood transfixed by the magnificence of the building before her and the activity of dozens of men scurrying about on the grounds.

The new hospital was now almost complete. Maisie had seen it when the family had visited Jack in the old hospital on the hill behind, but her thoughts had been so focused on him that she'd failed to appreciate the enormity of it. Now, at five storeys high, it was by far the largest building in Broken Hill and she thought it far too grand for a mining town.

It was indeed grand. With a 376 bed capacity, it was the biggest hospital in Australia outside the capital cities, and the Broken Hill and District Hospital would be the first in the nation to be fully air conditioned. The £250,000 example of modern engineering had been funded by contributions from the Hospitals Commission, the local mining companies and almost every man, woman and child who lived in the city. Unionists had agreed to have their pay docked by one penny in the pound to contribute to the new building; women had baked and knitted and sewn for fundraising stalls; and children had spent their pocket money on the goodies.

For months, people had been talking about the marvels to be

found inside the new building and rumour had it that the kitchen features were so wondrous and out of place in Broken Hill that the cook had to travel to Sydney for training in how to use them. A series of later newspaper articles not only proved the rumours correct, but also provided intricate detail so that townsfolk felt satisfied their contributions had been well spent.

Barrier Miner Saturday 14 December 1940 (excerpt)

MORE ABOUT THE NEW HOSPITAL

The kitchen is all that could be desired in the most modern institutions. Provision is made for cooking by electricity, gas and steam. An idea of the labor saving devices can be obtained when it is known that among the plant are an electric potato peeler and an electric cake mixer.

The Hospital has its own refrigeration plant and all the food required can be stored so that it will keep as long as desired in freezing chambers. Throughout the building are many small refrigerators.

All washing of dishes is done in the kitchen. They are sent back to the kitchen by service lifts and cleaned in an electric washer.

A special room has been provided for milk storage. Huge containers can be set at any required temperature. The room is painted blue, because it is believed that flies have an aversion to the color.

The hospital had been under construction for almost three years on that day Maisie stood before it on her way to become a nurse (although the foundation stone was not officially laid by Governor-General Lord Gowrie until June 1939). It was meant to have been occupied by now, but there had been a series of delays.

Even before construction began, there had been issues. The Barrier Industrial Council (BIC) protested vehemently against the inclusion of a private ward in the new hospital. The unionists contributing to the Workers Contribution Fund Scheme through their pay deduction were to be entitled to free treatment at the hospital – but not in the private ward. This was against union principles.

Barrier Miner Friday 21 May 1937 (excerpt)

WORKERS' OPPOSITION TO PRIVATE WARDS

'A public hospital should know neither race, creed, color, religion, nor class. Once inside a hospital all things should be equal. Once we have private wards we sell these wards and they become privileged wards,' said Mr C. R. Hendry, workers' representative on the Hospital Board, when addressing members at last night's monthly meeting of the Board. He was afraid that if the Board continued with its policy of private wards the penny in the pound proposal by which the workers were to contribute their £15,000 would be withdrawn.

The Hospitals Commission was adamant it would not be blackmailed. Eventually the issue was resolved through a couple of mass meetings, where unionists voted to accept the private ward, but only if they were allowed access to it by paying the difference between it and treatment in a public ward.

Next came a series of strikes about pay and conditions. At one time the carpenters returned to work, but the bricklayers held out, seeking a pay rate of 26 shillings and 8 pence a day rather than the 25 shillings and one penny they were being paid. This meant the frame of the second storey was constructed (complete with concrete floor) before the ground floor had been bricked in. When the brickies returned to work, they couldn't remove the timber poles being used to prop up the second floor until the concrete on the ground floor had cured – so for a month passers-by were bemused to see a brick second storey balancing on a timber framed lower level.

Broken Hill Hospital, c. 1941. The hospital was demolished in 1999.

Other delays were caused by a union ban on using imported joinery, and the fact that materials which *were* allowed to be brought into town were often held up by transport issues.

Now, in October 1940, the hospital was almost entirely finished, and the workers Maisie could see were mostly involved with painting, installation of electrical fittings and putting the final touches to the mortuary, boiler-house and old x-ray block refurbishments. The only remaining major work was to connect the hospital to the Broken Hill Water Board's sewerage system (with this delay being addressed by a temporary septic tank funded by an extra £200 grant from the Hospitals Commission).

The first 100 patients would not be transferred to the new hospital until 6 September 1941, but they would then express 'total contentment' with the new facilities. The private rooms – outfitted at a cost of £11,343 – were deemed to have come from the Hospitals Commission's contribution rather than workers' pay packets.

Maisie found it easier to make her way around the construction site to the old buildings at the back than to find the matron's office once she got there. Finally she was stopped by a pretty nurse in a green uniform with a starched white apron and a perky starched white hat with two green stripes on it.

'Have you lost your mother, sweetie?' the nurse asked. Maisie solemnly told her, no, she'd lost the matron's office.

'I've come to be a nurse like you,' she said.

Once the nurse was able to confirm that Maisie was indeed at the hospital on her own and hadn't just wandered away from her parents, she decided the best place to take her was to the assistant matron. She took Maisie's hand and hurried along hallways, occasionally shifting the weight of the linen she had looped over her other arm. When they reached the appropriate door, she knocked tentatively and received a sharp 'Enter' in response.

'Wait here,' she told Maisie before disappearing inside.

Maisie was glad of the short reprieve. She had removed her outer housedress and left it folded neatly in the basket on the front of the bike so she could present well in her Sunday-best when she asked the matron for a job, but her ringlets were looking decidedly dishevelled from the bike ride and she took the few minutes to capture the stray wisps stuck to her face back in her slides and brush down her skirt. Her instinctive action to pull up her white ankle socks was quickly reversed when she noticed this displayed red stripes from the dust. Her dismay at this was short-lived when the nurse emerged and ushered her into the office.

Sister Irene Drummond tried to look stern. This was never easy for her because she was a plump woman with a round face and double chin, round spectacles that sat in front of warm brown eyes and (though she tried to create a formal style with slides and a roll at the back) her long brown hair stubbornly waved and curled to further soften her face. Certainly Maisie wasn't afraid of her and was impressed by her beautiful red cape, white uniform and soft white veil that flowed past her shoulders. Maisie thought she looked like an angel.

'I know you need new nurses because lots have gone to war. It said so in the paper. And you said the new hospital will be "all that is necessary to make a girl happy and contented". I know that because my mother told my sister Dulcie. And the matron said in the paper she would accept "any young girl who is desirous of joining the profession". I'm desirous.'

Sister Drummond gave up all effort to look stern and tried as gently as possible to explain Maisie was too young to be a nurse now, but if she studied hard at school she would be welcome when she was older.

'I'm very nearly ten. And the training course is four years it said in the paper. That would make me 14. Dulcie has been working since she was 14 so that makes me plenty old enough!'

When that seemed to have no impact on the assistant matron other than a broadened smile, Maisie tried a different approach.

'My father has just died and I nursed him very, very well. I get picked on at school because I'm German and I get picked on at home because I'm a girl so I don't get on at all well with my mother. I want to come and live with the nurses. The paper said being a nurse meant you could "work with the heart, the hands and the mind". I'm very good at that right now! Please don't make me wait until I'm older.'

By this time Maisie was in tears and there was a glistening in the kind eyes of Sister Drummond too. She spent far longer than she had intended with Maisie and assured her she knew she would make an excellent nurse one day. She explained carefully about the need to continue to go to school and work hard, and suggested Maisie should bring in her school reports each year to show she was working at an appropriate level for a would-be nurse. Then she spent some time making a show of writing down Maisie's name and address and talking to her about the loss of her father and listening to what a wonderful man he was.

Sister Drummond arranged for a porter to deliver child and bike back to Patton Street. While Maisie was disappointed at the way the interview had gone, she was heartened at least to have a firm plan for life after Jack – and an ally to implement it.

It was this belief that kept Maisie reading the Broken Hill newspapers. The habit had become entrenched when she had read to her father every day on the side veranda. She had continued to draw comfort from it after his death because it was now a solitary exercise and didn't require her to talk to Rose – but now she scanned for news about the hospital opening. Shortly after her visit to the hospital, her disappointment in its outcome deepened. She read Sister Drummond had left.

Barrier Miner Monday 14 October 1940

FAREWELLS TO SISTER DRUMMOND

In spite of the shortest notice, medical and nursing staffs of the Broken Hill Hospital could not let popular Sister Irene Drummond depart without a due measure of farewells and expressions of regret. Sister Drummond leaves tonight to take up duty with the A.I.F.

Yesterday the sisters and trained staff set about busily transforming the Sisters' sitting-room in the new quarters, which has not yet been occupied, but which by evening was a bower of roses, larkspur and broom. Between 20 and 30 sisters and members of the trained staff offered their good wishes, and on their behalf Matron Hunter presented the guest of honor with a leather writing case.

Later in the evening Dr. Dorsch, on behalf of the resident medical staff, presented Sister Drummond with a travelling rug, and this afternoon the trainees gathered to add their expressions of good-will together with a fountain pen.

On Friday evening Sister Drummond entertained the sisters and trained staff at the Grand Hotel.

Although Maisie was alarmed at the thought of Sister Drummond going off to war, she consoled herself with the thought that only men were killed in wars and that, by the time her new confederate returned to Broken Hill, she would have good school report cards and test results to show her. There might be quite a few of these, she realised, because the war was far away and many of the boys in the neighbourhood who'd gone off early in the war hadn't come back yet, so she set about creating a receptacle to hold them.

First, she found pieces of calico in Rose's duster bag which she carefully cut into two equal rectangles. These she stitched together on three sides using a big needle and wool from Rose's darning box, proudly using the backstitch she'd just learned in sewing class, rather than simply tacking. Next, she created what she thought was a rather clever solution to keep the top closed. After soaking some scraps of fabric in a flour and water paste as a stiffening glue, she added them to one of her mother's dolly pegs – scraps of white for a skirt and veil and a lovely piece of red for the cloak. The peg didn't sit well on the loose fabric, but Maisie knew it would work once there was enough paper inside to thicken it. Finally, she wrote in ink on the front, FOR SISTER DRUMMOND. This wasn't entirely successful either, because the ink ran and splotched on the fabric, but Maisie decided it was more striking that way and was quite satisfied with her afternoon's work. She couldn't wait to fill the bag with her school results and was confident the assistant matron's pleasure in them would be equal to that previously shown by her father.

Chapter 4

Safe places

October–December 1940

Developing a plan for life without Jack was a titanic step for Maisie. She had been so entirely occupied with getting through each day that she had been detached from anything so crushing as a month or a year. Now, however, her path was so connected to her father that she thought he was guiding her toward a new life. Despite this, she thought her mother a bit quick to resume her old one.

Rose missed only two fortnightly meetings of the Housewives' Association following Jack's death before reclaiming her role on its social committee. Maisie had little understanding of the type of loneliness that could send a woman out of the house seeking social companionship within a month of widowhood. As long as the meetings took place when Maisie was at school, she chose not to think about it – but on 24 October 1940, an afternoon tea meeting was to be held at the Schuster home.

'I don't *want* those women here!' Maisie stormed when she heard. 'Some of them were really mean to Dad sometimes – and their kids are mean to us at school. How would you like it if they called you a Hun?'

Rose didn't tell her that some had. The Broken Hill Housewives' Progressive Association had almost 1000 members by this time – and this led to broad representation on the various sub-committees. Rose had been exposed to everything from whispered comments just loud enough for her to hear, to blatant derogatory remarks (and not always about her German husband; sometimes comments were made about her Wilcannia childhood living among the Aboriginal community). But Rose also had good strong friendships – and cousins – on the committees, so she refused to let the snobbery get the better of her and satisfied herself with a reply spirited enough to raise more than a few eyebrows.

Mostly she was very popular among the women. Her feistiness was part of her vibrancy – and her vibrancy was part of what made her so successful in leading the social committee. Meetings were generally held in the Band Room at the Trades Hall, but Rose had previously hosted both the main committee and the social committee in her home and now saw the quick return of 25 South Street to the meeting calendar as a form of acknowledgement of her value – and validation that her enforced enemy alien registration was not going to interrupt her life.

There were other wives of German men prominent in the association, but (to Rose's knowledge) none had sustained the indignity of being fingerprinted, measured and photographed at the police station. The fact Rose's home remained as an optional venue meant the other 'British' women didn't care about the alien registration – or didn't know. The issue was more likely consciously ignored. Rose had been a founding member of the association, and her outspokenness was certainly not a shortcoming. This group of women were a little feared by most of the men in the city and many a politician, businessman or council alderman had been on the receiving end of the group's quite militant actions. Rose's assertiveness only added to her value.

The Broken Hill branch of the national and state-based organisation had formed in 1935 but, by November 1939, the women had taken a lesson from their unionist miner husbands and developed their own set of rules. It was no baking club!

Broken Hill struggled with wildly fluctuating unemployment due to the vagaries of the mining industry and the local Housewives' Association decided its principal role would be to reduce the cost of living across the community. As secondary objects it would:

Educate women to a sense of their duties and powers in the life of the community and as citizens, and to give every child adequate food, clothing, shelter, education and amusement,

and:

Arrange lectures and demonstrations to help women to become more efficient citizens, to arrange and assist direct distribution from producer to consumer wherever practicable, and to demand cleanliness in the handling of food.

The association would remain non-sectarian and unaligned with any specific political party, but would:

Make use of any and every political, industrial or any other organisations to forward its aims,

which included:

Raising of the school leaving age, compulsory education in domestic science for girls, the opposition of profiteering and the operations of trusts and combines, the appointment of women to all boards and tribunals affecting the home, and the establishment of machinery to elect women to parliaments and municipal councils.

These were not empty words. The women were accustomed to seeing what the power of numbers could do for their men on the mines and so the branch wrote to – and received responses from – the Prime Minister's Department and Premier's Department about the high cost of water in Broken Hill compared to metropolitan Sydney; the town clerk to protest the cost of electricity, seeking for it to be reduced to four pence a unit for light and a penny a unit for power; all local cinemas to reduce the cost of tickets; and the Metropole Theatre to introduce a Saturday matinee session for south residents. The mayor, town clerk and every alderman received letters protesting a proposed increase in municipal rates.

A deputation confronted the managers of the Broken Hill Ice

and Produce Company and A.H. Grant & Son to reduce the price of milk – with a letter sent to the Master Dairymen's Association demanding a reduction in the price of pasteurised milk below five pence a carton – and another deputation delivered a preferred price list to the Master Butchers Association.

All bread depots were boycotted for a period of time (and the Premier's Department called upon to intervene) when the women thought it necessary for bread to be 'wrapped in a special paper' to keep it clean and fresh – but they decided to drop their push for a reduction in the price of sugar after receiving comprehensive information from the Prime Minister's Department about difficulties in the industry.

The Housewives' Association also took a specific interest in, among other things, the price of potatoes, butter, tinned fruit, and bus fares; the service cost for gas; compulsory military training for young men; and increases in wage taxation.

Membership fees were set at one shilling a year (with men allowed to become associate members if they also paid one shilling) and the branch regularly made donations of one guinea (one pound, one shilling) to worthy causes such as purchasing cots for the children's ward at the hospital, providing the young patients with ice cream at Christmas, or furthering the work of the Youth Welfare Movement.

There were 3680 men working on the Broken Hill mines at the end of 1940, but almost 400 jobs had been lost between November and December and the remaining total employed was about 1000 less than the previous December. At least 2500 men were unemployed and seeking food relief for their families. They queued in long lines – gaunt men in fat men's suits bought for happier occasions. The huge unemployment list was not a hangover of the Great Depression, but more an example of the cyclical whimsies of mining. The men were waiting on new developments along the line of lode which would have them back in their jobs earning at least £250 a year, but meantime needed to feed their wives and children.

Petrol rationing had started, but was slow to be implemented, and a scarcity of other goods at that point was more due to rumours and panic purchasing than the reservation of food and clothing for the troops.

Food relief coupons distributed by police provided the unemployed with a number of commodities at a discounted fixed price, but medicine (strangely) and tobacco (considered by the men essential) were excluded and special application needed to be made for assistance with boots and clothing.

There were complaints the clothing distribution wasn't being handled appropriately and a deputation of the Housewives' Association took up the matter with Inspector Homann at the Central Police Station. When this failed to produce the results they required, the women decided to find their own way of clothing the poor.

A large basket was placed in the foyer of the Town Hall and the pages of the *Barrier Miner* (known as 'the establishment newspaper' in contrast to the union-owned *Barrier Daily Truth*) repeatedly cajoled residents over an eight-week period to support an appeal for clothing for the needy.

Barrier Miner Saturday 2 September 1939 (excerpt)

APPEAL FOR USED CLOTHING

With unemployment growing alarmingly the need for such a charitable effort as this becomes more evident and needs all the public support possible.

If you are so fortunate as to have frocks, coats, suits, shirts, or any other articles of clothing for which you have no further use, just wrap the parcel up and drop it into the basket in the vestibule of the Town Hall.

It is best that some poor person should have the use of it than to leave it lying idle. There are many little children and grown ups, too, who will be grateful for those shoes your family has discarded.

Do your part of the kind act today, and the Housewives' Association will do the rest.

Broken Hill responded. Within a short time there was sufficient clothing and shoes for children, women and men, but repeated calls for older boys' clothing couldn't meet the need (it was said because boys typically wore out, rather than grew out of, their clothes). The Silverton Tramway Company provided the collection basket, the WIU Band stored the clothing and provided a room for sorting and distribution, Pellew & Moore and Dryens provided cases for parcelling and a lorry was obtained from the Unemployed Union to transport goods and assist collection where people were unable to take clothes into Argent Street.

By the end of the appeal more than 400 families had been clothed – with an allowance of 'at least two of every article required for each child or adult'. Queues had formed on each of the four distribution days such that the process began earlier than advertised. In addition to the thousands of clothing items, the association was able to distribute several 'perambulators' (prams), a double bed, blankets, rugs, curtains and handbags. So great was the response to the Housewives' appeal that, after all the unemployed applicants had been accommodated (and even those employed people with large families and low incomes), two large parcels of clothing were sent to the orphanage, three to the Pensioners Association and three to the Aboriginal camp at Menindee.

It was good works such as this that enabled Rose to persuade a grieving young Maisie that it was indeed appropriate for the Broken Hill Housewives' Progressive Association to hold a meeting at the Schuster home just weeks after Jack's death. Maisie knew her father would have wanted it so – and the next day's newspaper reported that she delivered a delightful tap dance item to entertain her mother's guests.

Rose could be thought to have been resilient to grief. Her successive losses had at least brought her to a point where she understood it. Surviving loss requires a safe space to deal with it and, for Rose, activity was her safe place. For the children, she chose the Lutheran Church. In the next months, the church became a haven for Jackie, Maisie and Maxie – a sheltered space where they could feel their grief, remember their father and celebrate their German heritage without shame.

Given the rancour directed to all things German and the difficulty the children were having at school, Rose's determination to maintain and strengthen their relationship with the Lutheran congregation could be thought foolhardy. But Rose had no intention of lessening ties to the German community – she was as dedicated to committee-work in her husband's church as she was in the Housewives' Association. Jack had found his God in the fellowship of the church rather than its formalities, so she was determined the children would take their place among the congregation heading off on a sunny morning for a church picnic some nine weeks after Jack's death. She couldn't save her German children from the taunts at school – or the violence that sometimes marked their way to and from – but she could create for them a space where it was safe to grieve. All three Schuster children were therefore prominent participants in the annual Lutheran Church Picnic on 19 October.

Barrier Miner Tuesday 22 October 1940 (excerpt)

LUTHERAN CHURCH PICNIC

The annual Sunday School picnic arranged by the Women's Guild of St. Paul's Lutheran Church was held on Saturday at Kurnell Gardens. The picnickers, about 120 in all, travelled in lorries and cars. A good road made for pleasant travelling. Because of the warm weather, the distribution of cool drinks, ice blocks, oranges and sweets was welcomed. The Women's Guild is grateful to Kurnell Gardens for supplying a case of oranges.

A programme of sporting events was arranged for the children in the morning and for the adults in the afternoon.

The Schuster name was conspicuous in the published list of sporting successes – both among the children in the morning and the adults in the afternoon. Jackie won the shoe scramble for the boys and Maisie for the girls; Maisie won the three-legged race with a friend; Maxie won the match guessing competition; and Rose won the cotton winding race. The Schusters also featured in the skipping, sack, wheelbarrow and egg and spoon races; threading the needle; driving the nail; and guessing the length of a piece of string. So soon after Jack's death, the family would have been excused had they stayed home. That they went may have been in honour of Jack, but that they were so competitive once there came from the example set by Rose.

Rose's stoicism continued as Christmas approached. This would not only be the first Christmas without Jack, it was to be their first Christmas without real gifts. Jackie was due to begin at the Broken Hill High School in the New Year and his uniform and supplies would take all they had.

Jack had been awarded workers compensation of three pounds six shillings and sixpence weekly in 1934. This was the amount estimated he could have earned in a non-mining job if one was available in the Broken Hill district. Adjudged to be only partially incapacitated, he was awarded much less than other miners considered fully incapacitated by their pneumoconiosis. The unions had used Jack as a test case on behalf of another 151 men judged to be only partially incapacitated by lung disease in an appeal to the Workers Compensation Commission. He may have been a poor choice as representative because, while other men appearing before the commission were noted to be 'unhealthy looking, somewhat pale and short-winded on exertion', His Honour Judge Perdriau seemed overly impressed with Jack.

Barrier Miner Saturday 24 November 1934 (excerpt)

SCHUSTER'S APPEAL FAILS

"The appellant impressed me as being honest, intelligent, and hardworking, in fact, of a very fine type. He was quite willing to undertake any class of outdoor work, but his failure to do so is due solely to the prevailing slackness in the labor market. That he has any disease is not self-evident.

"There is no doubt the appellant suffers a material degree of partial incapacity for work as a whole and is no longer fit for underground or indoor work. He suffers no disability whatever for outdoor work in a rural district and can perform well known branches of outdoor labor in the city.

"The appellant's incapacity for work is not such that it can be deemed to be total.

NO REVIEW

"Application for review cannot be entertained unless there has been a change of circumstances in the case since the weekly payment was awarded. The onus of proving the change of circumstances rests upon the person alleging it. For the reason stated I hold that the Joint Committee did not err in law and the appeal therefore fails."

By the time Jack's lung disease had progressed to a point where he could substantiate total incapacity, he was physically unable to take on the task and Australia was again at war with Germany. As an enemy alien, he was powerless to fight for an increased award. Rose and the children were always to pay the price for this. As Jack's widow, she continued to receive only the 'weekly living wage'.

So Christmas at the end of 1940 for the bereaved Schuster family was without 'proper' gifts or Christmas fare, as well as without Jack. There was no heart in the Schuster children to make the Christmas marzipan they had made with Jack and no interest in stringing up decorations of chained coloured paper. There was some joy though, again in the arms of the Lutheran Church. All three children celebrated along with the rest of the congregation in the Christmas service on 17 December. Maisie and Jackie opened the singing with the first two stanzas of 'Little children can you tell?'

> *Little children, can you tell,*
> *Do you know the story well,*
> *Every girl and every boy,*
> *Why the angels sing for joy,*
> *On the Christmas morning?*
> *Yes, we know the story well,*
> *Listen now, and hear us tell,*
> *Every girl and every boy,*
> *Why the angels sing for joy,*
> *On the Christmas morning.*

Maxie was not left out and he and Maxie Baum delivered a recitation together about the Christ child in the manger. All the Sunday school children received a book as a present from the church, a small bag of sweets and a larger bag of uncracked nuts. Maisie duly collected these gifts from her brothers and handed everything to Rose for re-gifting on Christmas morning. She didn't at all mind there'd be no special gifts, treats or decorations for Christmas this year. Christmas was about family and her family was broken. She was in no mood to make 'special occasion' memories, because the ones she had already just hurt.

Chapter 5

Capitulation, conflict and consumption

February 1941

Rose spent the early part of 1941 in trepidation. Six weeks after she had registered as an enemy alien she had also reluctantly begun the process of becoming a naturalised Australian but now, months later, she'd yet to hear any progress on the matter. That she had capitulated and submitted to the indignity upset her. She remembered how stoic Jack had been when faced with discrimination or maltreatment. She also remembered her own hot words when the regulations had been proclaimed, so she felt some shame at 'giving in' to the authorities. Now the shame was joined by fear that increasingly clutched at her as time passed.

'I've let the bastards get to me,' she told Tommy. 'They never got to Jack. Not once! He held his head high no matter what they bloody did. He never fired up, but he never cowered neither. Now look at me. I might have told them what I thought of them once, but in the end I'm toeing the bloody line, aren't I? And sitting here waiting for them to come take me away or take the bloody house from the kids.'

Rose was outback tough. She was Wilcannia tough. She was Broken Hill tough. But she wasn't tough enough for this. During the naturalisation interview at the police station on 2 October 1940, she'd been an emotional mess. What frightened her so much about the process was the nonsense of it. If it had been a sensible or reasonable thing to do, she would have had nothing to fear. But she knew from Jack the cruel and unreasonable things that had happened to German people in Australia during World War I – and there were plenty of examples of it in this new war – so she didn't feel she could rely on the Federal Government or police to do what was reasonable and right. Unreasonableness was evident in the process. If you accepted that it had to happen at all, she reasoned, it should have been a case of simply filling in a form to prove you were born in Australia. But it wasn't.

There were more than 45 questions on a five-page questionnaire and Rose found it gruelling. Even Constable Ford, who conducted the interview, struggled with the complexity of it. Many of the questions were impossible to answer because of the circumstances – and at other times the pair made answers fit what they thought the Department for the Interior meant to extract. For example, in response to 'Did the alien have any relatives or friends in Australia prior to arrival? Who were they? (names and addresses)', they wrote:

(Mother) Mrs. James, 87 Morish St., Broken Hill; (brother) W. Seward, 67 Patton St., Broken Hill; E. James, cnr. Patton and Bonanza Sts. brother.

Rose's application would be helped, she and Constable Ford thought, by these relatives who were 'natural British subjects' and also by the fact she had five children born in Broken Hill of a first marriage to an Australian – four of whom (at the date of the application) had gone on to marry 'British-born subjects'. All this was added to the form.

Character references were required from 'friends of British Nationality'. Mrs Cherry and Mrs Lawson of 27 Bonanza Street were chosen and Constable Ford noted these women were known to him and spoke very favourably of Mrs Schuster's 'attitude'. 'Associates and places the alien frequents' were listed as:

Mr and Mrs W Thone, Patton Street; Mrs Ellis, Boughtman Street; and Mrs Bates, Patton Street.

'Property held by the alien' was noted as including the house at 25 South Street (valued at £320), furniture (valued at £150), Jack's old ute (unregistered), £2 cash in hand and £4 in the bank. No, Rose had no explosives, firearms, camera, wireless transmitting apparatus, motor boat or row boat – but the wireless radio receiver Dulcie had bought for Jack (seized in the 1939 raid on the house, but returned when Dulcie had gone into the police station to show the licence was in her name) was noted and the licence number 6396594 (current to May 1941) duly recorded on the form.

In response to a question that asked 'What do reliable neighbours think of the alien's general conduct?', Constable Ford typed:

> Sergeant Costello, who was stationed at South Broken Hill, has known Mrs Schuster for years and gives a good report of her.

They hit a stumbling block when Rose was required to produce her signed parole form. Question 42 related directly to it: 'If the alien has not already signed a parole form have one signed at once and attach hereto. Any refusal or disinclination to do so should be reported at once for action'.

Rose's capitulation on this issue was especially humiliating and she was grateful the interview was being conducted by Constable Ford rather than Constable Munro. She angrily signed the form with its long list of forbidden items and its commitment to not frequent any place of public amusement. She rationalised there would be no need of it once the naturalisation process was complete, and surely the process would not take long, given her Australian birth? Constable Ford simply typed 'Parole Form now signed' and made no reference to Rose's disinclination to do it.

Question 43 sought Constable Ford's opinion about the security risk Rose might provide:

> The police investigating this case will hereunder furnish a report setting out the opinion they have formed from the alien's attitude as to whether or not any action should be taken to restrict his movements from a national security point of view. Give reasons.

Now this presented an issue for Constable Ford. If he truly wrote on the form about Rose's 'attitude', her application was likely to be rejected – and even he could see such a rejection would be ludicrous. He wrote:

This person was a natural born Australian, her marriage previous to this one to the late Mr Schuster, was with an Australian. Her family are all born in this Country and having children to both husbands her natural ties will definitely be with this Country, which she knows; whereas, not with a Country – Germany – which she knows nothing of so far as the political make up of the present time, as talking to her showed. She is a very nervous type, the fact of being questioned in regard to the Aliens Registration matters was very upsetting to her and worried her a lot, so she would not be the type to cause trouble if she wished to, which in my opinion is extremely unlikely. She keeps very much to herself. All her relatives are Australians and live in this city.

No one had ever called Rose 'a nervous type' before – and she was *exactly* the type to cause trouble if she wished to! It can only be assumed Constable Ford was trying to find a tactful way of describing Rose's quick reaction to some of his questions and her behaviour when she finally had to sign her parole form.

To the next question, which asked: 'Do the reporting police believe that this alien can be safely left in his present employment, having regard to national security?' Constable Ford wrote:

She is in her own home and all right there.

Rose's application for naturalisation was stamped as having reached 'Intelligence Services, Government Services – Military Police Investigations' on 4 November 1940, but she had heard nothing. Now her disposition really was becoming 'of the nervous type'. She played over in her mind her attitude to the Sydney police when they had raided her home at the beginning of the war and her stubbornness with Constable Munro in refusing to sign the parole form. The police had such power. The local coppers had liked Jack, and saved him, but she'd done nothing to engender the same respect from them. She feared her hot temper and hotter words would see her taken away and she worried for her children. At every knock of the door she imagined police had come to take her for internment.

Coupled with that, she was struggling financially. In mid-February she came home from a church meeting to find a municipal rates account for eleven pounds four shillings and ten pence in the letterbox. It was still clutched in a shaking hand when she moved through to the kitchen to find Maisie had not set the table for tea and there were no simmering vegetables on the stove. The potatoes, pumpkin and carrots were still sitting on the bench and Maisie, who was meant to have prepared them in her mother's absence, was nowhere to be seen.

'Maisie!' she called to the backyard. 'Get in here this minute!'

The shrillness in her mother's voice frightened Maisie. She'd been sitting on the white rocks in the backyard thinking of her father and, now that she was brought from her trance-like state, could see the long shadows cast on the ground meant it must be quite late. She sprang up and ran to the back door.

'Get in here!' Rose repeated.

'No! You'll hit me if I do,' she replied with a defiant lift of her chin.

'I'll bloody well hit you if you don't!'

This little exchange was quite common in the Schuster household – and had been long before Jack's death. But now there was no one to protect Maisie from what came next. Her father was gone, Dulcie was living with Topsy and even Jack's tame magpie was no longer there to ferociously fly at Rose if she raised a hand to her daughter. Maisie decided to chance it. She would run in quickly past her mother and pick up the crockery for the table and then her mother wouldn't hit her for fear of breaking it. The plan didn't work.

Rose was coiled with fear and frustration and Maisie had been adding to that by her increased withdrawal since Jack's death. She struck out hard as Maisie tried to run through the lobby and Maisie landed hard on the linoleum floor. But if Rose was strung tight, so was Maisie. She'd had enough of violence from the schoolkids and by now her reactions were sharp. She kicked her mother – hard. The retaliation stunned Rose, but not enough to stop her. Mother and child continued to hysterically hit out and kick at each other in a frenzy of movement until Rose came down hard with her knee on Maisie's stomach.

Maisie woke to find herself on Jackie's bed, with Dulcie crying above her and Rose administering teaspoons of brandy between her lips. She immediately threw up the brandy, but received no admonishment from her mother when it splattered Jackie's quilt. She was astounded by this – and by Dulcie's presence. Had she been there long enough for Dulcie to be called? This episode was to stay with Maisie all her life (and certainly the smell of brandy always brought waves of nausea) but the fury and intensity of it shocked them both at the time. Somehow, though, the extraordinary violence made things a little better between them. It was as though there had been some release to a pressure cooker of emotions and resentfulness.

The resentfulness would slowly rebuild for Maisie as she brought home her school reports and test results to only a summary glance from Rose, so that eventually she didn't bother and instead only carefully installed them each week in the pouch she had made for Sister Drummond.

Rose, however, no longer had any reason to resent Maisie. That had been steeped in her failure to penetrate the close bond between her daughter and her husband. With Jack gone, there was no longer any competition for him. Rose continued her busy life in the Lutheran Church and Housewives' Association, while waiting apprehensively for news of her naturalisation. She had still heard nothing by the time she attended a Housewives' Association meeting on 27 February 1941.

Mrs Cherry and Mrs Lawson had been visited at their Bonanza Street home by Constable Munro to confirm the verbal references Constable Ford had claimed they'd provided, but this had been prior to Christmas so there was some conjecture now among those present as to what that might mean. Rose was unsettled by perceived pitying looks from the other women.

They must have had more confidence than Rose that all would be resolved favourably, for she was elected at this meeting to lead a house-to-house membership drive in South Broken Hill. It can only be speculated what Constable Munro may have thought about Rose being commissioned to wander the streets to diligently knock on every door.

But the busy Housewives' Association had much business to conduct this February meeting and soon moved on from Rose's troubles. First there was the need to elect two members to sit on the newly formed prices committee in response to a request from the BIC. Having appointed Mesdames Wakefield and Williams, the women went on to discuss 'the low price of commodities in Sydney compared with Broken Hill'. A newspaper cutting was read to the meeting about a man, his wife and three grown-up children who lived on less than £2 a week and another woman reported on a female baker in Sydney who was supported by 4000 housewives when she sold bread at four pence a loaf and made a comfortable living from that. Mrs Wakefield was instructed to use these examples when giving a speech at the Don Corner that night on the high price of goods in Broken Hill. The women then resolved to send a letter of congratulations to the BIC for 'maintaining its stance in the beer strike'.

This was not a strike in the normal sense of the word. The men hadn't downed tools at work – they'd downed their beer glasses! The Federal Government's November 1940 War Budget had significantly increased the excise for licensed premises, but when publicans responded by increasing the price of beer from ten pence a pint to one shilling, the Broken Hill miners protested vehemently. On Sunday 2 February 1941, a BIC mass meeting (although not especially well attended) had voted to initiate a 'black ball'. This meant unionists were banned from drinking beer in any hotel that refused to return to the pre-budget prices of ten pence a pint or sixpence for a ten-ounce glass. It was a serious move. Real men didn't drink wine and few in the town paid out for spirits. 'Having a beer' was sustenance – a natural consumption as necessary as food or water.

Given the importance of the thirsty miners to the hoteliers' livelihoods, no one had thought it would last very long, but it was now some weeks and the Housewives' Association was keen to encourage the men to stand strong. Ostensibly, this support was steeped in the women's goal of reducing all commodity prices in Broken Hill, but it's easy to believe they were also very happy to keep their husbands out of the pubs.

The day after the Housewives' letter of support to the BIC appeared in the *Barrier Daily Truth*, Maisie came home from school to find two rickety bicycles leaning against the front fence and was excited at the thought that meant Tommy and Jimmy were inside. Their almost daily visits immediately after Jack's death had become less regular and she hadn't seen them in the two weeks she'd been back at school following the Christmas break.

'Where are they?' she challenged her mother when she found they weren't in the kitchen drinking tea as expected.

'Don't you go out there with them, my girl!' Rose snapped. 'There's things need doing here for tea.'

Maisie locked eyes with her mother and inched toward the back door.

'Maisie, I mean it. You go out there and you'll be for it.'

Maisie hesitated. Today she'd been elected Captain of her Grade 5 class. Yesterday, her teacher had asked her to help one of the other girls learn her spelling words. The day before, she'd been given a gold star for her composition in English. She hadn't told anyone all these things yet because she wasn't seeing Dulcie until the weekend. Tommy and Jimmy would be so pleased to hear her news. But the look on her mother's face was enough to hold her firm. Then she heard her father's voice, 'You can only be brave, *Liebchen*, when you're first afraid.' And with that thought, she headed out in search of her brothers.

When she found them sitting on the side veranda drinking her father's home-made wine, her excitement turned to distress.

'Stop! What are you doing? That's Dad's wine!'

'It's okay, Maisie. Really it is.' Jimmy immediately put down the long bottle from which he was drinking and moved toward her with a purposeful encircling arm extended. She shrugged him off.

'All the garden's dead, Jimmy,' she said quietly as though he should understand why that was relevant. 'All the vegetables have gone to seed and even the trees are dropping their fruit because there's been no water.' Tears threatened. 'This is all that's left living of Dad. And you're drinking it.'

They hadn't drunk it all. A few bottles were still in the wooden crate, with curved wooden chocks under the bottoms to keep them at a slight angle so the wine kept the corks plump. But many more were scattered around on the concrete floor. Some of these were empty, but others were still upright with only the cork and a small amount of liquid missing. Maisie knew these were the bottles where the wine had become vinegar. Rose would make the decision later as to whether they were useful to her.

'We're sorry, Maisie. We know you helped to make it, but it won't be any good by the time you're old enough to drink it anyway,' ventured Tommy.

They just didn't get it. It wasn't that Maisie wanted to drink the wine herself. She wanted to keep it. To her, it really was a 'living' thing. She and Jack had toiled together to create something beautiful (at least, in some of the bottles). She loved the two men before her almost as much as she loved Jack, but no amount of remorse now would have her feel kindly toward them.

'You don't even like it,' she said, and it was true. They were beer drinkers. They had never liked Jack's wine, nor the alcoholic cider he'd made – although they'd drunk more than one glass of both with him on the side veranda, rather than let him know it. Now, though, they weren't game to go to the pub. Tommy had already been fined a pound by the union for drinking 'black' beer and they reasoned if they were going to drink alcohol they didn't enjoy, it might as well be free.

Maisie had no heart to argue with them further. She picked up the hammer they'd used to break into the crate and began to nail the slatted top back on to enclose the few remaining bottles. Neither Tommy nor Jimmy moved to stop her. Tommy hugged Maisie's shoulders without interrupting her work and Jimmy tousled her curls before both men headed sheepishly back inside to Rose.

Maisie picked up one of the 'vinegar' bottles, recorked it, and held it tight against her chest. She knew that she really should go back into the kitchen and face the repercussions of her defiance to Rose while her brothers were still there. But she didn't move. She pictured herself and her father sitting on wooden boxes with a wide-necked two-gallon crock between them, chatting away to each other as they pulled the plump grapes from the stems and carefully brushed any grit from the surface of each grape.

Most winemakers will wash the fruit before crushing, but Jack's preference for the fermentation process was to use a combination of air and the natural yeasts on the surface of the skin. It was a bit trickier to do it this way, rather than wash the fruit and add a controlled amount of yeast later, but Jack thought grapes were a gift from God and one shouldn't meddle too much with divine creation (despite the fact that wild yeast could sometimes produce quite a foul flavour for no explicable reason).

Even in her current sombre mood, Maisie smiled as she remembered taking turns with her father to use the long-handled masher to crush the grapes in the crock. Next came the honey, produced in hives at the bottom corner of the big backyard. The sweetening recipe was never particularly accurate. Jack used a hand-made big wooden honey wand and the number of wands per brew he pre-estimated from the taste of the fresh grapes. However, it was Maisie's task to hold it steady while the honey drizzled into the crock (which meant sometimes Jack had to add extra honey or brown sugar at a later stage, because a little tongue had sneaked one or two licks of the wand when her father was distracted). Apart from sweetness, the honey also provided food for the yeast to aid fermentation and sometimes when this process was a bit slow to begin, Maisie wondered whether her sneaky treat had had some impact.

The first night of fermentation, the big crock would be left in the warm kitchen – warm enough to encourage the yeast to grow, but not warm enough to kill it – covered by a cloth stretched across the top to keep the mozzies out, but let the air in to do its work. The next day was busy. Jack and Maisie would lift the cover and stir the 'must' every three hours (Jack even getting up to do it during the night) but over the next three days the crock would require only an occasional stir and father and daughter would take turns. The first bubbles always caused much excitement (wild yeast wasn't as reliable as packaged yeast) and, if they happened to appear on Jack's shift, he never revealed it.

'Dad, Dad! It's working!' would bring him from the backyard to marvel at the popping bubbles and deliver a 'Good job, *kleine Tochter*'. Over the next three or four days the bubbles would first increase to gurgling and then gradually reduce until Jack made the call to strain the liquid and siphon it into a glass carboy for longer term storage.

During this secondary fermentation, it was important to let

the gases escape from the liquid without letting oxygen enter the container, so a rubber balloon was fixed on the neck of the carboy. The noise the balloon made when the gases were released brought a giggle from Maisie as she thought of it now, while remembering the time a neglected balloon took off for a farty zig-zag around the kitchen brought outright laughter.

The time spent ageing and mellowing in the carboy could be anything from one month to nine, usually dependent on how much honey had been needed to adjust the taste or whether the batch had other berries added to the grapes. Now as Maisie caressed the bottle held to her chest she remembered how long she and Jack had spent making sure the bottles were scrupulously clean before bottling (even this she had enjoyed as they worked together) and how she had held the funnel still for her father and called out, 'Stop' at just the right moment, both of them laughing if she misjudged how much was still in the funnel, so that wine escaped the bottle over her small hands.

Again Maisie smiled as she immersed herself in the scene. For just a little while, she could be with him again. She could talk to him and he could answer. Rose called her from the kitchen. She knew she had to come back to the present but she tried hard to stay. Then he was gone.

As always, the high of again being in a moment with him was followed by a crushing low. She didn't want happy memories of him. She wanted him. Now there was an added emotion. She needed to face Rose's ire for having so openly defied her to go and search for the boys.

When her dragging steps finally led her into the kitchen she was dismayed to find Tommy and Jimmy had already left – and then more than a little surprised when Rose said nothing, but gently removed the still-held wine bottle from her arms.

'Go and wash your face for tea,' was all Rose said, and the look of sympathy on her face was enough for Maisie to decide she *would* tell her the exciting news from school. Later she wished she hadn't. Rose was clearly proud that Maisie had been elected class captain (and said it might mean Maisie could end up being President of the Housewives' Association one day) but the academic achievements received little attention. Maisie took the composition with its gold star and the spelling test with its bold red 20/20 and tucked them into her makeshift folder for Sister Drummond.

Chapter 6

Pubs full of beer

Tommy and Jimmy weren't the only Broken Hill men to be struggling to find ways around the union blackball on beer. Men all over Australia had protested at the increase in beer prices following the Federal Government's War Budget and some areas (especially in Sydney) had tried boycotts to get price increases reversed, but the action had been short-lived. However, Broken Hill's Barrier Industrial Council had extraordinary power because it brought all local unions together under one banner and could therefore exert pressures in a number of different ways. This power meant the battle could be protracted.

At the time of the 2 February mass meeting, it was assumed the resolution to prevent unionists from drinking beer in any hotel which refused to charge pre-budget prices would be enough to get the pubs to back down. However, hoteliers made a case that said they couldn't afford to. At 500 pints a week, they argued, the new cost of beer would only achieve increased income of eight pounds six shillings and eight pence a month, whereas the increase in excise for one month was more than £80, so they would already be significantly out of pocket.

The registered clubs were in a better position to absorb the increase, the hotels told the BIC, because they only paid 2% licencing fees on purchases, while the hotels paid 5% – and hotels also had to pay rent, while clubs were freehold. The BIC had little sympathy for the hotels and affirmed its position that all unionists were forbidden to buy beer at the new price, reminding members across all unions a fine of a pound would be added to their union dues if they did.

Clubs and any hotel prepared to charge pre-budget prices were initially excluded from the ban, but the Registered Clubs Association decided its five clubs would also not sell beer during the blackball.

Barrier Daily Truth Tuesday 4 February 1941 (excerpt)

FIRST DAY OF THE BEER BAN

Unionists Avoid The Hotels

Broken Hill drinkers had their first taste of a beer strike yesterday and it was a complete ban that was applied. The hotels in the town were deserted and at one prominent hotel in Argent Street the bar was closed in the afternoon. There had not been a customer there all day.

The usual crowd of men who generally frequent hotels and lounge outside of them were, for the most part, absent and the streets and hotel corners presented a strange and peaceful sight. The hotels were not picketed and if the present response keeps up, it does not look as if it will be necessary.

Discussions around the town centred mainly on the ban and at the moment it seems more important than the international situation so far as the beer-drinking population of Broken Hill are concerned.

As the unionists complied with the ban and the usual thriving pub trade was decimated, hoteliers responded by laying off staff in the Town Employees Union – including domestics that cleaned the rooms of hotel guests. This saw 250 people out of work with only 48 hours notice. At the end of the first week (when temperatures were reaching 91 degrees Fahrenheit by 10 am) the city's registered clubs rethought their position and said they were willing to sell beer at pre-budget prices.

However, a 9 February mass meeting (of 600 unionists this time) decided this would only result in men shifting their 'drinking holes' and do nothing to hurt the breweries, which is where the BIC now thought the new costs should be absorbed. To add further pressure, this meeting also extended the ban to include all intoxicating liquors (later it would even include soft drink). This inflamed the minority non-beer-drinking unionists, who were already complaining they would eventually be asked to contribute to a levy to support the now unemployed staff, but with no benefit to come from any subsequent shift in beer prices.

The United Licenced Victuallers' Association (ULVA) responded to these heavy-handed tactics by closing down all the city's hotels for a fortnight – but then capitulated and re-opened on 22 February to serve non-unionists and visitors to Broken Hill (although these visitors were still required to fend for themselves in their rooms because the hoteliers refused to re-employ the domestic staff they'd retrenched along with the bar staff).

By early March the Silver City Workingmen's Club again offered to sell beer at pre-budget prices, but also offered to close its book to new members and allow union pickets at the door to prevent non-members from entering. Hoteliers suggested an investigation should be undertaken to resolve whether it was reasonable for the hotels to sell at pre-budget prices (advocating representatives from both the ULVA and the BIC conduct the investigation). As a further move toward middle ground, they offered to sell pints at 11 pence for the duration of the investigation. All offers were rejected.

Representatives from the South Australian Brewing Company from Adelaide and Tooth & Co from Sydney arrived in Broken Hill to negotiate with the BIC, but can't have done it well – because now it was ruled no fresh supplies of their beers could be brought into town for local consumption (although supplies would be allowed for the outback pubs). The Registered Clubs Association immediately sent representatives to purchase bottled beer in Queensland and others to try to negotiate with other brewing companies in Adelaide and Melbourne for draught beer.

Hotels continued to open for non-unionists, but only the licensees and their families could serve in the bar or collect supplies from storerooms at the ice-works because the transport union refused to handle their goods. Stocks were running low.

On 25 March, publicans turned up en masse at the Railway Town Goods Shed and at the Tooth & Co warehouse in Beryl Street to load fresh supplies from the cargo to be sent to the outback. They loaded crates of bottled beer into sedan cars and six barrels of beer (300 gallons) onto the back of a utility, but were followed back to their premises by pickets and reported to the BIC. The hotels were told if they sold the beer at more than pre-budget prices a total boycott would be called, which would have pickets at their doors and no one (including non-unionists or visitors) allowed to enter their premises.

Barrier Daily Truth Wednesday 26 March 1941 (excerpt)

PUBLICANS COLLECT BEER

Considerable Amount Of Liquor Unloaded

Last night the secretary of the Barrier Industrial Council, Mr. J. G. Polkinghorne, made the following statement; "Some hotel licensees were observed today (Tuesday) getting beer and all unionists know what their position is in regard to this procedure.

The B.I.C. Executive advises that the fight is on in earnest following this latest move of hotel keepers, and calls upon all unionists to take up the challenge made today.

It is every unionist's fight and every unionist is expected to do his or her job. The prestige of unionism is at stake, so refrain from buying beer till it is sold at the price asked.

A taxi-driver lost his income on 1 April, after being reported for carrying 'black beer', and two days later the BIC announced food deliveries would be withdrawn to any hotels caught taking delivery of 'black beer'. This didn't mean they could no longer buy food for their guests, only that no one would deliver it for them. Members of the Horsedrivers' and Wholesalers'; Butchers'; Bakers'; Dairymen's; and Shop Assistants' Unions were affiliated with the BIC and supported the stand.

Correspondence from the Deputy Prices Commissioner to the BIC advising that 'a thorough examination' had been made into the price of beer in Broken Hill and that the increased prices were 'only sufficient to give hotel keepers a reasonable return for the services rendered' had little effect on the BIC's resolve. On 9 April, after 66 days, the hoteliers agreed to an 'indefinite trial' of selling beer at pre-budget prices and the blackball was lifted.

On the same day, Yugoslavia's Belgrade was reduced to a mass of debris and Germany captured Salonika, which had the largest population of Jewish people in Greece – but the Broken Hill beer battle had taken longer.

After such a protracted and volatile campaign, the announcement the blackball was lifted was surprisingly relegated to page 2 of the unions' newspaper the next day. The BIC had been shaken by the hotelier's stance, which it saw as a threat against unionism rather than an issue of maintaining income. Although the BIC resisted a front page article proclaiming, 'WE WON!', it left no one in any doubt it had retained its power – and would use it again if required.

Barrier Daily Truth Thursday 10 April 1941 (excerpts)

SETTLED

The liquor dispute has ended. That is fortunate, irrespective of any views held in regard to either prices or liquor merits or demerits. That is said advisedly for the reason that, the dispute, as pointed out on Saturday in this column, had obviously assumed fundamental aspects that involved unionism itself.

The hotelkeepers found themselves in the position of being the spearhead of such an attack, more particularly after their declaration that they were buying 'black' beer. That challenge was alarming as it was unique ...

The dispute may or may not be permanently settled, but it is something to know that the hotelkeepers, a section of our business community, have demonstrated that they are really not actuated by the motive of wrecking the organisation that in the field of common industry is the protective force of their own customers.

However, when action is taken that is calculated to smash this defence line, unionists are forced to protect it, come what may, irrespective of the actual motive for the attack, or challenge. The dispute has been declared off and the hotelkeepers have decided to give pre-Budget an indefinite trial ...

What the hotelkeepers do in the future is a matter for that future. If they continue to sell at present prices it is very clear that there will be no dispute. There will be no basis for it.

The hoteliers later made a half-hearted effort in July and again in August to say the trial hadn't worked, but quickly dropped the case when a new boycott was threatened. Meanwhile, the hundreds of pounds that should have been saved during the two-month beer blackball did not find its way into shops struggling with a depressed economy.

Barrier Miner Saturday 15 March 1941 (excerpt)

EMPLOYEES NOT MISSED

The mystery of what is being done with money not being spent in hotels remains. Although crowds thronged city streets today, there was still no easing in the depression that is sweeping through the city shops.

Indicating the extent of this, the manager at one city store said eight of his staff were now taking their annual holidays, and seven were on part-time. Business was so slack that these employees had not been missed.

Unless the position improved, the whole question of staffing and over-head expenses would have to be reviewed.

Other city stores have dismissed some of their employees, because it is not their policy to put anyone on part-time.

The president of the Chamber of Commerce (Mr. R. K. A. Kitchen) said that businessmen described the slump as the worst for all time.

Although money that would normally be circulating through hotels was now being saved, bank deposits had not increased, and businessmen were not getting the trade they had expected to follow.

The lack of additional commerce or savings gave rise to some suspicion the union blackball had not been followed. A number of unionists were fined their one pound when reported for drinking beer during the dispute. However, the unions had other evidence to suggest, in the main, they had been supported.

Barrier Daily Truth Tuesday 18 February 1941 (excerpt)

LIQUOR BAN DECREASES COURT CASES

The influence of beer on the public is clearly evidenced by the lack of cases on a Monday morning at the Police Court. There were customarily several drunk and language cases, but yesterday the only business was an examination order or two, a case in the Children's Court and only one man was fined for drunkenness. However, he did not flout the B.I.C. mass meeting's resolution, as he was under the influence of wine. That one man was charged with being found drunk in Bromide St. on February 14. He did not appear and so forfeited his recognisance of 10/.

In the midst of the beer conflict Rose at last received some news of her application for naturalisation. Constable Ford called at the house to advise she had first to advertise in local newspapers that she was applying for naturalisation and then, if there were no objections received from the community within 14 days, to pay a fee of five shillings at the police station. She was livid. It had taken five-and-a-half months to reach this point.

Added to her anger was embarrassment at having to so publicly advise of her pursuit of naturalisation when she had been so broadly outspoken against it. Then there was the matter of her Wilcannia birth, which she preferred not to own. Rose placed the advertisement, but with a small token of rebellion.

Barrier Miner and Barrier Daily Truth Tuesday 18 March 1941

NATURALISATION NOTICE

I, ROSINA MARY SCHUSTER, of German nationality, born at Broken Hill and resident fifty (50) years in Australia, now residing at 25 South Street, Broken Hill, New South Wales, intend to apply for NATURALISATION under the Nationality Act 1920–1936.

On 31 March (one day early) she stormed into the Central Police Station and slapped her five shillings on the counter, expecting there would now be a quick resolution to the matter. She was wrong.

Chapter 7

Nature's friends

Rose dealt with trauma, stress and frustration by keeping busy. Both the Housewives' Association and the Lutheran Church had benefited after she buried her husband and then throughout the process of registering as an enemy alien and applying for naturalisation. But, apart from these diversions, she had not left the South Street house in weeks, with Maisie sent 'to do the messages' in Patton Street. On the Wednesday after paying her five shillings at the police station, she kept the three children home from school and had them dress in their Sunday best.

Initially, none were happy about it. Dressing up was always an ordeal for Maxie (who dreaded the constraints certain to be imposed lest he soil or damage his 'good' clothes), while Maisie was concerned about missing the weekly spelling test and Jackie protested he would miss his lunchtime soccer training. Nonetheless, excitement began to build about this mysterious midweek outing. Jackie and Maisie postulated their mother was finally going to rebel against her parole and take them to the cinema as a special treat, but when Rose herded them aboard the bus heading into Argent Street, Maisie was delighted to think maybe they were going clothes shopping. Though not yet 11, she had developed early and was embarrassed about budding breasts emphasised by the strain of a too-small best dress and a worn-thin house dress. On arrival at their destination, only Jackie was happy with it.

Hundreds of people were already massed at the front of the imposing two-storey Technical College building (the crowd swollen because it was one week prior to the end of the beer blackball). The college's front picket fence had been gradually replaced in recent weeks by an imposing, but low, concrete wall with intermittent turrets. Jackie had taken interest in the progress of this work on the occasions he had been forced to walk from the high school to catch the bus home (because training for one or another of his sports had kept him past the time when Rose thought it safe for him to walk the two and a quarter miles over the hill to the south). More intriguing than the fence was a structure set back a little in the centre of a concrete path. It had been wrapped in hessian for months (well before the construction of the wall began) and Jackie, along with the rest of Broken Hill, was keen to see what was hidden.

'It's a fountain,' Maisie told him with some superiority. 'Just like the one we had in Semaphore. It's for Uncle Bert and it's got angels, just like ours did.'

Maisie was only partially correct. She still read the local newspapers, though her daily attention to the task had progressively slackened since Jack's death, and she had followed with interest the regular reports of growing donations to build a memorial fountain in honour of Albert Morris.

Albert was a world-renowned botanist and naturalist who had many claims to fame in the scientific arena, not least of which was a personal collection of some 7000 arid plant species. He had rooted many examples of these at his Railway Town home and in the Zinc Corporation plantations, the cemetery, hospital and schools. Another 4000 seedlings had been planted in the Penrose Park at nearby Silverton. But his most remarkable achievement was a series of regeneration reserves (gazetted in 1937) established across 1715 hectares forming the perimeter of Broken Hill.

This land had been denuded due to long years of miners harvesting the Mulga scrub for steam engine fuel; townspeople scavenging for fencing and firewood; goats, camels, cattle and horses grazing the remnants; and destructive rabbits with their indiscriminate warrens. The result was huge red sand drifts whipped up regularly to billow horrendous dust storms over the city and its residents. Albert's encyclopaedic knowledge of arid plants and their preferred cohabitations had transformed the area (under the umbrella of the Zinc Corporation) into a desert oasis – not in the usual sense, but in thriving old-man saltbush and mulga and succulents. They were still young, but were already beginning to hold the sand in place.

The early success of Albert's work had him pursued to address similar issues in Port Pirie, Whyalla and Iron Knob, as well as more exotic locations in South Africa and the United States. But the most extraordinary aspect of Albert's achievements was that he was self-taught. Born at Bridgewater in South Australia, Albert had arrived in the Broken Hill district by horse-drawn cart as a four-year-old in 1890 where his stone-cutter father worked on a Thackaringa mine. Albert's interest in arid plants developed after a childhood accident left him with one foot so badly damaged that he couldn't play with other children. He spent much solitary time examining the various species of saltbush he found in the bush and carefully propagating seeds and cuttings. He later trained at the Broken Hill Technical College in metallurgy and worked at the Central Mine for more than 36 years (for some years as chief assayer). But he never lost his interest in arid plants.

Albert formed the Barrier Field Naturalists' Club in 1920 with Dr W.D.K. Macgillivray in an effort to encourage others to see the beauty in native flora rather than the popular imported exotics that simply couldn't cope with the local climate, the sandy soil and toxic drifts from the mine tailings. He was a regular visitor to hundreds of Broken Hill homes, encouraging the use of local flora in rockeries to green barren yards that quite rightly rejected the favoured but futile English cottage gardens.

Maisie had many happy memories of 'Uncle Bert' and Mrs Morris in the Schuster backyard when they had lived in Hebbard Street close to the skimp dumps. She could picture him now in his sturdy dungarees, shirt sleeves rolled up and a big broad-brimmed canvas hat to protect a balding head of white hair. He wasn't handsome, Maisie recalled, but had a kind face and a rather portly shape, which rocked a little as he moved about the garden because of his limp. He wasn't really her uncle, but she loved him as though he were (and he was known as Uncle Bert to many of the city's young people).

Mrs Morris was always with Uncle Bert and Maisie openly admired her, partially for her beauty. Mrs Morris was slender, with shiny dark hair smoothed into buns coiled demurely at the nape of her neck, and a pair of spectacles perched on her nose which, to a young girl, made her look very learned. Mostly, though, Maisie admired her simply because she was there. Maisie was inspired by this stylish woman who preferred to be in the yard with the two men rather than sipping tea in the kitchen with her mother. She felt vindicated for all the times Rose had chastised her for spending time outside with Jack rather than developing housewifely skills inside.

Maisie had listened intently as the three adults discussed Jack's geraniums, his grafted fruit trees and his techniques for subsistence vegetables. Mostly the conversation was around her father's use of co-planting and rotational planting. Bert was interested in what Jack had to say about timing the planting of specific vegetables so that their flowers attracted 'good insects', which would then devour other insects attacking immature seedlings of other species. Jack was interested in *anything* Bert and Margaret had to say.

When Albert Morris died at 52 on 9 January 1939 after a long battle with an inoperable brain tumour, he was lauded by the general manager of the Zinc Corporation:

Barrier Miner Tuesday 9 January 1939 (excerpt)

PASSING OF MR. ALBERT MORRIS

Career Of Service For Broken Hill; Famed Botanist

A career of outstanding botanical service ended today with the death at Warrawee Private Hospital of Mr. Albert Morris, of

Railway Town. No keener student of botany could be found anywhere in the Commonwealth, and the fame that this self-taught botanist earned for himself carried beyond Australian shores.

His death will be mourned by thousands, old and young. Prime mover in the successful regeneration projects inaugurated some years ago, Mr. Morris's work will be long remembered.

Mr. Morris always believed in making field naturalists' work more interesting by acquainting the more humble members of the society with the common names of all species of plants, reserving the highly technical names for appropriate occasions.

There goes to his eternal rest today one of the finest citizens of any community in which it has been my lot to live. In this community of varied persuasions, both political and religious, I am sure that there is no-one whose passing will be regretted so collectively.

The Schuster family was living in Semaphore at that time, so there'd been no goodbye from Jack and Maisie to their gardening friend. Now Maisie decided being present at the unveiling of Uncle Bert's memorial was a fitting thing to do and she felt guilty at her earlier resentment and desire to instead be buying a new dress.

As the speeches droned on, however, she wished they would hurry up so she could see the angels. First came the President of the Albert Morris Memorial Committee, Mr M.A. Mawby, who spoke at length about Albert Morris's background and achievements before concluding:

'His mind turned frequently on the problems of soil erosion, which in those days made buried and abandoned homes a common sight. He was convinced that the preservation of natural trees and shrubs would do much to remedy this, and besought the interest of Broken Hill people.'

Mr Mawby went on to congratulate all concerned in the 'magnificent' fundraising effort for the memorial, which had 'caused it to be built without any drain on government departments'. The public subscription, which had included pay-day contributions of two shillings from Broken Hill workers and donations from distant universities and naturalist societies, raised £390. Only £310 had been required for the fountain, so the remaining £80 had been given to the Education Department to contribute to the cost of the concrete fence, funding half.

Four ornamental lamps on steel pillars to be placed around the fountain had been donated by the Zinc Corporation, while the Department of Works and Local Government had funded the planning and design of the monument and would provide water free of charge. Maisie thought this last contribution wasn't very generous, for she couldn't imagine it would take very much water to fill up the fountain, judging by the size of the hessian-draped structure.

Next came the President of the Barrier Field Naturalists' Club. Mr. A. Wiggins also spoke at length and, after extolling the virtues of Albert Morris, went on to castigate those who had not had his vision:

'Mr Morris fought hard for many years, against great opposition and some ridicule to get people to pay attention to what they were doing to the environment. The citizens of today are at fault because they have not cultivated the necessary environment of park and gardens for the benefit of youth. I appeal to the youth of Broken Hill to take an interest in field naturalist activity, for their own uplift, and for the benefit of all. We have paid heavily for the sins of our fathers in this city, and I hope the children of today will not have the same experience.'

'Well,' Maisie thought, 'He obviously didn't know my dad! And he doesn't know how hard I worked in the backyard either. Maybe that's why Dad didn't join his club.'

She sighed audibly when she saw yet another speaker stepping up to the podium and received a stern look from her mother. Maxie had given up paying attention long ago. He was sitting on the footpath playing with the shoelaces he'd removed and which were now imaginary snakes attacking each other. The 200 schoolchildren assembled on the steps of the building had begun to fidget, too.

The next speaker was Mr P.D. Riddell, the Superintendent of Technical Education, who'd come from Sydney to accept the memorial on behalf of the Education Department. Mr Riddell was equally verbose, but at least his speech was more interesting. He'd previously lived in Broken Hill and been Principal of the Technical College and he spoke about how, when he had planted lawns and palm trees at the front of the building, Albert Morris had been the only one to encourage him and show faith that one really could grow lawn in Argent Street (if one stuck with kikuyu). Mr Riddell was also the only speaker to acknowledge the help Mrs Morris had given Albert in his work. Maisie looked over to where Mrs Morris stood with her husband's mother, brother and sister and felt sure she saw Margaret swell with pride.

At last it was time for the unveiling. After one minute's respectful silence, the Burke Ward School girls choir sang 'Trees' set to the words of Joyce Kilmer's poem and Mr Wiggins began to unwrap the hessian.

Maisie was sorely disappointed. There were no angels. In fact, it wasn't really a fountain at all – at least, not as Maisie had imagined. She had vivid memories of two fountains set in the front yard of the Schuster home in Semaphore guarded by angels with beautifully crafted wings. She and her brothers had spent many hours filling the pools at the base with seawater and created a microcosm of the ocean with beach sand, little fish, shells, crabs and seaweed. She had been expecting something similar. Nowhere in the newspaper coverage she'd read had it said *drinking* fountain!

Maisie may well have been disappointed, but others weren't. For its time, the Albert Morris Memorial Drinking Fountain was really quite magnificent. Standing on a raised concrete base was a perfect block of polished red granite about five feet tall, three feet across and two feet deep. It was levelled at the top to form a squat blunted pyramid. The fountains were attached on either side of this granite memorial, with water flowing from taps into beautiful smooth bowls.

The fountain, which had been built in South Australia, carried a bronze indented tablet which simply read ALBERT MORRIS – NATURE'S FRIEND. On the back, another bronze tablet bore the immortal lines:

> I expect to pass through this world but once. Any good, therefore, that I can do, or any kindness that I can show to any other fellow creature, let me do it now. Let me not defer it, nor neglect it, for I shall not pass this way again.

Maisie was right to feel some compassion for Margaret Morris and the lack of acknowledgement for her. While the fountain at the Technical College is one of many memorials to Albert scattered throughout Broken Hill, there is little recognition for Margaret and her significant involvement in his achievements. A dressmaker with a naïve interest in botany when they married in 1909, Margaret was with him every step of the way, travelling thousands of miles in search of species and often taking on the heavier work because of Albert's physical impairment.

Margaret wrote of protecting the bole of saplings by planting them in kerosene tins (with the bottoms removed and the sides slashed to facilitate rusting and allow the roots to escape). She was very much part of the collecting, pressing, documenting and photographing of all Albert's specimens and often hand-painted her husband's black and white glass slides to show the colour of species they identified.

Her beloved Bert's premature death meant he didn't get to see his regeneration reserves in mature bloom, but Margaret did – and helped to get them there. After his death, Margaret managed the Zinc Corporation's nursery and took on the role of 'Botanical Adviser to the Plantation', working with the new Plantation Foreman and Ranger Jack Scougall to continue Albert's work. She was later to say of her husband's legacy:

> This is the first town in Australia, and probably in the world, to attempt to improve the living conditions for a whole city by surrounding it with a belt of scrub to break the force of sand-drift and prevent houses and fences being buried with it.

Margaret was right. Mining is castigated for its negative impact on the environment, but Broken Hill is the first example of green action in Australia – and it was a mining company that took it. The test grounds for Albert's regeneration reserves were huge tracts of land established as a series of plantations around the Zinc Corporation's leases – developed by him with progressive support from three of the company's senior executives.

Zinc mill superintendent and metallurgist Sir Maurice Mawby (also a member of the Barrier Field Naturalists' Club) was first to understand the potential in Albert's talents to address issues the company had with sand drifts and dust storms on their leases. Albert assured him rabbit-proof fencing and support in the early years for new trees, shrubs, sub-shrubby plants and grasses could do the job.

The Zinc Corporation's managing director William (W.S.) Robinson had the foresight to believe in Albert's vision and, when he recruited A.J. Keast to manage and restructure the Broken Hill operations, he included the task of planning and providing for Albert's experimental plantations.

These fenced plantations across many hectares hosted many thousands of trees, saltbush shrubs and grasses (86 recorded species in 1939 and more than 200 by 1944). They thrived with the help of furrows dug to create new topsoil and watering in their early years by

Albert and Margaret Morris, c. 1935.

An early example (1907) of the rolling dust storms the Morrises'
regeneration work addressed.

effluent from the city's sewerage treatment works, gravity fed from an elevated tank. The scheme included an extensive nursery which developed seedlings until they were at least one foot high; adjacent orchards which grew oranges, lemons, mandarins, grapefruit and olives; avenues of trees to line entrances to the operations; and magnificent rockeries to adorn the various residential and guest houses on the mine leases. All this was achieved with mine labourers who had no gardening or horticultural experience and has stood the test of time.

The regeneration reserves surrounding Broken Hill followed the Zinc Corporation's plantation pilots and were developed with support from the other local mining companies. The National Trust listed them long before the city as an entirety became Australia's first National Heritage List city in 2015.

The fact neither Margaret nor the Zinc Corporation receive as much recognition for the green belt surrounding Broken Hill is likely due as much to Albert's selflessness and popularity as to the vision he realised.

Barrier Miner Editorial Thursday 3 April 1941 (excerpt)

ALBERT MORRIS IS NOT FORGOTTEN

Of Albert Morris, probably the greatest thing one can say is that the respect with which he is remembered today is no greater than the esteem in which he was held during his lifetime.

Although his fame outside Broken Hill was limited to scientific circles, Albert Morris had many attributes of the truly great. He was an altruist. The honor in which he is remembered has nothing to do with personal power or wealth. He is honored as a citizen whose concern was the welfare of the community in which he lived. He sought neither praise nor reward. He struggled against ridicule and opposition because he believed his work would be useful to others. He gave freely of his energies in the service of an ideal and begrudged nobody the benefit of his toil. Is it any wonder that where his work is known he is held in the highest regard?

We all appreciate the beauty and the value of the preservation of natural vegetation, but few of us have the passion, the forethought, and the faith that drove this man to expend his whole energies on a work we all admire. Not many of us have his modesty or his courage either.

Future generations, whose heritage might have been the barren plains and hills that were Broken Hill, will have cause to think gratefully of Albert Morris. Those who knew him well have been wise enough to make sure that his name and his deeds shall not perish.

It had been more than two years since Albert Morris's death at the time of this memorial unveiling, but less than eight months since the Schuster family had lost their own 'nature's friend'. Their grief was still raw. Rose's determination to take her children to witness the ceremony may have been another act of defiance, since the Technical College was next door to the Central Police Station and the family stood on the footpath outside it. Maisie would later think her mother had taken them because she knew Jack would have gone if he were alive. Whatever the reason, the outing left a lasting impression on all of them.

The immediate impact, though, was a pall of misery. During the rattly bus trip back to the South, Rose reflected on how people had once spoken about her husband with the same admiration they now spoke about Margaret's; Jackie was regretful about time not spent with his father tending plants in the backyard; while Maisie was lost in memories of angel sentinels above pools of delight in Semaphore, her father building them seaweed beds to sleep next to the ocean, and mad dashes across the road the next morning for his pancakes drizzled with lemon juice soaking spoonfuls of sugar. Maxie was miserable because he had lost one of his shoelaces and was in trouble with Rose.

Chapter 8
Winning tactics
April–May 1941

Within a week of the unveiling of the Albert Morris Memorial Fountain, Rose regretted the decision to go. Maxie was ill – very ill – and the symptoms frighteningly pointed to diphtheria. It began with a sore throat and raspy voice, and Rose could clearly see the glands in his neck were swollen. He was having difficulty swallowing – and breathing. Nothing seemed to shift the fever.

'I shouldn't have taken him out in that crowd,' Rose told Maisie as the two worked to change the sheets on little Maxie's bed for the third time that day. 'We *knew* diphtheria was around again. All those people jammed up together and no fresh air for him, sitting there on the ground.'

'It's not your fault, Mum. It's everywhere at school, too.' She watched Rose twisting her hands over in her apron. 'There're lots of kids away and two are in hospital. He could have got it anywhere.' Despite their discordant relationship, Rose and Maisie were at one in their love for Jackie and Maxie. She knew how her mother felt.

'It might not be diphtheria. Maybe it's just the flu, or even strep throat,' Maisie offered. She knew her mother would be thinking of the sons she had lost to childhood diseases.

Two of Rose's boys to Thomas Vale had died early and her first-born son to Jack, baby Reinhold, had died from pneumonia at eight months. Maxie, also at eight months, had been stricken with pneumonia and had been near-death when surgeons removed a rib to ease pressure on his pus-filled lungs. Later medical opinion condemned this practice as not only futile, but dangerous. Maxie had survived it to become a robust little boy, but Rose still feared every childhood disease as it cycled through the town.

'Will I go for Dr Funder?'

Rose hesitated. There was no doubt Maxie needed attention, but there'd been recent appeals for people to refrain from calling doctors out for treatment at home. The Liquid Fuel Control Board had cut the petrol allowance for doctors by another 25% and the townsfolk were being asked to take sick patients to surgeries or the hospital rather than ask doctors to use their precious fuel for other than emergency situations. She looked at her wheezing son. Was it an emergency? Diphtheria was a common childhood disease. There wasn't a house block in Broken Hill that hadn't had more than one of its children afflicted with it, but it was such a horrible disease and many children died of it. Two weeks ago it had taken Dorothy Bennett's daughter. Jackie and Maisie had been immunised during an inoculation program at Alma School, but Maxie had been too young.

'Yes,' she nodded at Maisie. 'Go into Mrs Denham and ask her to use the phone to call him. Maxie's too sick for me to take him in and, if he hasn't got it now, he soon will if I take him to the surgery while he's weak like this.'

The prevalence of diphtheria in Broken Hill had initially reduced somewhat due to a succession of immunisation campaigns, but there was a good deal of fear and resistance to the inoculations, so the disease was building again. A recent spate had had 13 children in hospital (four of them critical), a toddler had died of the disease in March and Mrs Bennett's young girl in April. Rose was terrified. Her fear was only mildly mollified when Dr Funder arrived and reassured her he could see no membrane stuck to Maxie's tonsils. Then she was angry.

'The bloody council's got a lot to answer for,' she told Dr Funder. 'Maxie's been registered for immunisation, but the bloody town hall says there's not enough on the list to warrant another round. There're 30 on the list, for God's sake. How many more do they need? I shouldn't have to live in bloody terror while I wait. I've got enough on my plate right now.'

Rose would usually have been more respectful toward Dr Funder (though she never shied from speaking her mind), but the stress from having believed she might lose her last-born son found its own release. Dr Funder wasn't fazed.

'I wish more people felt like you about immunisation, Mrs Schuster, but it's not the council's fault. The machinery's all in place. We just need sufficient numbers. There're a lot of scaremongers out there turning people off. All this talk about blood poisoning and immunisation making children ill is a nonsense, but people believe it.'

'Well, I've heard that too, but I still put his name down. Jackie and Maisie had the shots and it didn't do them any harm – but I understand why people are frightened of it. They reckon you're actually putting diphtheria into them and, I have to say, that makes me think twice.'

Dr Funder spent some time with Rose explaining about the tablets and mixtures he was leaving for Maxie, who did indeed have 'a strep throat'. It was a severe infection on top of his tonsillitis, with the inflammation causing the swollen glands and stertorous breathing. But the kindly doctor spent even longer talking to her about the immunisation process, reasoning he not only needed to keep her committed to the campaign, but that Rose would make a good ally in the fight to convince other mothers to inoculate their children.

'The serum *sort of* has diphtheria in it, Mrs Schuster, but it's called an anatoxin because all the power of the bacteria has been removed by a chemical, so it's not toxic anymore. There's just enough there to stimulate the body to develop resistance to it and, at its most successful, this resistance becomes immunity. In the worst case, any dose of diphtheria picked up will only result in mild illness.'

'But you're still injecting diphtheria? Some say the kids get sick with it after they get the injections. My two didn't, but I believe my friends when they say theirs did ...'

'Look, I'll explain it this way. When children are in hospital with diphtheria, we inject them with an antitoxin to help them fight the disease – and we've been doing that for 40 years! All the immunisation process does is give children a little bit of the weakened bacteria over three injections, weeks apart, so they can create their own personal antitoxin. Sometimes they might show some of the symptoms of diphtheria, that's all. And, as you know, we do the scratch test first to identify any children who might be sensitive to the anatoxin and adjust their dosage.'

'It's all gobbledygook to me, Dr Funder. But it doesn't matter, I've got his name down and he'll have it just like the other two. You just need to get the bloody council to give it out and Maxie'll be there.'

'Mrs Schuster, listen to me. *Without* immunisation Maxie has a one in ten chance of contracting a decent dose of diphtheria in the school yard – and one in a couple of hundred of dying from it! *With* immunisation, the chance of getting a serious dose of the disease will be less than one in a thousand and the chance of him dying is about one in a million! Tell your friends that!'

Maisie was spell-bound by Dr Funder. Although she only understood about as much as her mother, she was busily storing away what information she could comprehend for when she became a nurse (and imagined herself expounding her new-found knowledge to Sister Drummond when she came back). Rose, meanwhile, was planning to ask for a change to the agenda of the next Housewives' Association meeting. Dr McMeekin had been booked to deliver a lecture to the special Housewives' Ambulance Class about Air Raid Precautions, but Rose now thought Broken Hill children were far more likely to die of diphtheria than bombs. She asked Dr Funder whether he would be prepared to deliver a lecture and he agreed, but Rose's questions had led him to develop his own plan.

Within a week, a lengthy educational article appeared in the *Barrier Daily Truth*. Under a large heading, AN APPEAL AND A WARNING, Chief Health Inspector Mr S.J.J. Davey stated the imperative for 'every parent in Broken Hill to know the scientifically established facts about diphtheria and immunisation'. The article to deliver those scientifically established facts stretched across several columns and down much of the length of the page, with bold headings and at least some attempt in the many paragraphs under each to use language that the general population could understand. Simplifying the language also strengthened the message.

Barrier Daily Truth Thursday 1 May 1941 (excerpts)

DIPHTHERIA CASES REPORTED

Health Inspector Stresses Need For Immunisation

AN APPEAL AND A WARNING

Diphtheria is one of the most frequent and fatal of children's diseases ...

One in every 270 will die from it, often from slow suffocation due to the spread of the membrane down the air passages ...

57 out of every 100 infections are contracted by close association, such as in schools, with apparently healthy children who nevertheless harbor the causative germ in their throats without developing symptoms of diphtheria ...

People should not allow themselves to be misled by non-medical busybodies who falsely state that serums and anatoxin injections cause 'blood poisoning,' etc. On the contrary, they are nature's own method of producing cure and resistance, or immunity, to infection. This immunity can now be safely produced, and will protect their children from this terrible disease ...

Parents will therefore only have themselves to blame if – through following the advice of agitators without medical qualifications or experience, against that of 'the greatest experts' in the world – their beloved child quite unnecessarily suffers from, or even dies of, diphtheria.

Mr Davey's harsh words did the trick. On 28 May he supervised a new diphtheria immunisation campaign at the Town Hall. Maxie was among more than 500 children who turned out for the first stage of treatment, having recovered fairly quickly from his strep throat, though whether that was hindered or helped by the number of potions and poultices Rose added to Dr Funder's regime is open to conjecture.

A month after the unveiling of the Albert Morris Memorial Fountain and Maxie's feared brush with diphtheria, Maisie got her new dress – purchased at Martin's the Block Corner for the princely sum of 15 shillings.

This was an extraordinary amount for the meagre Schuster purse and Rose had not shopped at Martin's since Jack had been alive, healthy, and bringing home a full mine wage. The imposing store was the 'quality' draper in town (with some competition from Pellew & Moore and Dryens) and, even during sale time, its wares were unaffordable for the bereft Schusters. However, the timing of Maisie's need was perfect for a mother trying to prove her support for her country. The store was giving an entire week of cash sales to the next war loan to be paid to the government.

Barrier Miner Saturday 3 May 1941 (advertisement)

Announcing

WAR LOAN WEEK
At
MARTIN'S

The Whole of the Takings from Every Cash Sale made at the Block Corner between 9.30 MONDAY and 1 p.m. NEXT SATURDAY

is to be Invested to the present War Loan.

NO DEDUCTIONS WILL BE MADE FOR COST OF SALES

– OR ADMINISTRATION EXPENSES –

THE ENTIRE TOTAL TO BE SUBSCRIBED.

This will afford a golden opportunity for
thousands of Broken Hill shoppers to aid the War Effort
and the same time receive more than their
money's worth in return.

This is YOUR easiest and most effective way to help!

You obtain full value for your money, and you have
the gratifying knowledge that every penny you've spent
has helped to swell the War Loan.

It's one more reason why, next week,
you should especially shop at

MARTIN'S
THE BLOCK CORNER

To this point Broken Hill had contributed more than £12,000 in donations to patriotic funds and the government had been given £585 as a gift and £27,248 in interest-free loans. There was no sign of the resistance to war exhibited in the mining community during World War I and the extraordinary measure by Martin's to commit to lending a week's total cash sales (not just profits) was indicative of its prestigious position in the city. The store and its owner, J.P. Martin, were held in high regard, both for bringing a sophisticated capital city presence to the mining town's main street and for breaking a 'hoodoo' that had hung for many years over the pre-eminent commercial position on the corner of Argent and Oxide streets.

This site had been razed during the great Argent Street fire of 1888, which had demolished the entire western side of Argent Street between Chloride and Oxide streets within a six-hour period. The speed and ferocity of the fire was due to the fact most of the buildings were constructed of timber and iron, lined with tinder-dry matchboard and papered hessian. Four years later, another fire that raced along Oxide Street to Gawler Place collected the new wood and iron buildings reconstructed on the corner site. Then came a succession of stores that failed to succeed in the rebuilt premises – furniture and ironmongery, drapers and grocers – despite almost all the city's traffic passing by its doors including almost every suburban bus.

J.P. Martin bought the failing business of Drapers Ltd in 1922 for stock of £4,800 and pushed landlord Mr H. Krantz to substantively rebuild the string of shops from Argent Street to Gawler place with sturdier materials. He would later tell of selling a piano worth £90 on a Saturday morning for just £38 – so he could have a cash float for his store's opening on Monday morning. With external renovations completed by 1925 and business thriving (to the extent he had repaid the capital he had raised to buy the business), Mr Martin travelled to Melbourne and Sydney and brought back to Broken Hill emporium ideas that had previously not been seen in the city.

Maisie, along with the rest of Broken Hill, had watched in awe during the months just prior to Jack's death as the exterior of the block corner was again remodelled, this time with a new concrete parapet and stucco finish, moulded on horizontal lines. A futuristic tower on the corner facing the intersection included a grandiose 'M', with MARTIN'S displayed three times along the parapet in large stainless steel lettering rumoured to have cost £37. But Mr Martin had also spent more than £3,000 to revamp the interior.

By the time Maisie came in with her mother to buy her new dress and finally saw inside, she thought Mr Martin's store was simply the most glamorous thing she had ever seen. There were large mirrors inset at regular intervals around the walls and on columns, reflecting glass counters displaying haberdashery, hosiery and small decorative gifts and knick-knacks known as 'fancy goods'. Everything was lit by powerful electric lamps which gave the effect of bright daylight, while tasteful 'easy chairs' were scattered around the store, some next to writing tables topped with beautiful containers of Martin's the Block Corner stationery, so customers could write letters while they waited for fittings or rested in comfort during a busy day in town. A few tables also held a telephone so customers could make appointments or tend to other business. Everything sat on beautiful carpet which stretched wall to wall. The basement had been expanded by the removal of some 600 tonnes of soil and converted into a spectacular showroom of corsetry, millinery and mantles (loose capes or cloaks), as well as accommodating administration offices.

More than 30 employees conducted business across 11 separate departments – Manchester and Furnishings; Dresses and Silks; Clothing, Mercery, Men and Boys Wear; Hosiery; Fancy Goods and Perfumery; Haberdashery; Underwear, Corsets and Children's Wear; Mantle; Millinery; Window Dressing and Ticket Writing; and Office. Mr Martin's war loan sale celebrated 19 years of successful trading.

Maisie and Rose moved about the store speaking to each other in hushed tones and even ventured downstairs, though they had no interest in hats or capes and Rose had never been a fan of corsets. Here Maisie stood mesmerised by the little cash railway that brought dockets and cash from the upstairs sales people to the cashier and returned change for customers. When she stood for too long watching this, there was no sharp reprimand from Rose, who instead placed a hand under her daughter's elbow to gently lead her away.

Maisie realised her mother was every bit as awed by the ostentatious store as she was, though no one else would have noticed it, because there was no battle on the selection of the new dress. Maisie and Rose were at odds about most things – and *always* about clothing – but Rose readily accepted Maisie's choice and they moved to the fitting room to be sure of the sizing. It was here that the argument began. Maisie refused to take it off.

'I want to wear it home on the bus,' she told her mother firmly, though still in hushed tones.

'You can't do that, Maisie. We need to pay for it first. And I need the parcel. Get changed at once!'

'No.'

'I'm going to wait for you outside and I'm going to give you exactly one minute to take it off and get back into your own dress. If you're not out of here in one minute, there'll be no new dress.'

Maisie thought about this. If she didn't take the dress off, she couldn't see how she could possibly miss out on owning it. Rose would have to pay for it before they could leave the store. If she did take it off, Rose could return it to the rack.

Meanwhile Rose, when she emerged from the fitting room, had been met by a small queue of waiting women. She knew how stubborn Maisie could be and this was not the setting for her to physically remove the dress from the child. She reached a hand back into the fitting room to lead Maisie out, retrieved the now crumpled too-small best dress from the floor and held her head high as she moved past the waiting shoppers. There was no pride to be had, though, when she asked the snooty shop assistant to wrap Maisie's old dress.

Maisie had been smug at the defeat of Rose in the fitting room but had compassion for her mother at the sales counter. Rose's pink cheeks exposed her embarrassment and Maisie felt a stir of remorse as she noted that the pink suited her mother and she hadn't seen colour in her face for a long time.

She was surprised when, instead of waiting at the bus stop on the corner outside Martin's, Rose chose to walk the block and a half of Argent Street to the police station. She wondered for a moment whether she was to be reported to the police for not having removed the dress, but rationalised that couldn't be it, because it was paid for now.

Rose bustled to the front counter and pointedly placed the brown paper parcel on the high counter separating her from the constables. The paper was stamped in several places with Martin's stylish 'M' monogram, but there was also a new and very large ink stamp, which she deliberately turned to face Constable Munro. It said, 'WAR LOAN WEEK. THANK YOU FOR YOUR CONTRIBUTION'.

Neither Constable Munro, nor Constable Ford, was able to give Rose the information she sought, however. It had now been nine months since Jack's death, eight months since she registered as an enemy alien, seven months since she had applied to become a naturalised Australian and six weeks since she'd advertised her intention and paid her five shillings. Constable Munro looked at the brown paper parcel and kindly told Rose he would make enquiries.

Though it was what she set out to achieve, Constable Munro's changed attitude brought little comfort in the coming weeks. She had recently heard of two Italian men being interned for no other reason than annoying their neighbours. This was on top of the German friends who had already gone. There wasn't quite the World War I hysteria toward enemy aliens Jack had told her about, but it seemed it was easy enough to manufacture 'evidence' that someone posed a threat to the security of the country. Rose knew how much influence the local police had in this. Constable Ford had been supportive of her, but Constable Munro? Rose wasn't sure. He wasn't a bad person, but he was obsessive about ensuring aliens didn't step out of line or pose a threat to his country. By her extravagant purchase, Rose was only hoping to convince him of her patriotism. But something else had happened as she strode back along Argent Street with Maisie at her side. Her daughter was skipping.

The royal blue rayon–wool blend dress with its double breasted gold buttons and Peter Pan collar would remain in Maisie's memory into adulthood. It was only later that she had an appreciation of the burden that dress imposed on a severely limited Schuster household budget. But in that moment, for just a little while, she was happy.

Chapter 9
Triumphs and tribulations
June–August 1941

Fifteen shillings spent on one new dress at Martin's the Block Corner was remarkable enough for Maisie to remember it for a lifetime, but the Schusters weren't impoverished. The family in 1941 fared better than many in the town: bills were paid; food was on the table (though Rose's pasties rarely contained much meat); and the children always had reasonable clothes for school and 'best'. Socks and woollen jumpers were darned to make them last a little longer; long pants often had patches on the knees (invariably on Maxie's); and all three children wore shoes with cut-out cardboard inner linings when thin leather soles wore out – but these were economies some in the town would have felt privileged to make. The Schusters lived in a good home at a time when Chief Health Officer S.J.J. Davey was petitioning the council to serve closing notices on almost one-third of the city's housing stock in a campaign against 'slum houses'.

Maisie grudgingly understood the need for the economies and the only one she seriously resented was the cardboard inner soles in her shoes. It seldom rained enough to cause water to seep in through the holes, but it was more than the trifle it should have been. The cardboard was a constant reminder her father was no longer with them. Jack had skilfully re-soled the family's shoes on a big old iron last in the backyard and, because he was so willing to help friends and neighbours, it became a regular activity, another they had enjoyed together. Perhaps in preparation for his death, he had gently trained her for the job and she'd become quite competent at it. Now, though, Rose wouldn't trust her with pieces of expensive leather. Maisie felt the cardboard not only screamed out her father was dead, but also that she had let him down.

Rose's refusal to buy the leather wasn't about being deliberately mean-spirited. She had spent a lifetime in forced frugality and was relentless in teaching her children not to be wasteful with food, clothes, toys or time. (This also applied to grandchildren – I remember my mortification when severely reprimanded as a young child for adding both butter *and* jam to a piece of toast at my grandmother's table.)

So, while there was not often money for new clothes, and never for extravagance, the bereft little family managed to get by quite well on Jack's 'living wage' workers compensation payments and NSW Child Endowment payments, now topped up by a partial NSW Widow's Pension. However, in the second half of the year, federal changes designed to bring relief to struggling families in a war-strapped economy brought instead additional financial pressures for the Schusters.

To increase its power to coordinate the war effort, the Federal Government in April 1941 rushed through a bill to take full control of (and substantially increase) income taxation, which had hitherto been partly the preserve of state governments. The increased revenue enabled a greater role in social security, so a national Child Endowment scheme was introduced concurrently. The payments of five shillings per week for second and subsequent children under the age of 16 were set to begin from 1 July, with the NSW State Child Endowment payment (in place since 1927) to cease on the same day. The endowment was not means-tested, nor taxed, and was paid directly to mothers to care for their children, regardless of the economic circumstances (or predilections) of fathers. The change to a national endowment scheme should have made no difference to the Schusters, but at the end of July when Rose called at the bank to withdraw her first payment for the preceding four weeks, she found the NSW payment had indeed stopped, but the federal payment had failed to start.

Maisie had been taken along for the visit to Argent Street so she could help to carry the shopping and was not happy about it. The boys were at home playing footy with Tommy and Jimmy and that's where she wanted to be, too. Her petulance turned to embarrassment as her mother castigated the poor man behind the metal grille in the bank when, try as he might, he could find no injection of funds to update in Rose's bank book. At his suggestion, Rose and Maisie headed across the road to the post office.

Recipients had an option to receive the endowment monthly in cash at either the bank or the post office rather than have the payment directly credited to their bank account each quarter. The teller suggested maybe there had been an error and Rose's payment might be waiting for her there. Maisie thought the man just wanted to get rid of her mother from the bank. She cringed at the curious looks from other customers as Rose intermittently raised her voice or let fly with one or another of her best expletives.

As they crossed Chloride Street, she stubbornly refused to hold Rose's hand and then stood back from her a little when Rose waited in the post office queue for attention. As the intensity of the conversation between Rose and the post office assistant heightened, the distance between mother and child progressively lengthened. By the time a manager was called to deal with the incensed little woman who loudly insisted she needed the endowment to feed her 'poor little children', Maisie was well hidden behind one of two wooden writing pillars in the centre of the room.

'You're best to take it up with the Town Hall, madam,' she heard the manager say.

'I'll bloody well do that – and be right back here for my bloody money!' Rose retorted.

On hearing they were about to visit the Town Hall, Maisie sprang from her hiding place to take her mother's hand. The Town Hall was her favourite building!

Most Broken Hill people were justifiably proud of this centrepiece to the main street. It was constructed in 1891 from garnet-encrusted sandstone blocks quarried from the Block 14 mining lease, and its ornate filigree work, rows of arched windows and distinctive orator's balcony above the front entrance were exceptional in an outback mining town. A tall watchtower on the side adjacent to the post office was used for fire spotting and the fire service was located at the rear of the building, so it was certainly a place of some prestige. The importance of the building wasn't lost on Maisie but, for her, its true beauty lay in the gargoyles that adorned it.

They were part of a delicious memory of sitting on her father's shoulders as he stood among a crowd being addressed by a man in a small group on the first floor balcony. She didn't remember the purpose of the gathering, but savoured the pleasure of being hoisted high on Jack's shoulders, with his hat on her head, and his subsequent kind ministrations when she became frightened of the gargoyles. Small effigies at the base of the watchtower were ugly, although not alarmingly so, but a larger winged dragon on the side of the building had terrified her.

The grotesque face looked down, with sharp teeth and a protruding tongue bared in a wide-open mouth. He was poised to pounce, with extended wings attached to a thorny body and webbed feet with long talons seemingly ready to push off from the wall and fly down on her. Maisie's distress at the gargoyle had caused her father to lift her down gently and lead her to the yard in front of the police station so she could see the sculpture more clearly.

'There is nothing to be frightened of, *kleine Tochter*. That ugly little fellow has a very special purpose. He protects this whole building,' he had told her, crouching so he could look directly into her tear-stained face.

'From the devil?' Maisie had hiccupped. She'd thought that would be a little peculiar since, to her, the gargoyle looked exactly as she thought the devil might look, including the long spiked tail which curled around to a point.

'No, from the rain.'

The Town Hall was constructed in 1891. Most of the building was demolished in the 1970s, but the façade has been retained and preserved.

This had seemed even more peculiar, since rain was a rare but always welcome visitor. She had listened intently as her father carefully explained that gargoyles were designed to capture water run-off from the rooves of masonry buildings and direct it out through a spout in the elongated face so the rain fell away from the building rather than coursing down its sides and eroding the mortar between the blocks. Broken Hill's average annual rainfall of just 8 inches meant there were few gargoyles on local buildings, so the Town Hall always seemed a little special to Maisie, quite apart from its strong association with the lovely memory of her father. Her love of gargoyles would remain throughout her life and, in her eighties, one of her prized possessions was an ugly concrete gargoyle attached to her back fence which directed water into a bird bath below.

Now, as Maisie crossed the small space between the post office and the Town Hall with her mother, she dallied for a moment to admire the gargoyles and revisit that scene with her father. She was enjoying the conversation with him until her hesitation brought an extra hard yank from Rose, and then he was gone again. This time she didn't mind so much. Coupled with her excitement to at last see beyond the magnificent iron gates that barred the entrance to the Town Hall was more than a little admiration for her mother for being important enough to take her through them.

Once inside, she marvelled at the intricate pattern of the tiled floor, the resplendent staircase curling up to secrets above and the rows of beautiful wooden doors which seemed to disappear into infinity down a long hallway. She was devastated when told to wait on a chair while her mother went through one of those doors to consult with the taxation officer, but consoled herself watching a receptionist pulling and pushing corded plugs in a switchboard.

When Rose emerged, her face was red and she strode determinedly toward the front door, without pausing to see whether Maisie fell into step behind her. Her destination was the police station next door. Here Rose initially used surprisingly measured tones to explain her predicament to Constables Munro and Ford. The omission of the Child Endowment payment, she had been told, was due to her enemy alien registration and application for naturalisation.

The federal scheme specifically addressed the issue of payment for children of enemy aliens. Under general rules, both the mother and child had to have been resident in Australia for twelve months previous, but children of enemy aliens were excluded from eligibility unless they were born in Australia or the mother was a British subject. Maisie and Maxie should have been eligible for the payment regardless of Rose's status, since they were both born in Broken Hill, but somehow her registration as an enemy alien (which meant she was certainly not British) had seen her excluded. Her unresolved naturalisation left her in 'no man's land'. The taxation officer agreed it was a mistake, but insisted the quickest way to resolve the issue was for Rose to complete her naturalisation.

'So can you bloody help me get this done or not?' Rose demanded of Constable Munro.

Rose's tale had both policemen looking a little uncomfortable. Even Constable Munro had come to admire the spirit in the tough little widow and, after Rose's patriotic purchase at Martin's, he had followed through on his promise to look in to the matter.

He gave Rose a copy of a letter.

Box 45a, G.P.O., SYDNEY

3 May, 1941.
Ib. Subsection,
I.S.G.S.
4th Military District,
Keswick Barracks,
KESWICK, S.A.
Mrs. Rosina Mary SCHUSTER

The abovenamed who was Australian born and who resides at 25 South Street, Broken Hill, is an applicant to make a Declaration under Section 18A of the Nationality Act. She is aged 50 and is the widow of a German National. She is favourably reported upon in Eastern Command and advice is requested as to whether there is any objection in 4th Military District to her making the Declaration.

G.H.V. NEWMAN, Lieut.,
Intelligence Section (Ib.),
EASTERN COMMAND

'I've only been able to establish that Keswick has no objections, Mrs Schuster. They replied a week after this letter. I can tell you nothing else.'

Maisie was stunned to see tears well in her mother's eyes. Rose rarely cried. Certainly she never trembled as she did now.

'But this is nearly three months old,' Rose whispered. 'Why has there been nothing else? It's not just a matter of pride now. It's money – money we need. In two weeks' time it'll be a year since my husband died. What did I do? What did I ever do but stand by him when you hounded him? He was a good man.'

All colour had drained from Rose's face and Maisie feared the quietness in her voice more than she had ever feared her yelling. She saw her mother's hands twisting in an imaginary apron and stepped up to the tall counter.

'Get my mother a chair,' she told Constable Munro. When he obeyed, she moved to stand next to Rose and placed a little hand on her mother's shoulder so she might feel the comfort Maisie had always drawn from Jack's touch.

'And some water, too.'

No more was to come from the police station visit that day, than this new connection between mother and daughter – and the constables' consensus that the mother's spirit was well present in the daughter.

It would take some months before the Child Endowment error was rectified and Rose by that time had run up sizeable accounts at both the butcher and the grocer. She felt shame at this, as did Maisie when she did the messages and had to ask the shop owners to 'put it on the tick'. Ten shillings a week was not something the Schusters could manage easily without.

Rose had been a little broken that day in the Central Police Station and cracks opened by unfairness are always the hardest to mend. Sometimes they are simply glazed over. Rose's glaze was to ensure she and her children were kept busy.

Both the Housewives' Association and Lutheran Church served their purpose in keeping Rose active during the first crushing year without Jack. Perhaps she simply chose to put her grief aside until she felt better able to take it out and look at it. The children, though, had no choice. Maisie sometimes felt like a dry leaf in the wind, buffeted this way and that by her mother. She felt so shrivelled by the loss of her father that she no longer sought control over how she spent time without him. As the year unfolded she continued to work diligently at school so that Sister Drummond's folder had a satisfying bulge, but she had no interest in the extracurricular activities her mother planned – yet not enough soul to battle against them.

Apart from serving and entertaining when Rose hosted Housewives' meetings and being involved in church and Sunday school activities, there was also the Rechabites

Rose had joined Broken Hill's Independent Order of Rechabites during her first marriage to Thomas Vale. Tommy and Jimmy had also been enrolled in the temperance lodge, with the hope the required abstinence pledge would prevent them following in their alcoholic father's footsteps. The boys' participation had lasted only as long as Rose's tenuous control of them, but she had been determined to try again with Jack's children and each had been enrolled promptly on their fifth birthday. Their participation up to the point of Jack's death had been spasmodic. When he was well, being at home with him was far more entertaining than the parlour games of the Rechabite gatherings, and when he was ill, they had no heart for it. Now Jackie, Maisie and Maxie were turned out for the fortnightly meetings regardless of their inclination.

The temperance movement was strong in Broken Hill – unsurprising given the fabled 'hotel on every corner'. The miners' propensity at the end of a long shift to down beer as fast as their elbows would allow meant wives were ready members and enrolled their children so they could be indoctrinated from an early age in the evils of drink. All the temperance lodges required members to sign a pledge to abstain from any form of alcohol and also to spread the word about the dangers of alcohol consumption. But these organisations also acted as 'friendly societies' – providing financial assistance in times of illness or unemployment, assisting families with funeral costs, and helping widows and orphans with welfare support. Many of the men of Broken Hill, who could foresee an early death from the mines or the booze, were therefore willing members too.

The International Order of Good Templars, the Barrier Temperance Alliance and the Sons and Daughters of Temperance all enjoyed good membership, but the Rechabites were pervasive, with seven 'tents'. Branches were known as tents in deference to the founder from biblical times, Jehonadab (a descendant of Rechab), who not only forbade his followers to drink wine, but also to live in cities where they might be exposed to debauchery, so they lived a nomadic lifestyle in tents criss-crossing deserts. Broken Hill's Rechabite tents were in every corner of the city – Star of the Barrier in the central area and at Railway Town; a centrally located Sturt tent; Hope of Picton in the west; Samuel Bonsall and Willyama Lily in the north; and the Star of Alma in the south.

Apart from the strictly teetotal organisations, there was also a strange assortment of other friendly societies in the town – 'the Lodges' that so frustrated Pastor Zweck – including the Grand United Order of Oddfellows, the United Ancient Order of Druids, the Manchester Unity Order of Oddfellows, the Independent Order of Oddfellows, and the Masonic Benevolent Fund of the Broken Hill Freemason's Company. And then there was a range of religious organisations – including the Protestant Alliance Friendly Society of Australasia, the Catholic Young Men's Society, and the Hibernian Australasian Catholic Benefit Society. There were so many that a United Friendly Societies' Council was formed to ensure everyone was working toward a common good for Broken Hill and its mining-dependent population.

Most of the organisations began as strictly fraternal societies, but gradually and reluctantly admitted women and children to various levels or in separate lodges. The secrecy and rituals of each society were closely guarded and each had a rich and colourful culture, with office bearers holding titles such as 'Grand Master', 'Right Worshipful Grand Master', and 'High Chief Ruler'.

The grieving Schuster children may well have been turned out of their home to reluctantly reconnect with their Rechabite tent after

Jack's death but, once there, even grief could not dampen their inherent competitive spirit. Increasingly it was one or another of the Schuster names (sometimes all three) that popped up in the daily newspapers for having won a sporting competition or parlour game and (in the case of Jackie and Maisie) having led a particular meeting or study group. Jackie was quickly appointed chief ruler of the Rechabites' Alma juvenile tent and later Maisie would attain the same leadership role for the girls' tent.

In March, the high chief ruler had announced there was to be a Champion of Champions competition across all Rechabite divisions in Broken Hill, with each tent to select their representative champion for the major competition. As the first anniversary of Jack's death approached, the children were distracted by the task of ensuring the Alma Rechabites were represented by Schusters.

Each fortnight's gathering since the March announcement had been dedicated to internal competitions to decide the respective skills of tent members. The specific format of the championship was to be kept secret until the event, so good all-round skills and an overriding competitive drive were required. The junior division was set at 11 and under, so Jackie was excluded, but he coached Maisie and Maxie during practice at home – skipping, cotton winding, bottle-fishing, quoits, and various forms of darts. In early August it was announced 10-year-old Maisie would represent the girls and eight-year-old Maxie would represent the boys.

A triumphant Maisie ran all the way home after the gathering to break the news to her mother, careless about the fact it was Maxie's news too and he was unable to keep up with her. The next morning, to atone for this, she added a fictitious couple of sentences when reading aloud the *Barrier Daily Truth* article that announced the competing champions, pretending there was special mention of Maxie's extra young age.

This new energy in the Schuster household gradually dispersed over the next days as the little family prepared for the first anniversary of Jack's death. On Thursday 14 August 1941, Maisie again read from the newspaper to her mother and brothers:

Barrier Daily Truth Thursday 14 August 1941

SCHUSTER – In loving memory of our dear Husband and Father, Reinhold (Jack), who passed away on August 14, 1940.

You are not forgotten, dear Dad, for true love never dies;
For we who loved truly know,
How much we lost a year ago.
If all the world was ours to give,
We'd give it, yes, and more,
To see our darling father's face,
Come smiling through our door.
— Inserted by his loving wife (Rose) and children Jack, Maisie, Max.

SCHUSTER – In loving memory of our dear Step-father, who passed away on August 14, 1940.
A loving father, true and kind,
His equal on earth you'll never find.
For each of us he did his best,
May God grant him eternal rest.
—Inserted by his loving step-children (Dulcie, Eve, Tops, Tom and Jim).

Later they all went to the cemetery – not just Rose and the children, but also Eve (who cycled 340 miles from Murray Bridge for the occasion), Topsy, Tommy, Jimmy and Dulcie. The Vales may well have been Jack's step-children (most quite grown by the time he married Rose) but they had loved him dearly. They stood in a sombre group thinking of Jack and all that had happened in the twelve months since he had left them. For each, there was a different story, but common among them was the overwhelming sense of loss. Maisie was dry-eyed during the graveside visit, which surprised them all.

'That's because he's not here,' she told Dulcie. 'Dad's at home in the backyard. I talk to him all the time.'

Dulcie discussed the issue with Rose when they all returned to the house. Jack's name had not been added to the wooden cross at the head of the grave, which still bore only the inscription:

LILLIAN SCHUSTER
1893–1920
26 years

REINHOLD WALTER
1928
8 months

Visits to Jack's grave were never as regular as either Maisie or Rose would have liked. With no car (except Jack's old broken down utility), they had to rely on family or friends to drive them. There were few with operating vehicles and very restricted access to petrol. The cemetery could be reached by first catching a bus from the South into Argent Street, then another to Railway Town, followed by a significant walk. Once, in the first few months after her father's death, Maisie had ridden the boys' bicycle as far as the cemetery gates, but failed to muster sufficient courage to go in. Her father's grave was at the back of the cemetery and reaching it meant walking past too many unattended graves with sunken dirt tops (some seemingly in the shape of a body) so that Maisie found the experience confronting even when accompanied by her mother and too daunting to tackle alone.

But it's not likely Rose hadn't updated the cross just because it was difficult. Either of the boys would have done it for her. It may have been because it was his first wife Lillian's grave that she didn't want to add his name, although she had been prepared for her own son with Jack to be buried there with her. Perhaps, again, it was because Rose found it was easier to cope with Jack's death by pretending it didn't happen. There was no longer any pretence for Maisie though. While the rest of the family sat in the kitchen that night and discussed Maisie's strange comment at the graveside, she went into the backyard to talk with her father – and found he was no longer there.

On 4 September, three weeks after the first anniversary of Jack's death and one day after the second anniversary of the commencement of World War II, Maisie became Broken Hill's Rechabite Junior Girl Champion of Champions. She had won the skipping, hand darts and deck quoits. Maxie was disappointed he couldn't match his big sister but, given he was three years younger than many competitors, had to be content with the fact he had been good enough to compete.

Maisie was proud of her win and even prouder when she overheard her mother boasting to friends. There were almost 400 junior Rechabites in Broken Hill at the time, so to have a daughter Champion of Champions brought some prestige. Topsy, Tommy, Jimmy and Dulcie were among the hundreds of people there to enthusiastically cheer on the competitors and Maisie loved that they came, but keenly felt one person missing. The next week she overcame her fear of the cemetery and rode the boys' bike to leave her little trophy with her father. It had a beautiful maroon solid base with a silver goblet on top engraved with:

Independent Order of Rechabites
Broken Hill
Juvenile Girls
Champion of Champions
Maisie Schuster 10 years

When she went next, the trophy was gone.

Chapter 10
The war at home
September 1941

That the Schuster family should be so fiercely focused on battling for parlour game supremacy at a time when thousands of lives were being lost daily in battles for European supremacy is not as curious as it may appear. Only one-quarter of the eventual 4000 Broken Hill men and women who served in armed forces and paramilitary organisations during World War II had left the city at this point (from a population of 28,000) and there were no members of the family off fighting. They were yet to learn the fate of acquaintances who would never return. So, in many ways, the war existed on the radio and in the newspapers rather than in their reality.

Maisie still deliberately skimmed over articles (just as she had when reading to Jack on the side veranda) because they proclaimed German atrocities or victoriously announced German deaths. There were likely uncles and cousins among these casualties. Jack had been unable to resolve the emotional turmoil of his beloved adopted country and homeland killing each other during all the years of World War I and the months he was alive at the beginning of World War II. The task was impossible for an 11-year-old. So Maisie refused to undertake it.

Rose was so angry at her enemy alien status, so frustrated by the naturalisation process, and so fearful of the harassment of German and Italian friends, she found it easier to hate the Australian authorities than the enemy overseas. She had loved one of them – her kind and gentle German – and she believed there were many more like him being killed by Australian bullets.

During this pre-Holocaust period there was less victimisation of the children at school, largely due to their ubiquitous success in all manner of sports – athletics, swimming, basketball, netball, soccer, cricket and boxing – but they felt the prejudice keenly through what was happening to their mother and what they saw happening in the families of their friends. Several of Jack's friends had been sent for internment early in the war and his remaining months alive had been spent in guilt that he escaped it. The torment of those not yet 'captured' was continual. There were repeated raids on family homes; confiscation of trivial items such as family photos with a German inscription on the back; cars parked outside homes so that friendly visitors were nervous to enter; and 'interviews' that constantly sought denunciations of any alliance to Germany and proclamations of allegiance to the King. The most difficult aspect of the interrogations was when people were asked to give up the names of German people they knew. This made innocent people feel traitorous if they provided them and fearful if they did not. So, the Schusters' war had the Australian Government as opponents.

This explains why Rose was so apprehensive about the delay of her naturalisation. She knew it took very little for hysteria to overcome common sense – and proof of treason was not required. In correspondence from the 4th Military District to the inspector of police in Broken Hill regarding one of Jack's friends, Major R.H. Perkins wrote:

> Where it is difficult or inadvisable to produce any witness or document, strict legal proof will not be insisted upon, but heresay [sic] and other secondary evidence will be accepted.

More than a hundred Broken Hill homes housing enemy aliens were raided by police during the early years of World War II. Based on surnames alone, it appears Italians fared less well than Germans and accounted for more than three-quarters of the investigations now stored in the National Archives. This may well be due to a propensity for miners to target southern Europeans rather than northern when decrying their jobs were being taken by foreigners, but is more likely to be due to Italians forming a larger proportion of the city's population than Germans.

Discrimination at the mine face heightened in direct correlation to unemployment numbers. Immediately after Italy entered the war in June 1940, 46 Italian men working at the North Mine were sacked from coveted and lucrative contract positions they had earned through long-term hard work. These roles were given to other North Mine employees, with their respectively vacated trucker and mullocker roles passed on to British subjects made redundant from a depleted Central Mine. There was concession for enemy aliens who had been naturalised, but this only meant the bigotry was less blatant and other reasons were found for turning them out of underground work. They were accepted as shopkeepers and town labourers, but wartime austerity measures meant these jobs provided limited income.

That a lead-mining town should be struggling to provide work for its labour force during a time of world war may seem odd, but Australian manufacturing was significantly reduced due to a sorely depleted national workforce. Thousands of young men now spent their days in battlefields rather than factories. All overseas contracts for the sale of lead had been suspended at the outbreak of war and, while a newly negotiated contract with the British Government to supply a fixed tonnage of lead meant jobs for 3680 local men, more than 2000 were out of work. The mining companies 'topped up' the wages of locals joining the forces, but this wasn't always an option. Mining was a designated 'protected industry' so permission from federal manpower authorities was required before mine employees could enlist. It was usually given because there were so many men waiting in the city to step into vacated jobs.

Broken Hill tried to wage its own war at home to address its unique unemployment issue. In January 1941 first steps were taken to build an annexe to the Technical College, specifically to train young men in trades useful to both the mining industry and the war effort. More than 100 subsequently undertook munitions production training at the annexe under an unemployed youth training scheme and were shipped off to work in munitions factories across the country, but mostly in Adelaide (with the NSW Government providing them the cost of train fare as a loan to be repaid in instalments once they had started work).

Meanwhile unions agitated for construction of Broken Hill's own munitions factory to absorb the unemployed miners. A June announcement by the Federal Government confirming its approval excited the city. The mining companies contributed £25,000 of the £100,000 required to construct the factory and 60 lathes were manufactured locally in mine workshops ready for the work. Talk was constant about the training to be offered through the Technical College and the promised basic wage to be paid even during this training period. Men battered by the daily struggle of providing for their family impatiently awaited their return to work, but ultimately the Broken Hill Munitions Annexe would not open until November 1942 – and then employ mostly women.

Petrol and tobacco rationing added to the stresses. The town boundaries were easily covered by 'Shanks' pony' (on foot) and bicycles, but petrol was required to access the bush on the perimeter of town to trap rabbits and shoot kangaroos to put extra food on the table. Long queues formed at the police station to get the required consumer licence and then at the post office on monthly allocation days for coupons. Many in the city had long since relinquished vehicles, but petrol coupons were pooled for bush trips and, on the occasion someone needed to travel to Adelaide, a hat would be passed around to gather sufficient two-gallon tickets, which couldn't be hoarded because they bore an expiry date.

The men were less generous with tobacco rationing. This was unregulated and many complained they were being treated unfairly by shopkeepers who might allocate four to six ounces a week for regular customers who spent other money in their stores, two ounces to regular tobacco customers who spent less on anything else, and found they had 'run out' for others. Some British-born miners lamented they were being discriminated against as foreigners in this regard.

However, Broken Hill was not a town to focus on doom and gloom if there were highlights to be had. The city celebrated as the first patients moved into the new hospital on 2 September (days before Maisie's big Rechabite win) and again three weeks later when it was officially opened by the Governor of NSW, Lord Wakehurst, who visited with Lady Wakehurst. From 12 September thousands turned out for the Silver City Show held over three days at the Western Oval. The Schuster children weren't among them.

The show had always been the highlight of the year for Jackie, Maisie and Maxie, even superseding Christmas. They hadn't gone the previous year because it had come too close upon their father's death. Their collective memories were too raw of walking home with Jack weighed down by the various prizes (donated by local businesses) for his entries in the fruit and vegetable section. Maisie thought this year she would just avoid that pavilion and excitedly looked forward to the dog competition and the wood-chopping, although this too was inextricably linked to her father because of their wood chopping ventures into the bush together. She had always been undecided about the buckjumping and the 'horses over hurdles' events, fearing the beautiful animals would be harmed, but she had fond memories of jumping up in unison with Jack to cheer together for a horse when its leaping and plunging dislodged a rider and cringing into his chest if a horse fell at a hurdle.

Maisie was stunned to learn they were to stay away again.

'But we have to go, Mum. I have an essay in the competition, and it's really, really good! There won't be another one like it.'

Tears and tantrums had little effect on Rose. She was determined to abide by her parole – having decided church, Housewives'

Association meetings and Rechabite gatherings were *not* 'places of public amusement'. Maisie tried a different approach.

'Jackie's sure to win in the cycling events – both the one lap and the half-mile! And this year it's at night. All the arena and the track will be lit by electricity for the first time. Don't you want to see him win?'

Seeing her mother unmoved, she tried again. 'And there's cooking this year. You would win that for sure!'

Nothing would change Rose's mind, not even the other new entry to the program – a thrift section. This was a clear acknowledgement of austerity measures, offering 'salvage-minded women' cash prizes for the best article made from a sugar bag or an old felt hat; the best darning on socks or stockings; and the 'most satisfactory home-made soap'. One division in the section called for the best fruit cake made without eggs, butter or milk and Rose wondered whether she might send an entry in with someone else, until she learned the recipe needed to accompany the cake. *Her* recipe would be disclosed to no one. Instead she sent in entries in Topsy's name for the soldier's section, which awarded bags of wool for the best entries in knitted socks, mufflers, gloves, scarves and sleeveless pullovers. Tommy and Jimmy offered to take the kids to the show, which just brought laughter from Rose, but she also refused offers from Topsy and Dulcie. The show was renowned for drunken brawls and she feared beer-fuelled hostility to her youngest offspring.

'This is one time you can thank your lucky stars you had the father you had, rather than theirs. Those kids are German. They're not going anywhere without me where people have got bloody drink in.'

Maisie *did* win the essay competition that year. The Broken Hill Ice and Produce Company donated a cash prize of five shillings for the best essay from a child under 12 on the topic of 'The Best Use of Apples'. Maisie's entry gave a detailed description of how to turn apples into cider, meticulously recounting her father's stories of how he had done just such a thing on the Schuster farm in Saxony. The judges commended the entry for its uniqueness. Maisie wasn't sure whether she was more delighted with this win, or that her mother hadn't even received a special mention for her knitting.

The 1941 Silver City Show attracted record entries and record crowds and raised record profits. Earlier wartime shows had donated profits to the Fighting Forces Comfort Fund and the Red Cross Prisoner of War Fund, but the 1941 profit of £380 was directed immediately into the Barrier District Spitfire Fund. This had been launched by the local police force in March, led by Inspector Homann, with an initial contribution of more than £85 from policemen's pockets. The city was intent on purchasing one or more planes for the war effort and there had been a succession of fundraising functions, including a two shilling Art Union, with a £275 Ford 'eight horsepower touring car' as the drawcard prize.

Maisie sulked all weekend about missing the show, although much of her disappointment was tied up in the thought she could have had a whole day out with Topsy and Dulcie without her mother. On the Monday, however, her spirits lifted when she was presented at a school assembly with a first prize certificate for her essay and a promissory note for five shillings.

Maisie was first out the gate at home time. It wasn't in excitement at showing the certificate and voucher to Rose, but because she wanted to write a little note to attach to the certificate to record that it had been for essay writing and for finding something different to do with a healthy apple. She thought Sister Drummond would be impressed at that, but she also knew there would be little time for the annotation before she had to peel the vegetables for tea. Maxie was dawdling as usual. After several calls of 'Hurry UP Maxie!' she decided to leave him to it and go on ahead. When she reached the corner, though, she hesitated. Would she leave him to cross the road on his own? She turned to look and saw him standing stock-still mesmerised by the sky. She lifted her eyes and for just a moment wondered at a beautiful and deepening red glow in the north. It took only an instant to realise.

'Maxie! Dust storm!' she yelled and started to go back for him, but it was too late.

Thunderous sound washed over her first, then horror as she saw the rolling wall of red dirt block out first the sky, then the distant houses, then the school, then her little brother. 'Maxie!' she yelled again, but the wind took her voice as swiftly as it snatched the papers in her hand and the satchel from her back. It threatened to take her, too, before she clung to the cyclone wire of the fence.

The sand stung her face and body. She couldn't breathe. She needed to cough. But she needed to inhale to do that and there was no air to suck in, only dirt. She tried to force open her eyes to look again for Maxie, but there was no point. It would just let the dirt in, and there was nothing to see anyway. It was as dark as night. She was choking. Her face hurt. Her legs stung from the sharp gritty sand of the skimp dumps the rolling dust had collected on its way. Her scalp throbbed as it fought to keep the long hair the wind wanted to take with it. Then it stopped. The vicious wind biting them suddenly lost its teeth and rolled on, but the next stage would last for hours.

There was still scant visibility because the air was thick with red dust, but it just hung there rather than whipping against her. A newspaper came out of the gloom and hugged her legs and in the distance now she could see car lights. But she still couldn't see Maxie. Then she heard his howls.

By making her way gingerly along the wire fence she found he was really only a few feet from her. She had made good ground during her initial run to get him. He was sitting on the ground, the pudgy fingers on both hands wrapped so tight around the wires of the fence the whiteness was apparent despite the covering of dirt. Even though the wind had passed, he wouldn't let go.

Maisie prised his fingers off one by one, but by the time she worked on fingers two or three down, the others had curled back around again. She gave up and just sat behind him cuddling his back. Finally his rigid little body relaxed and when he looked over his shoulder at her, his face broke into its usual broad gap-toothed grin. Maisie knew then her face must look as funny as his, with white rivulets from tears washing down an otherwise thick coated red-brown face.

Both children dawdled on the way home after that. Maisie now had nothing to put in her folder for Sister Drummond and she knew the foul mood her mother would be in – and the work that was to come. Rose, like most Broken Hill women, would be in a decidedly grumpy mood for days after a big dust storm. It meant walls and floors had to be swept and washed, curtains taken down and shaken, carpets dragged to the line and whacked, and the outer covers of beds washed out-of-turn, so it upset the routine of the housework which had regular jobs for each weekday.

But ruination of the weekly housekeeping schedule wasn't the only damage this particular dust storm left behind. The region was in the midst of a severe drought that would see the River Darling stop flowing within three months. This drought would ultimately last for six years, so that the period 1940 to 1945 saw Broken Hill average only 5.5 inches of rain per year. Albert and Margaret Morris's semi-mature regeneration area could do little to protect the town under these conditions.

The 22 September 1941 dust storm left laneways cluttered with smashed outhouses; sheets of iron torn from rooves and fences scattered about the streets; big canvas blinds used for cooling verandas ripped to shreds; and the mining companies' huge expensive surface machinery clogged and inoperable. Trains in and out of the city were delayed while tracks were cleared of mounds of dirt and the Royal Flying Doctor Service planes were grounded. More alarming for those on outer properties, the RFDS base communications were down too – the aerial was out and took some days to repair.

The city's doctors, however, were happy. They believed the occasional monumental dust storm was good for 'dispersing germs', thereby stopping the spread of diseases – good timing with so much diphtheria in the town. But some must have had concern for the miners and former miners suffering from pneumoconiosis from their work underground.

Chapter 11

Expulsion, extermination and exodus

September–December 1941

Maisie hesitated before opening the back door. She wasn't sure what she dreaded most – the furious work she knew she would be dragged into to rid the house of dust that would be in every nook and cranny; her mother's reaction to her filthy uniform on a Monday night; telling Rose about the lost five shillings; or Maxie telling Rose she had left him behind to deal with the dust storm alone. That all changed when she found her mother, not busy with the broom, but sitting slumped at the kitchen table with a cup of tea in front of her and obvious signs of spent tears on her face.

'We're all right, Mum ...' Maisie began.

'No, I don't think we are, love'. The uncommon endearment filled Maisie with dread. 'They've been at Uncle Herman again. And this time they think they've got him.'

This had even the perpetually overcharged Maxie rooted to the ground. Herman Schipanski had been a close friend of Jack's and the three Schuster children were so close with Herman's sons Harold and Ron they were considered cousins. Both Maisie and Maxie began to cry again. They couldn't bear the thought of Uncle Herman being sent to gaol. Herman was one of the last to remain in Broken Hill of a circle of friends that had been targeted for internment since the beginning of the war.

Wilhelm Bertram, Andrew Munster and Frederick Schroeder were arrested on 14 September 1939, just four days after the police raided the Schuster home. Their crime was to have 'associated' with August Menz who was a travelling salesman attached to the

Irish Linen Spinning and Weaving Company in Adelaide. August Menz was accused of 'distributing badges and other pro-Nazi propaganda' along with his wares and having tried to draft Robert Lohmann into 'German activities' when he heard Lohmann had applied to be naturalised. Menz would ultimately spend more than five years in detention – at the Gladstone Gaol in the South Australian Flinders Ranges, in an unlined tin hut at Tatura in Victoria and at the Broadmeadows Internment Camp attached to the Australian Army during an unsuccessful appeal against his internment. He would not be released until December 1944.

There was little authorities could claim against Wilhelm Bertram, Andrew Munster and Frederick Schroeder, other than they knew Menz, regularly met other German people at the house of Herman Schipanski, and were friends with Harry Taylor and Jack Schuster, both of whom had been found to have German literature in their possession. This was enough to mark their papers 'strong Nazi sympathizers' and pack them off to Gladstone with Menz.

The nonsense of the investigation and internment process was exposed two months later when Wilhelm, who had in fact fought in the German army during World War I, was released on parole back to Broken Hill. Both Andrew and Frederick were held a little longer, but released three weeks later on 7 December 1939. It was the irrationality of the whole process that was so frightening to people like Rose. They *knew* innocent people were being incarcerated for no real reason – and without even any pretence at requiring proof.

On the day of the dust storm, Wilhelm's wife Ellemaria Bertram had been to visit Rose to return a letter she had been translating. Mrs Bertram was the 'go-to' in the German community for translations, particularly for documents written in High German. The letter proved to be inconsequential, but the news she brought with her was not.

'They're pinning the aerodrome fire on Uncle Herman! And Max Bohm too!'

Rose was incredulous.

'Mrs Bertram says it's not the local coppers – it's come from Sydney. She says they want all Germans and Italians off the Zinc whether they've been naturalised or not. And they want all Germans out of town that might be friends with men on the Zinc. Mrs Bertram says it's got to do with stuff they're making for the munitions factory. She says they've been told to get Herman even if they can't find proof or witnesses prepared to speak against him. She says they reckon they *have* got evidence about the fire … He's in trouble for still being friends with Mr Bertram and the others – even though they got sent back here. Mrs Bertram says Uncle Herman *refused* to sign a statement. And that Mr Menz is in it again too. Mrs Bertram says …'

At this point Rose stopped. She was breathless from trying to get as much of the news out as quickly as possible, but she also had suddenly realised she was unloading to an 11-year-old girl who probably didn't understand and certainly couldn't help.

'Let's go down and see them, Mum. C'mon. The dust will wait until tomorrow and I'll stay home to help you.'

Maisie was stunned when Rose agreed. Never had she known her mother not to start work immediately after a dust storm, and she would never see it again. They left a note for Jackie and set off with Maxie in the still-thick air to walk the two miles to Knox Street.

Herman Schipanski at this time was 65 years old. He'd lived in Australia for 34 years, the last 31 in Broken Hill, and had taken steps to become a naturalised British subject just a few weeks into World War I though authorities now were claiming they could find no record of it. His wife Mary had been born in Adelaide of German parents and together they had produced nine Australian-born children. The five oldest were adults and three had Australian-born spouses. But it appeared none of this would save him from accusations of being pro-Nazi, even though he had told his interrogators he thought Hitler should have his throat cut.

However, just as Mrs Bertram said, he stubbornly refused to sign a statement about his interview.

'It took me ten years to live down information given to you in the last war,' he told the constables.

The only 'evidence' police could claim in regard to the aerodrome fire was that Herman and his large family lived on the last street of South Broken Hill 'in a very lonely part of the district' and that he regularly had German people in his home. Even this had become less regular and less obvious since the internment of his friends.

Maisie spent the trek to the Schipanskis' looking for her certificate and promissory note among the papers strewn about. Maxie had been reluctant to come at first, but had settled when he found the fierce wind had passed through the southern end of town and was now only a spectacular rolling wall in the distance. By the time Rose and Maisie reached the corner of Central and Knox streets, he was half a block ahead.

Mother and daughter froze when they turned into the street. Up ahead, just a couple of houses before 267, sat a big black car containing two men in hats and coats on a hot day. Maisie recalled her father's lesson that 'you can only be brave if you are first afraid', but she thought she had already been brave enough – and afraid enough – for one day. Without any discussion between the two, Rose ducked back into Central Street while Maisie ran on to catch Maxie and drag her confused young brother back to the corner, loudly admonishing him for running away.

That terrible day would remain with Maisie all her life. While hot and windy August days drowned her in the sorrow of her father's funeral, dusty September days brought the taste of dirt in her mouth and the shame of having put her fear before her friend. She knew her father would have continued on to visit Herman if he had been with them that day – and probably stopped to pass the time of day with the policemen on his way. She so wanted to live her life according to her father's moral compass, but it was hard for an

11-year-old. She wasn't to know it then, but there would be many times throughout her life where she asked herself 'What would Dad have done?' to guide her through a challenge – and more than once she would feel incapable of fulfilling the response.

There was another enduring sadness from that day – Rose never asked about the essay certificate or the five shillings. That the win was so unimportant to her mother was far worse than the hiding she had expected from losing the rewards.

Ultimately, Herman Schipanski wasn't interned, although papers clearly and determinedly calling for it remained. Max Bohm was. He was arrested in March 1942 and spent two years at the Loveday Internment Camp at Barmera in South Australia.

Three weeks after the dust storm, on 14 October 1941, Maisie came home from school to find her mother sitting in the dirt of the front yard with her back against the fence near the letterbox. At her side was a string bag of groceries and two of the wrapped parcels had spilled to the ground. Rose held a large buff-coloured envelope in her right hand and two sheets of buff-coloured paper in her left.

'Mum! Are you alright?' Maisie was alarmed to see her mother sitting in the dirt, but then terrified by her white face and bluish lips. Her dazed eyes were set deep in shadowed sockets and her slackened mouth had a little dribble at the corner. Rose didn't answer, but eventually gave a little wave of the papers.

'Commonwealth of Australia Certificate of Naturalisation ...' Maisie read aloud. And it was. Duly signed by the Minister of State for the Interior, Joseph Silver Collings, the document renounced Rose's allegiance to the Republic of Germany and entitled her to 'all political and other rights, powers and privileges ... of a natural-born British subject'. It had been too much for poor Rose after walking home from Patton Street in the afternoon heat, to so suddenly find her long-held fears unfounded. She hadn't ever expected the certificate to come in the post – and emotional shock from good news can cause as much damage as bad.

By the time Rose had had a cup of tea and a Bex powder, Jackie was home from high school to look after Maxie, so Maisie went with her on the bus to Argent Street. The correspondence accompanying the certificate advised Rose that she remained an enemy alien until such time as her declaration was duly signed and registered with an appropriate officer, who could be found at any post office licenced to issue money orders, and accompanied by a completed Form R.A.7, which could be obtained from said officer. When those formalities were completed, Rose needed to take her stamped naturalisation certificate with her Alien Registration Certificate to the Central Police Station so the Register of Enemy Aliens could be amended.

Rose was determined to be an enemy alien not one day longer than essential so, despite her continuing wooziness, she and Maisie completed the tasks. Both were a little disappointed to see neither Constable Munro nor Constable Ford on duty at the police station. It had taken more than 12 months, but at last Rose was British again. In April 1946 Parliament would pass a 'Nationality Bill' which allowed Australian women married to aliens to retain their nationality while they remained within the Commonwealth, but it came too late for the thousands of women like Rose.

Rose and Maisie headed home without the shopping that usually accompanied a trip to Argent Street and Rose took to her bed. She remained there for two weeks with her 'heart-turn'. Maisie stayed home from school to care for her and, for the first week, she was miserable. Missing out on schoolwork always brought some concern, but this was different. Maisie felt she was missing out on being German. She rationalised if her mother was now British again by virtue of her naturalisation certificate, this meant her children were also British.

'The German part of me is Dad's part,' she wept to Dulcie.

Dulcie had been coming at night to help with Rose, but their mother had been fairly demanding about care for herself and care for the house, so the first opportunity for the sisters to sit and talk came on the weekend when Rose was asleep. Maisie was pleased for her mother that the certificate had come at last, but she was distressed at personally giving up any small link to her father. There was still occasional nastiness at school and in the community, where she was often called a 'little Hun' by grown men she passed when doing the messages, but Maisie would never trade peace for a connection to Jack.

'You silly thing,' Dulcie consoled her. 'You *are* German. You will *always* be German and I wish I could be too!'

Perhaps neither of the girls would have made the claim if they had known what was happening overseas. Sometime earlier that year Adolf Hitler, Heinrich Himmler and Reinhard Heydrich had hatched a plan to not only expel the Jewish people from Germany and its domains, but to exterminate them. This was to be 'the final solution of the Jewish question' that became the horror Holocaust and claimed more than six million lives. Around the same time as Rose received her naturalisation and Maisie cried because she felt her heritage was being stripped, the systematic brutalisation and persecution of Jewish people had already killed more than 100,000 civilian men, women and children through mass shootings, starvation, lethal injection and failure to treat diseases in the ghetto concentration camps into which they had been herded. However, a new method was being tested. The first gassing experiments using Zyklon B had begun.

The Broken Hill newspapers gave little space at this stage of the war to the plight of Jewish people overseas. As with elsewhere in Australia, there were pockets of prejudice toward Jewish beliefs and customs. Local businessman Aron Feldman was initially refused naturalisation because he was 'not a fit and proper person and never will be'. He was accused of 'selling menswear onto the black market', though there were other, more substantiated, claims – including that he lived in sin with a mistress for whom he deserted a young wife in England, and that he assaulted a former Australian girlfriend by grabbing her arm at a Melbourne beach. But the damning aspect of the records left behind is the use of the phrase 'whining oily Polish Jew' to describe him – on official documents.

Broken Hill, however, had quite a significant Jewish population and an active congregation of more than 250 people that beautifully maintained the handsome stone synagogue they had built just before World War I. This congregation was also a major contributor to the general community, with local 'machers' (a Yiddish term meaning 'big-shot' or someone who 'makes things happen') such as Frank Griff and Albert Dryen building retail businesses that would survive several generations. These people must have wondered at the tiny amount of newspaper space allocated to atrocities that would have filled pages had the victims not been Jewish.

Barrier Daily Truth Friday 31 October 1941 (full article)

Massacre of Jews
Shootings in Poland

A.A.P. London

Reuters learns from Polish sources that German troops massacred over 1,000 Jews near Lomza. They were ordered to descend into trenches where they were forced to kneel in rows three abreast. Troops then machine-gunned them. A similar massacre of several hundred Jews is reported from Rzeslow, in south Poland.

Juxtaposed on the same page, several column inches were given over to how difficult it was becoming for Broken Hill people to get 'excursion tickets' on trains to Adelaide for Christmas.

Each year there was an exodus of more than 5000 people (about 3000 adults and 2000 children) from the Silver City to the South Australian capital city, which is much closer than Sydney, for the annual three-week mine shutdown. The usual practice was for the South Australian Railways to put on an extra six trains to accommodate the travelling miners and their families, with a special 'picnicker fare' of 30 shillings return. This year the miners and unions were incensed to learn that not only would there be no special trains at subsidised prices, but also only about half the holidaymakers would be able to book tickets in advance for the regularly scheduled daily trains.

A deputation sent to Adelaide found the SA Railways traffic manager unmoved. Mr S.H. Watson told them the military had first call on rolling stock and his staff had been decimated by call-ups for camp enlistments, to the extent his remaining personnel were exhausted from overtime shifts. The regular trains would need to keep seats available for travellers from Sydney, so only three of the seven carriages for each train could be pre-booked, allowing for 2500 Broken Hill people in the weeks prior to Christmas Eve. Last-minute seats might become available, Mr Watson told the deputation, but those wanting to travel would have to queue and take their chance. There was bad news on fares too – second class tickets would be two pounds eleven shillings and sixpence and those desperate enough to pay first class would part with three pounds six shillings and sixpence.

Escaping the outback heat for some Christmas seaside relief was more important than cost, and long queues formed at the Sulphide Street Railway Station in preparation for the opening of priority bookings at 10 am on 31 October. Those first in line arrived at 2.30 am and the queue soon stretched for many blocks, with the *Barrier Daily Truth* offices across the road providing reading material from 5 am onwards, which included a photograph of the waiting mob. It took only until 1 pm for all pre-bookable seats to be sold, apart from a small number available for those willing to travel on Christmas Day.

From mid-December the queues began to form again – this time for the seats not taken up by Sydney travellers that could be purchased one week before departure. Hundreds camped out

The annual Christmas exodus, 1946.

overnight each night. Men good-naturedly kept the place of others who had gone elsewhere along the line to join in a card game illuminated by an acetylene lamp; women brought along large urns of tea to share along the line; hampers were opened each morning to serve breakfast; and children who waited with them were given ice-blocks as the day progressed.

Ultimately the NSW Railways saved the day by providing nine additional trains to carry holidaymakers to Sydney. They offered return tickets at the one-way price to offset the difference in cost between travel to Sydney and the usual trip to Adelaide, allowing another 2800 holidaymakers to escape the town. A number of travelling families were without their menfolk when the Prime Minister announced the holidays should be cancelled. The North and South Mines complied, but the Zinc Corporation forged ahead with its scheduled shutdown.

It's not surprising that the lack of rail transport out of town caused such furore. There was no petrol to travel by car, air fares were extraordinarily expensive and reserved for the privileged, and the city itself shut down with the mines. Each year when the mining companies forced their workforce to take synchronised holidays, other businesses and shops did the same, because there was simply no one around to require service.

The annual en masse seaside holiday was such an integral part of Broken Hill's culture that in 1947 the Zinc Corporation spent £25,000 to construct a huge tent city on 26 acres of land adjacent to Fort Largs at Largs Bay to provide subsidised holiday accommodation for its workers. Facilities included a mess hut called 'the canteen', ablutions blocks, laundries, playgrounds, and more than 1000 tents equipped with stretchers, tables and chairs and ice chests, supported by daily ice deliveries. This highly subsidised accommodation came with coupons for breakfast, lunch and dinner in the canteen, and ice creams for the women and children.

[*Author's aside: Few Broken Hillites aged 40 or older would be able to say they did not have memories of holidays spent at the 'Zinc Camp' at Largs Bay. Those who weren't eligible for access by working on the mines always knew another family who did, and an extra child was readily accommodated. Maisie grew up without childhood memories of the camp since her earliest recollections were of Jack on workers compensation, but she created wonderful memories for my sister Jenny and me, and a sense of importance once we were old enough to have our own tent next door to Mum and Dad's. In turn, I have happy memories of taking my own girls on holiday to the Zinc Camp and appreciated the good nature of administrators who happily erected a tent for us on my childhood site of B1.*]

Chapter 12
New reasons for fear
December 1941–March 1942

Everyone's frenzied bid to get out of Broken Hill for Christmas 1941 was interrupted briefly when Japan bombed the American naval base at Hawaii's Pearl Harbor on Sunday 7 December. More than 2000 assembled soldiers and sailors were killed and another 1000 wounded. The obstinate United States was finally forced to enter the war. Its declaration on Japan the next day was followed three days later by Germany's declaration of war on the United States. The great power was now fully involved and the political storm that had been dividing the country since the beginning of the war was over.

Japan's relentless and rapid progress through China and other parts of Asia had been causing apprehension, but the audacious attack on American soil startled Broken Hill. City streets were scattered with groups of men huddled around radios to hear the ABC broadcasts. Others rushed to the area office at the Sulphide Street Station to enlist. Most of these were over-age and therefore rejected, but the office remained open around the clock to secure as many new recruits as possible. Telegrams arrived to cancel the leave of servicemen on home visits and, by Tuesday, 200 men who had had their call-up deferred at the request of employers were told to get ready to leave. These weren't mine employees, whose exemptions remained in place, but men in businesses where there were no ready replacements in the city. By August 1942 two of Broken Hill's oldest banks, the National and the Union, would close due to staff shortages caused by military service.

Impassioned editorials in local newspapers called for the community to listen to the dangers of a potential invader perilously close to Australian shores 'with well-cleaned ears'. Most in the city felt it was high time America entered the war to fight with the allies anyway and that the Japanese attack had only ignited an American response that was long overdue. Those well-cleaned ears, however, were shocked to hear Winston Churchill say he would dedicate British troops and equipment to defend Britain rather than help protect Australia against the Japanese in the Pacific. They were appalled to hear Australian Prime Minister John Curtin then call on America for help. This new allegiance did not sit well with Broken Hill's staunch British loyalists, but they were grateful for it ten weeks later when the so-called 'yellow peril' came even closer to home.

On Thursday 19 February 1942, Japanese forces bombed Darwin in two separate air raids – one from 10 am that dropped bomb after bomb for more than 40 minutes and another an hour later that lasted 30 minutes. The two raids killed 243 people and wounded another 400 but the government announced only 17 deaths to lessen the impact on national morale, as the fall of Singapore only days earlier had already had an effect. The bombs destroyed military aircraft, sank ships at anchor and demolished civil and military facilities, but these losses too were downplayed.

This attack was not entirely unsuspected, because Darwin was the established base for the Allies preparing to defend New Guinea from Japan's relentless march. Darwin would be bombed 64 times over the next 20 months, and there were attacks on other northern centres such as Townsville, Katherine, Wyndham, Derby, Broome and Port Hedland, but this first assault sent tremors of alarm throughout the nation.

The *Barrier Miner* was able to report the bombing briefly that evening and its posters scattered across town proclaiming 'Japs bomb Darwin' soon had a mob gathered at the front doors seeking more information. Men walked around waving rolled up newspapers as though swatting flies making crude comments about the stature of Japanese people. When they heard Curtin had called for 'every person in the nation to work like slaves to support the war effort' they laughed and said, 'We've been working like slaves for years, mate!'.

The jocularity covered a rising fear. Broken Hill people had been assured by Town Clerk Con Crowley at the end of 1940 there was no need for air-raid shelters in Broken Hill because there was nothing in the city that would attract an enemy attack, but the bombs landing on Australian soil now had people unsure.

Until this point the Silver City had adopted a Dad's Army approach to the war. Demonstrations were held on ovals (and attracted thousands of spectators) about the different types of bombs that could be dropped; the Fire Brigade demonstrated its competence in extinguishing flames to similar crowds; and the Housewives' Association regularly had guest speakers to explain how they should behave to protect their children in case of an air raid (which was basically to take them to non-existent shelters). The city complied with regulations to black-out outdoor entertainment and sporting facilities at night – which caused a howl of protest when the City Baths closed at 7 pm on a string of days above 107 degrees Fahrenheit – but streetlights remained stubbornly ablaze. Children now unable to enjoy their Gypsum Street playground after dark simply congregated in the halo of light on street corners.

In March things stepped up a notch. People talked of digging a 200 foot long tunnel from the Block 14 hill to connect with the upper levels of the mine, so that the whole population could shelter underground if required. Construction began on air-raid shelters at the schools, hospital and the mines. Some schools (such as the Marist Brothers College and St John's School) were fortunate enough to have cavernous concrete basements that only needed minor modification, while other schools dug a criss-cross of deep trenches lined with sand bags.

Maisie was more terrified of the trenches and shelters than she was of the bombs. On her ninth birthday an initially harmless game with her brothers in the backyard had ended with her tightly wrapped in a woollen blanket that gave her no air. She had felt on the verge of suffocation before her father rushed to unwrap the parcel. Now she was claustrophobic (an affliction which remained throughout her life) and the thought of cramming into a dugout with hundreds of other children brought a rising panic. She decided when the mine whistles sounded to warn of bombs or a plane full of machine gunners, she would disobey the teachers and hide under the big pepper tree in the back quadrangle instead. There was also the thought that, because she was German, the other children might not let her in.

Then the authorities had the wisdom to distribute 'Air Raid Bags' to all local schoolchildren.

Barrier Miner Thursday 5 March 1942 (excerpts)

Children Now Carry Special Air Raid Bags

An extra item of dress for some hundreds of Broken Hill schoolchildren now is a dilly bag worn round the neck, which contains a piece of rubber and some cotton wool. During an air raid the children will put the rubber between their teeth to reduce the effects of bomb blast on the lungs and will stop their ears with cotton wool …

"Most of our children have them," he said, "and the girls in particular put them round their necks and like wearing them all the time."

Maisie *didn't* like wearing the dilly bag. She thought neither the rubber nor the cotton wool would do her any good if a bomb were to be dropped on Broken Hill. Wearing it was just an ever-present reminder they were under threat. The next 'wise' step from the school authorities was to have teachers advise the children that they should run in a zig-zag fashion if machine gunners came out of the skies, so the bullets would have less chance of hitting them. Maisie would not have been the only Broken Hill child to have nightmares following this little gem, but adults weren't spared either.

Barrier Miner (same article, but describing the school trenches)

... the ground is a mass of deep trenches with sand-bagged rims and earthworks looking as businesslike as if it was all part of the much-vaunted 'second front' of the Allies. Walking through this system of trenches is like wandering through a maze, there are so many turns and cuttings. This means, of course, that the children would have additional protection if some vicious minded raider swooped down to machine-gun the diggings.

Was this all part of some weird approach at inclusivity? So that every man, woman and child should feel part of a war from which they were so geographically distant? Was it not enough that husbands and sons and brothers and cousins and friends were now away fighting? Broken Hill sits more than 1500 miles from Australia's northern and western coasts, and more than 580 miles from the east. Enemy aircraft would need a special reason to fly those distances to attack it. Some argued the lead mines provided that reason, but others rightly countered the coastal factories that turned the lead into bullets were much more valuable targets – and much more accessible! Whatever the view, the ARP (air-raid precautions) campaigns were more alarming than reassuring.

Maisie lived in a state of perpetual fear. This puzzled her, since the one thing she had feared more than anything had already happened. Her father lay in the ground in Rakow Street and she had thought all emotion had been buried with him. Now, though, there was an unremitting flow of new fears – her mother's health; the threat of loved friends being arrested for no reason; the schoolyard bullying with only her left to protect Maxie now Jackie was at high school; the talk of bombs and bullets raining from the sky; the thought of being forced to cower with hundreds of other bodies in a small space in which she would find it hard to breathe; and that she should attempt that with a piece of rubber between her teeth. She lived in an increasingly fragile world at a time when her own personal fragility gave her no tools to deal with it. She was so forced to focus on just getting through each day that she no longer felt able to plan her future. Over the following months Sister Drummond slipped from her mind and her school marks slipped from their previous high levels.

There was no such shirking in the town. Now both newspapers ran regular articles giving advice on how to behave during an air raid; volunteers were called to help provide covers for the school yard trenches; and hoteliers began digging trenches in their backyards after having been warned their cellars were not deep enough, nor protected enough, to accommodate their customers safely from bombs. Rolling black-out tests were conducted across specific sections of the city to ensure residents were appropriately prepared and a succession of elaborate demonstrations on public ovals (often attended by more than 6000 people) put the emergency services through their paces extinguishing flames, rescuing people from rooves, and using bicycles, whistles and torches to search for people supposedly trapped under rubble. The newly acquired motorised ambulance was a big drawcard in these demonstrations. The old horse-drawn caravan (with the driver perched outside in all weather) had only been replaced the previous year with a disused motorised version purchased from the NSW Ambulance Transport Board for the princely sum of £40. Rather than being only for transport, this new unit was equipped for on-site first aid, which would be available free to citizens who became contributors at three shillings a year. Non-contributors would be forced to pay one pound one shilling on each occasion they used the service.

Construction forged ahead on a new aerodrome south of the city (heavily subsidised by the mining companies) to accommodate heavier planes, and more money was directed to the Broken Hill Aero Club to assist in the training of personnel ready for the Air Force.

Enemy aliens weren't left out of the frenzied preparations. Seven men and two women were brought before the court and fined £10, with five pounds five shillings costs, for owning a camera. The cameras were forfeited and each had to lodge another £10 bond to comply with the regulation in future. It was 'an alien's duty to find out what is required of them', the magistrate proclaimed. Broken Hill people, meanwhile, had a duty to report aliens who were 'subversive' – and they were assisted in that task by a clear definition.

Barrier Miner Friday 20 February 1942 (in total)

Subversive Activities

Definition Is Given

What constitutes subversive activities? Constable M. Ford was asked to give his definition as Aliens Registration Officer in Broken Hill and he gave the following reply: 'Any words, deeds, or actions likely in any way to assist the enemy whether done directly or indirectly, thoughtlessly or otherwise.'

The definition was placed on the notice board in the charge room at the Central Police Station and at the post office.

Broken Hill began to feel prepared. Then an article appeared in the *Barrier Miner* citing a Mrs Rhodes who had survived Japanese air raids in Malaysia and said people would be stupefied during a raid and not remember instructions, so they needed to take action now – by keeping a bathtub filled at all times, removing glass from windows, electric light bulbs from sockets and pictures from walls. 'Is this any time for keeping up appearances?' she asked. Mrs Rhodes also warned parents to ensure their children wore identification bracelets because in Malaysia it had taken days for parents to be able to identify the bodies of their children killed in school bombings.

Many speculated all the earnest activity on air-raid precautions meant something was afoot and they weren't being kept in the loop. Those that knew kept their secrets well. Still, little quotes kept appearing in seemingly unrelated articles, especially from Constable Ford – 'The tongue is the unruly member of the body – watch it!' and 'Be British – Be Silent'.

The *Barrier Miner* took these quotes one step further when it inserted a cryptic stand-alone message on its front page.

Barrier Miner Wednesday 4 March 1942 (No heading, bold type)

A little knowledge is a dangerous thing, particularly when it deals with ships. Gossipers who know only a little still may talk enough to furnish the enemy with the vital link in his chain of information.

Broken Hill definitely had a secret. How the secret could possibly involve a ship given its inland location was a mystery to most.

Chapter 13

The inconvenience of war
April 1942–August 1943

Maisie (and Broken Hill) calmed as the months of 1942 rolled on without any attack from above. As the second anniversary of Jack's death approached, life slipped into the mundane inconvenience of war. Bakers stopped delivering bread to homes, although the horse-drawn milkman continued. Sanitation collections for the many properties not yet connected to the new residential sewerage system, including all the South homes, returned to horse-drawn 'dunny-carts' rather than the big trucks that deftly negotiated back lanes. Winter had been difficult. Petrol restrictions limited the quantity of wood brought into town and regulations limited the use of other fuels such as kerosene.

Troops, at home and overseas, needed to be clothed at a time when both materials and labour were in short supply. More than 85% of Australia's wool was required to clothe the military. Conservative clothing limitations had been around for some time – men were restricted to buying only two shirts at one time and shops had been told to limit their turnover of garments to three-quarters of their usual trade – but there had seemed no urgency about it until an announcement on 9 May. Clothing coupons were coming. Rose joined the mad rush of fierce women assaulting local stores following the announcement but, with little cash to spare, there wasn't the hoarding of clothes in the Schuster household that was common in many others.

The clothing ration booklets were collected in June from local polling booths – 112 coupons for each man, woman and child aged between five and 16 years, with extra coupons for younger children and expectant mothers. Employees in some industries received extra coupons too, while uniforms and other industrial wear required less coupons to purchase. The city's hairdressers were happy to receive an additional six coupons for two uniforms, but the porters at the new hospital were told they didn't really need a uniform and wearing an appropriate armband should suffice for identification purposes. The local member, Mr J.J. Clark, scored the Broken Hill miners an extra 15 coupons apiece to cover extraordinary wear and tear on their clothes, but their 'denim trousers' and flannels remained in short supply.

In late August, the coupon system was more keenly felt by the Schusters when tea coupons were included in the front of the clothing booklet. Tea had been rationed since March, but shopkeepers were a little kinder to some than others and Rose had always been able to acquire enough for her several cups each day to support her Bex powders. Now it was closely regulated and Maisie had the tedious task of spreading tea leaves to dry once they had produced more than one pot (to become an emergency store in case stocks ran out entirely). When sugar was added to the regulated ration list, Rose became decidedly grumpy.

The clothing coupons were required to last 12 months, and marked to ensure only half could be used in any one half-year, but already 15 coupons had been snipped from Jackie's and Maisie's booklets for new jackets. Maisie's one pair of shoes with their cardboard inner soles were beginning to hurt her toes and she had nightmares of going to school with no shoes and being taunted by the children about the number of darns in her socks. This dream recurred periodically throughout her life.

In September, the miners provided some distraction. Daylight Saving Time had been introduced on 1 January, with the 'extra hour of daylight' designed to reduce the use of coal and electricity across Australia. There'd been a bit of a fuss locally, but by the time people were beginning to get organised in their protest, it finished again on 28 March. Now it was due to start again and this time the miners were prepared. A mass meeting of unionists resolved to have their own time on the mines. They would move the hands on their clocks as instructed, but would insist on changing their shift start times (midnight, 8 am and 4 pm) to coincide with 'real' time rather than Daylight Saving Time.

Maisie was amused at all the reasons they gave in the paper – and reading them aloud brought a rare shared laugh with her mother – but she agreed it *did* sometimes still feel too hot to go to bed when the clock said.

The whole city ran according to the mine shifts and, for awhile, it looked as though Broken Hill would have its own little time zone. It already had the distinction of operating on South Australian rather than New South Wales time. During the standardisation of Australia's time in February 1895, the Silver City had rail links with Adelaide but not with Sydney, so most business was conducted over the border. This anomaly remains today.

Howls of protest from business, particularly the banking sector, about the shift changes found the unionists immovable – until the cinemas pointed out they could not change their show times to accommodate the new mine shifts. The town's bus schedule was set by the Liquid Fuel Control Board (to ensure fuel was conserved) and movies needed to accommodate the schedule. Another mass meeting was called to reverse the earlier decision and the new resolution included comment that Broken Hill miners 'would not rat on a Labor Government'.

As Maisie's birthday approached on 7 October, she stubbornly refused to celebrate it, just as she had the year before, and earlier as an eight-year-old when her father had been away in Germany.

'My happy birthday memories have Dad in them,' she had told her mother then. There was no need to repeat it now. Rose, however, managed to persuade her it was an appropriate time for a new dress.

The two set off for Dryens in town, each expecting a heated

tussle. Neither was proved wrong. The ongoing difference of opinion between Rose and Maisie as to what was appropriate for a young girl to wear was exacerbated by the fact dresses were only ever bought one at a time in the Schuster household (even before there was such a thing as clothing rations). That meant each dress had to be worn repetitively over a lengthy period, so losing the battle had significant and long-term consequences. Each therefore took the confrontation seriously.

At 12, Maisie was well developed – both physically and in strategic combat with her mother. Her heart was set on a blue dress with a straight skirt and maroon trim diagonally across the bodice so that the dress had one blue sleeve and one maroon. Rose, on the other hand, preferred a brown frock that had royal blue workings through the band, pockets on either side of the bodice at breast level and tied demurely at the back. The inevitable stand-off between the two continued for some time, with Maisie declaring she would 'never, *ever* wear that thing' if she were forced to own it. Rose knew from past experience the threat was not empty. Eventually, a compromise was reached. Maisie would have *two* new dresses and she would wear her mother's choice as well as her own. It was to be the singular occasion Rose bought two dresses for her simultaneously.

The dresses were priced well enough at nine shillings and eleven pence each, but they meant an additional 18 coupons were clipped from her ration book. Maisie was therefore amazed that her mother also bought her two pair of Celanese pantettes at three shillings and eleven pence plus three coupons each and two pair of elastic top socklets at one shilling and sixpence plus two coupons a pair. She decided not to tell her mother about the shoes pressing on her toes.

When she wore her brown dress to play at the South Park (because she cared less about it being damaged) a young Tommy Carr told her, 'You shouldn't wear a dress like that – those pockets draw attention to things that they shouldn't'. Maisie was secretly pleased her mother's choice had entirely defeated its purpose. Even so, she removed the pockets.

That this little incident at the park remained so firmly fixed in Maisie's memories in later life shows she had at last reached a somewhat peaceful place. 'Little things' were again important. Her life remained traumatised at its core by the loss of Jack, but she began to attend to all the bumps on the surface too. The end of the war was only slightly closer to her than its beginning (though she didn't know it) but she was dealing well with the various ordeals it brought. Her soul had smoothed a little.

She began to enjoy school again and though not top of the class, she was close. Sport continued to play a big part. She did well at most sports, but especially running and swimming. Her key competition was Aileen Trembath. Sometimes it was Maisie with the blue ribbon, sometimes Aileen, depending on the day.

Maisie began to look forward to high school. She had stopped stuffing Sister Drummond's folder with the minutiae of her school days, but her goal to become a nurse remained. High school was a step toward that. But in October, the world tramped on her again.

Barrier Daily Truth Tuesday 20 October 1942 (in total)

SISTER DRUMMOND MISSING

It was stated in a nurses' Journal recently that Sister Irene Drummond had been seen on a boat which was escaping from the Singapore fighting, and that the boat had been seen under attack and that it had not made its rendezvous.

Mr. Clark referred the matter to the Minister for the Army and has received the following reply: "With reference to your letter of the 21st September, 1942, enclosing one from the Secretary and Business Manager of the Broken Hill and District Hospital, Broken Hill, in which he seeks information as to the whereabouts of Sister Irene Drummond, formerly of the staff of that hospital, I desire to inform you inquiries reveal that Sister Drummond remained with her unit in Singapore. I regret to say that no news has since become available in reference to those members of the Australian Army Nursing Service who remained in Singapore. However, as soon as there is information of a definite nature, you will be notified immediately."

Maisie wasn't alone in her distress at this news. Most of Broken Hill knew of, and admired, Irene Drummond – not just because of her untiring work at the hospital, but because of her kindness toward their daughters. She, like Broken Hill, would wait until the end of the war to learn Sister Drummond's fate.

Maisie had met her only once, but that one meeting had had a profound impact. Someone other than her father believed in the importance of education for girls, someone other than her father and Dulcie was interested in her school achievements and someone believed she had a future other than as a housewife. But it was more than that. During that one meeting Sister Drummond had agreed with Maisie that she would not 'get over' losing her father and that she would grieve forever. Somehow that made things a little easier. She didn't have to pretend. She simply had to get on with life because that's all there was to be done about it. So she thought she would.

Maisie graduated sixth in her 6A class at Alma School, with book awards for Citizenship, Diligence and School Spirit along with her share of the sporting blues. There were to be 322 new students starting first form at the high school on Wednesday 10 February 1943 – and students from the South would represent the smallest contingent. North School would send 144, Burke Ward 82, Broken Hill (later to become Central) 56 and Alma 33, along with a handful of students from Wilcannia, Menindee and Kinalung. It should have been intimidating.

Having a big brother already at 'the big school' made it a little less daunting, but Maisie clearly felt she didn't need much support.

Sporting houses for the newcomers were decided according to alphabet groupings, but this sometimes changed according to enrolments. Jackie was an active member of the Sturt house, but in 1943 the 'S' surnames were allocated to Parkes. Maisie was offered the opportunity to instead join Sturt (common practice so that sibling loyalties were united) but she quite liked the colour green so chose to remain in Parkes. It made for interesting debates in the Schuster household around sports days. Now basketball and softball were added to her repertoire. She was never short of friends, male or female, and this proved to be a benefit for Jackie's 14th birthday on 2 June.

It was a Wednesday and an afterschool party was planned. Rose had been baking for days to ensure that Jackie's friends were suitably impressed and the long sleep-out was prepared with a trestle and stools. As time wore on, however, those stools remained empty of young people, save Jackie and his young brother and sister. Jackie was disconsolate and Rose disappointed.

'Would you like me to find some friends for him, Mum?' Maisie offered.

'He won't want a party of just girls!' Rose snapped, believing the day could not be saved.

'I can get boys, too.' Maisie assured her. She dashed off to do just that and quickly returned with an eager bunch of party-goers: Maxie Delbridge, Jackie Davey, Ronny Davey – all closer to Jackie's age than Maisie's – and Robert Baum, a bit younger. To round out the party, cousins Delcie and Dorothy Baum, Velma Dinham, Joyce and Pauline Morrow, Dorothy and June Jenkins, and Margaret Maine, along with Maisie's best friends Amy Cox and Bonnie Oliver. The party was a resounding success and the quiet Jackie began to enjoy a new popularity at school, especially with the girls.

Two months later, however, things changed. Rose turned up at Maisie's classroom to tell her Jackie had been severely beaten at school and was at the hospital. The school had sent for her via a policeman on a bicycle. Rose had no other information and wanted Maisie to go with her to the emergency room. Never had a mile and a quarter seemed to take so long to walk! Maisie was at first convinced Jackie must be dead – or at least dying – or why would her mother have got Mr Lavers to drop her at the school rather than straight to the hospital? Perhaps not, she then reasoned, because Maxie wasn't with her.

When mother and daughter first pushed back the curtain to see Jackie they both gasped. No, he wasn't dead, but he certainly looked as though he had been beaten to within an inch of his life.

One eye was swollen tightly shut; his lip was split; there was a large blue bruise on his temple speckled with red from a graze; his nose was swollen and red and plugged by cotton gauze; and his left arm was in a big white sling with huge safety pins at the elbow fold and floppy ends tied at his neck. The policeman sitting next to Jackie was the first to speak.

'Mrs Schuster, your boy is in a spot of bother. He refuses to tell us who did this to him and you'd be wise to convince him otherwise.'

Maisie was appalled. Jackie looked dreadful. She watched as the gauze in his nose turned red and fresh blood began to trickle from his nostril.

'*My brother* is in a spot of bother?'

She was incredulous. Though she spoke to the policeman, she couldn't tear her eyes from Jackie. When she did, it was to look at Rose. Why wasn't her mother saying anything? Rose wasn't sure what to say. If Jackie wasn't giving information about what had happened, there was good reason for it.

Even once home Jackie refused to tell Rose what had happened. That night he made the front page of the newspaper, but it told no one anything.

Barrier Miner Wednesday 11 August 1943 (in total)

A pupil of the High School, Jack Schuster, aged 14, suffered an injury to the left shoulder in a fall at the school today. He was taken in the Citizens' Ambulance to the Hospital for X-ray and then to his home at 25 South Street.

The same article appeared in the next morning's *Barrier Daily Truth*, but still Jackie would not give up his assailants. It was more than a week before he revealed what had happened.

'They think I'm a spy!' he whispered to Maisie. 'I told someone about the gold.'

Chapter 14

Secrets and sixpenny seats

Gold was Broken Hill's secret. It wasn't being dug out of the ground along with the lead, zinc and silver – it was being brought into town by the trainload!

The first shipment arrived in February 1942 soon after the bombing of Darwin. The Commonwealth Bank had ample secure storage for its gold (and that in its care for Britain and the Netherlands) but the possibility of a Japanese invasion of Australia, which had hitherto seemed ludicrous, was suddenly less so. An inland repository was deemed appropriate.

The initial bullion arrived accompanied by a contingent of bank employees and military personnel and was stored in the cells of the Broken Hill Gaol after its only prisoner at that time was packed off to Long Bay Gaol. The next shipment came from Melbourne in April and thereafter periodic special trains brought the country's newly produced gold and 555 gold ingots salvaged from the *Niagara*, which had been sunk by German mines off the coast of New Zealand in June 1940. This was British gold on its way to America to purchase munitions from before the United States had entered the war.

Ultimately the gaol would hold £50,000,000 in gold ingots and its later transfer back to capital cities on 13 April 1945 (once Japan was in retreat) was the largest single movement of gold in Australia. The journey took 40 hours and carried a guard of 30 bank officers and 100 military personnel.

Prime Minister Ben Chifley delayed announcing Broken Hill's

secret to the world until April 1947, after gold belonging to the Bank of England and the Netherlands Government had been safely sent home. Six months later, Randolph Churchill, the son of Britain's war-time Prime Minister Winston Churchill, visited Broken Hill on a five-week Australian tour and announced the clandestine gold storage had been known to only a handful of officials. Randolph Churchill was a renowned journalist and lecturer, but perhaps more widely known across the world for his escapades and arrogance. He had deserted his wife and five-year-old son in England because he preferred 'bachelor ways'; been fined for reckless driving in Connecticut; and caused an uproar in New Zealand when he criticised Auckland's wharfies for their 'slow turnaround of ships'. On his visit to Broken Hill as a guest of the North Mine, he won friends for saying Broken Hill had 'more hustle than America', but was jeered for saying, 'Little did the miners of Broken Hill suspect as they did their daily stint in the lead and zinc mines that far more precious ore had been deposited in the local prison'. Of course they knew!

Within weeks of the first shipment arriving, a special strongroom was built within the gaol using large quantities of cement and other materials; several modifications were made to external fixtures obviously designed to keep people out rather than in; and an elaborate system of alarms was installed, connected to the Central Police Station and monitored every 15 minutes. A large body of Commonwealth Bank employees suddenly became permanent residents and gaol accommodation was refurbished to house the numerous onsite guards. With little to do because their charges weren't moving, these guards established gardens within the five-acre gaol grounds and donated excess fruit and vegetables to the Red Cross and other local charities. These things don't happen in a small town (down to 20,500 people at that point) without everyone knowing what's going on. Broken Hill was offended.

Barrier Miner Thursday 2 October 1947 (excerpt)

CHURCHILL TELLS OF GOLD
LEFT IN BROKEN HILL GAOL

Mr. Churchill gained much knowledge during his recent flying trip to Broken Hill. He tells a good story about the gold that was stored in the Broken Hill gaol. His reference to the people of Broken Hill not knowing that gold was stored here is much astray. This "secret" was common knowledge here.

The people of Broken Hill may have talked among themselves, despite cryptic warnings in the local newspapers, but it was a closed group. Police constables who travelled 175 miles from Wentworth with a handcuffed prisoner were stunned when told there was no room at the gaol. They were given no explanation and were directed to go on to Bathurst.

Comments about the gold in the gaol may have been whispered but, true to Broken Hill style, they invariably ended in an outburst of laughter. One miner thought Rudolf Hess should be brought to see it and catch up with Sadeek. Hess had been Hitler's offsider and was being held as a prisoner of war after he parachuted into Scotland in 1941 supposedly to negotiate peace, while Peter Sadeek had been hanged at the gaol in 1907. Many a miner found a good joke to be made in recounting how the first large shipment from Melbourne had stopped at Jerilderie, where Ned Kelly robbed the bank.

So poor Jackie wasn't doing anything extraordinary when he spoke about the gold to a schoolmate in August 1943. The difference was, he was German. There were two direct outcomes from that day he spent being patched up in hospital: two weeks later Maisie channelled the fear she had felt rushing to the hospital to win the girls' half-mile walk at the school sports carnival (as a first-former in an event open across the school); and Jackie decided to get serious about his interest in boxing, which to that point had been Maxie's sport. On 8 November he became champion for his weight class in the high school boxing tournament, with the front page of the *Barrier Miner* that night noting that his 'straight left beat the fast and aggressive, but less scientific' favourite.

The German community had hoped the attention focused on Japan would bring some relief from victimisation. But there were no Japanese living in Broken Hill. This left the Germans, Italians and Yugoslavs fair game. The treatment of Yugoslavs was harsh. The country had not voluntarily sided with Germany and its people were much divided about its surrender, but it mattered little to which ethnic group people were attached; they were considered to have 'sold out'. People were viciously treated and labelled as 'cowards'. It didn't seem to matter that more than a dozen young local Yugoslav men had enlisted to fight in Australian services, some early in the war and some after Yugoslavia's surrender to Germany.

Twenty-year-old Rudi Alagich, a local sporting hero (and later to become a much-loved Patton Street tailor) enlisted in May 1941 and, from February 1942, spent 12 months defending Darwin until damage to his left knee sent him home on a medical discharge. Despite surgery, the medical board found him to be 'no further use to the army'.

Maisie had so many Yugoslav friends the other kids began to call her 'Maisie Schusterovich'. It was meant to be derogatory, but the group of friends decided they liked it and thereafter happily used the nickname among themselves.

Rechabite meetings continued to play a huge part in the Schusters' social life and by this time both Maisie and Jackie were chief rulers of their respective tents. Newspaper reports of the fortnightly meetings almost always carried their names for having led a particular project or won sporting and games nights. However, the highlight of their week – every week – was the Saturday matinee at the Metropole theatre. At sixpence each, it was within Rose's budget and her memories of the family being denied this pleasure won her over easily, even without the children's pleas.

The cheaper sixpenny tickets only gave them access to front stalls (which meant the film was distorted a little because the seats were so close) but they didn't mind. For Maisie, the highlight of the outing was the hour-long wait in the queue for entry, as only the more expensive back stalls could be booked in advance. Far from an annoyance, this meant she could wander up and down chatting along the long line of children while Jackie held her place – and Maxie's hand. But this had all stopped in June when the BIC put a blackball on all the major picture theatres. Although the Schusters had no unionist in their home, they would *never* cross a union boycott.

By late 1943, the picture theatre war in Broken Hill had run longer than World War II. The Broken Hill Housewives' Progressive Association had been battling for years to get the duopoly that ran local theatres to reduce their prices and allow people to book seats in advance without incurring additional fees. In 1939, three live entertainment venues – the Palais de Danse, Skating Rink and Tivoli Theatre – individually tried to obtain a licence to screen films. Their applications received strong opposition from Johnson's and Ozone Theatres. They not only had the Broken Hill market stitched up, but also the film distributors. Metro-Goldwyn-Meyer, Warner Bros., 20th Century Fox and British Empire Films supplied the Ozone while RKO Pictures, Paramount, United Artists, Universal and Columbia supplied Johnson's.

The Italian proprietor of the Tivoli Theatre, Joseph Salvatore Guidi, was blocked from obtaining a licence from the Films Commission under the *Theatres and Public Halls Act 1908–1938* – until the BIC and local branch of the ALP took a deputation to the NSW chief secretary to complain of overcrowding at the existing local theatres and that proprietors would not provide a cheap ticket for children on Saturday nights.

With this intervention, Guidi won his licence, but Johnson's and the Ozone appealed it. Guidi's access to films was then blocked (only Paramount would supply anything – and then only re-runs) so the Tivoli continued showing the type of 'shorts' and documentaries that had been running prior to being granted a film licence. When Guidi finally found a way to access films, the big boys took him to court – and won.

In May 1941, Judge Barton ordered Guidi 'desist from showing cinemograph film'. The BIC, after hearing promises from him of cheaper prices and better films, again backed the Tivoli. Union leaders gave the other parties 24 hours to withdraw their objections and, when they didn't, blackballed them. So the parties again ended up in court in August, this time before Judge Shortland.

There were then six picture theatres operating – the Ozone's indoor and outdoor theatres and Johnson's in town; the Hillside at Railway Town (showing the Ozone's films); and the Metropole out the south with both indoor and outdoor theatres (showing Johnson's films). The suburban theatres opened only on Wednesdays and Saturdays while the town theatres opened every night of the week except Sundays and also included morning shows and matinees. There was also the Crystal Theatre which ran only Saturday night with cheap 'revivals'. That meant a capacity for 4690 patrons in winter and 5774 in summer. There was little live entertainment coming to the city and only a few local productions, so thousands of patrons turned out for the bi-weekly change of movies. On Saturday nights both the major theatres were almost always full, with those seats able to be pre-booked (with a threepence booking fee) sold out by Friday lunchtime.

The duopoly argued before Judge Shortland that allowing an extra film venue in town would be 'economic waste' and cause 'undue competition for available film'. The judge supported that view and after a four-day hearing Guidi was told his licence was not endorsed. Judge Shortland was particularly unimpressed with the

Tivoli allowing children to accompany their parents on Saturday nights.

'Matinees are specifically provided for children and the days when clamouring children are present at night performances in numbers is, I hope, gone forever!' he told the court.

Judge Shortland labelled the dispute 'an old stew' and, because Guidi had caused the issue to come again before the court so soon after the last time, ordered Guidi pay all costs for the case (including both the senior and junior counsel the appellants had engaged).

But nothing changed. The Tivoli continued to show movies and Broken Hill continued to watch them, albeit at reduced levels – the seats were hard, there was no heating in winter, no sewerage connected, and the films had already been shown in the town. And the BIC maintained the ban it had slapped on the other theatres.

While the Tivoli was never full, it fared much better than the others, who were getting five or six people to a showing. When they brought in successful new releases to tempt moviegoers, *Moscow Strikes Back* at Johnson's and *Blossoms in the Dust* at the Ozone, the BIC decided to make its point better felt. It called out staff from both companies and they had no choice but to close. Judge Shortland was livid.

The Mail Adelaide Monday 4 September 1943 (excerpts)

THEATRES CLOSE AT BROKEN HILL

Blackmail, Says Judge

From Our Special Representative

BROKEN HILL. — 'Blackmail of the worst possible kind' was the comment made by Judge Shortland on the activities of the Barrier Industrial Council and the district assembly of the ALP in the film theatres dispute here …

The Tivoli, right, at the centre of the dispute and, left,
one of Broken Hill's teetotal bars.

The Crystal, one of six theatres showing to packed audiences
before the union black ban.

Judge Shortland, after a hearing lasting four days, refused to endorse Guidi's licence. During the hearing he made strong comments, characterising the 'interference of the B.I.C. and the ALP with the course of justice as blackmail of the worst possible kind.' ...

It was reported here yesterday the New South Wales Chief Secretary (Mr. Baddeley) had promised a Sydney deputation that he would recommend to Cabinet that the Act be amended to allow the responsible Minister to issue an endorsement where it was considered necessary ...

The whole dispute is regarded here as one of the worst examples in the history of Broken Hill of the use of industrial might for political purposes. Union and political leaders who have fostered the boycott have been bitterly attacked by correspondents — mostly anonymous, because of obvious reasons — in the local newspapers. Tomorrow's meeting is expected to put an end to an intolerable position by making it possible for the boycotted theatres to resume screening of current up-to-date programs.

The anonymous 'special representative' who reported out of Broken Hill for the Mail in Adelaide may have had high hopes for a resolution to follow the next day's mass meeting, but it wasn't to come. Instead, the Tivoli increased to nine screenings a week; introduced ticket prices of one shilling and threepence for front stalls and two shillings and seven pence for back stalls; allowed children in on sixpenny tickets to all screenings (even on Saturday nights); and pre-sold numbered seat tickets for everything. For the next three months, the Tivoli enjoyed attendances of more than 1100 adults and about 150 children on Saturday nights and 600 children at matinees.

But as Christmas approached, Broken Hill people had had enough. They wanted their 'proper' theatres back and they wanted new release movies. A mass meeting on 20 December called on the union executive to go into conference with Johnson's and the Ozone.

In the end, the major theatres gave away very little. Of six claims, the only one they granted was to allow bookings during the week for Saturday night cheap seats to reduce the length of queues, and to allow the same option for weeknight sessions if it was an 'exceptional' movie.

On Monday 27 December, the first films for six months were shown at the major theatres. Broken Hill again had all options open for film-going and Maisie had her precious Saturday afternoons back at the Metropole. All she needed now was *Gone with the Wind* to come to town. It was showing all around the country, but Broken Hill had been deprived because of the dispute.

In January 1944 Guidi submitted a new application to the Film Commission for a licence and Johnson's and the Ozone again submitted objections. Later that month, 26 police charges for showing films while unlicensed were withdrawn, but he lost an appeal against the remainder in May. In June, he died suddenly in Adelaide at the age of 77.

Gone with the Wind didn't arrive in Broken Hill until May 1947 (four years after its debut in Adelaide) but the Ozone allowed bookings for all seats more than a week in advance.

Chapter 15
Dances and dreams
September 1943–October 1944

Maisie had an extra, secret, delight at the restoration of Saturday afternoon matinees at the Metropole. She had a boyfriend. She'd met Cleave Hands at the high school social at the end of September and that night was one she would remember all her life – not so much because of Cleave, but because she'd been one of only three girls to turn up at the dance in her school uniform.

Rose initially refused to let her go. Maisie was not quite 13, young for her class, and she was still trying to squeeze into the two dresses bought for her twelfth birthday. There was no money for a new dress; no transport to get her home; and no inclination to have her daughter 'gadding about'.

On the night of the social, Delcie Baum came to say her dad was going to take his kids to and from the social in his horse and cart – and there was room for Maisie too. The Baums lived in Boughtman Street, diagonally opposite the Schusters. The children were second cousins, but closer friends, and Maisie spent a lot of time with Delcie and Dorothy. There was safety in numbers. Rose's objections were beginning to be worn down, but there was nothing to be done about a dress.

'I'll just wear my uniform. It's at the school so I bet there'll be lots of kids there in uniform. Please, Mum …'

Rose eventually gave in. She agreed there would be many girls without money or coupons for fancy dresses. There weren't. When Maisie first stood in the doorway to the hall she couldn't see one other uniform there. But she had two choices only – get back on the cart and go home, or go in and make the best of it. And that she did.

Maisie danced every dance of that school social, the last several of them with Cleave. The fact she was in her uniform rather than a dress had no impact on the number of partners. She had such a wonderful time she even forgot to hide the gap in her teeth when she smiled. [*Author's aside: My mother had a gap between her two front teeth of which Georgia May Jagger would be proud. When she was little she used to break off the head of a small gold safety pin and use it to close the gap, but as she grew older, she just learned to smile with her mouth closed or push her tongue up behind her teeth. The gap is a Schuster trait that she shared with her brothers and few of us in the next generation have escaped it. We proudly own it as our little piece of Jack.*]

The weeks after the school social seemed to fly. Maisie was in a happy place. Occasionally she was panged by guilt that she could feel so happy without her father, but she reasoned he would want it so, and it wasn't as if she didn't still think of him every day. In December, her bubble was pricked. Rose refused to take the family into town for the high school speech night, despite the fact both Jackie and Maisie were to receive a prize.

Maisie was devastated – less at missing out on walking on stage to collect her Junior Girls Athletic Championship prize than missing out on the venue. The annual awards ceremony was to be held in the Town Hall and once again she was denied the mysteries she was certain the magnificent building contained. School next day kept the bubble deflated. There were to be no sport blues this year. They were unobtainable because of the war, stockpiles had already been used, and the principal was certain the children were prepared to make the sacrifice and be content with a certificate.

Maisie wasn't sure she was. She didn't think a certificate tacked above her bed would have quite the impact of Jackie's blue felt triangle from the year before. And there was more bad news. This year there also would be no trophy for the sports winners and no book prize for the academic awards. Both were off limits in a country dedicating all resources to the war effort. Instead, the children received War Savings Stamps.

War Savings Stamps were a way of ensuring every Australian man, woman and child contributed to the war effort. By June 1943, the cost of the war had reached more than £1,000,000 and only one third of it had been raised in taxes (at a time when the average male wage was five pounds five shillings and eight pence a week). The rest came from treasury bills or loans and the War Savings Stamps were part of that. The concept asked people to live as frugally as possible, use the savings to buy specially printed stamps and, when they had enough to fill an issued card, trade them for a War Savings Certificate. Early stamps were sixpence and there were 32 squares on a card, but the traded certificate (bond) was for £1, payable in seven years. The four shillings difference was interest payable by the Commonwealth to its supporters. Thousands of Broken Hill schoolchildren participated in the campaign by buying stamps through their schools and competition was fierce to be the most patriotic school. Pellew & Moore had a window display showing how many bullets could be manufactured with each £1 War Savings Certificate.

Maisie didn't have a card so was issued with one along with her two sixpenny stamps for her championship win. Across the top of the card big white flowing letters in a bold red box said, 'Spend Wisely – Save and Lend to Australia!' and at the bottom, 'Personal Sacrifice is the Measure of National Service!'. She thought she had made quite enough personal sacrifice for this war she didn't believe in and, though she had become more patriotic since Japan presented an alternative enemy to Germany, she didn't want the fact she had run fast to mean more bullets were produced.

However, while the prize stamps did nothing to inspire her to a new way of thinking, the assembly in which they were presented did. Thirteen students were acknowledged before 1009 of their peers for having passed their Leaving Examination after five years at high school. Suddenly there was a new goal. Two of these students were going off to university and two to teachers' college.

Maisie had never before considered the possibility of anything more ambitious than an Intermediate Certificate and a career as a nurse. But now she heard Jack's voice, '*Kleine Tochter*, you can do anything if you really want to and you put your mind to achieving it. If you want to be a doctor or a chemist or a dentist or a lawyer – you can! You earn the right to be these important things by dedication, hard work and education, not because you are a boy or a girl. The important thing is to choose the education that matches the talents and passion you have, not whether you wear dresses or trousers.'

Becoming a teacher now seemed a perfect match for her passion – which was that girls were entitled to as much education as boys. The school leaving age had been increased from 14 years in 1940 to 14 years and 4 months in 1941 and incrementally since, so that in 1944 children would be obliged to stay at school to the age of 15. This suited Maisie perfectly and meant only an extra two years to gain her Leaving Certificate. Rose, she thought, could be persuaded once she saw excellent school results – and, besides, teachers' college meant a move to Adelaide, while nursing only meant a move to the nurses' quarters at the hospital. The more distance she could put between herself and her mother, she reasoned, would suit them both.

For the first few months of 1944 Maisie was dedicated to her school work. Cleave was relegated only to Saturday afternoons at the Metropole, but she liked it when he inched his arm along the back of the seat until it rested around her shoulders. Sports days still received driven attention, though she gave no time to preparing for them, and she was delighted with several third-place wins in the March swimming carnival. She was less delighted to receive more War Savings Stamps. This carnival was, however, to create another unforgettable event.

Maisie's well-developed figure – and Rose's determination to hide it – had caused yet another battle between the two when Maisie asked for a bra. Rose would have none of it. She steadfastly proclaimed her daughter 'too young' – despite nature more loudly proclaiming otherwise. Maisie decided to make her own. She used a piece of plain material for the foundation and covered this with a piece of sheer fabric gathered in the middle. She was delighted with her handiwork and thought the garment quite beautiful – until she undressed to change into her bathers. The girls in their pretty store-bought underwear laughed uproariously at Maisie's efforts and even less endowed girls not yet presented with the problem found the scene amusing.

'This is just for me to get used to them,' Maisie yelled. 'I'm getting my real bras soon! This is just until then and it works just fine!' It was a valiant effort at not showing her humiliation, but burning cheeks gave her away and she ran for the toilet cubicle before tears did too. Whenever she later recounted the incident as an adult, Maisie would say her anger at the teasing (and at her mother) stripped seconds from her time in laps of the Zinc Mine Baths and triggered her triumphs.

Built in December 1933 for the use of employees only, the Zinc Corporation indoor heated pool was an engineering marvel for the day, noted as second only across the Commonwealth to the Athenaeum Club pool in Melbourne.

At 75 feet long by 20 feet wide, the pool was a standard short-course size but remarkable in its filtration system, which had it known as 'the crystal pool'. Sons of Zinc Corporation employees were allowed entry fairly soon after it opened, but wives and daughters had to wait two years before they were allowed to swim in the pool – and then only at specially designated sessions. Gradually the exclusivity restrictions lifted to allow the local schools to use it for carnivals when there was an issue with the City Baths for weather or other reasons and the two local swimming clubs were permitted to train there in winter, enjoying the luxury of water heated to 78 degrees Fahrenheit. Later, Dawn Fraser and Jon Henricks would be among six swimmers coach Harry Gallagher brought to train in the pool during the winter months leading to their 100 m freestyle gold medals at the 1956 Melbourne Olympic Games.

Jackie won more than a handful of War Savings Stamps at the March swimming carnival, showing true talent for the sport, and he was about to get more opportunity for training. In June, on his 15th birthday, he left school to take up a gardening apprenticeship at the Zinc Corporation. Maisie wasn't the only Schuster child to learn the joy of tending plants at their father's knee.

The swimming carnival was a small distraction for Maisie from her renewed dedication to schoolwork, but there was soon to be something much more diverting. The relationship with Cleave had gone the way of most 13-year-old's partnerships and there was a new beau on the scene.

John Dougherty was a fourth year student and school prefect. The pair sat together in the quadrangle every recess and lunchtime and Maisie was the envy of her classmates. School was now a heady whirl of social fun, exciting learning and sporting success. The escape it gave five days a week made evenings and weekends bearable. Confrontations with Rose came less often and were less volatile. Maisie longed for her father, but four years had mellowed the grief so it no longer sat at the back of her throat. Her 14th birthday, however, fractured her core as surely as Hitler's bombs splintered London.

Maisie had been home for a week to care for her mother, who had had another 'turn', when she came upon Rose wrapping her school uniform and some shirts in old newspapers ready for the Housewives' Association collection.

'What're you doing? That still fits. What are you *doing*?'

'You're not going back, my girl. You're 14 now and I need you here.'

Maisie tried to unwrap the parcel as quickly as Rose wrapped and the paper tore in the tussle. Panic was growing – although her mind tried to rationalise there was no need for it.

'But Mum, you need to be 15 this year. I've got another year and a bit. Did you forget?' Now some concern. Maybe her mother was as ill as she said?

Rose hadn't forgotten. She'd been an agitator (as part of the Housewives' Association) to extend the school leaving age, so she knew the schedule well – but thought it should only apply for boys. She'd been equally arduous in seeing girls taught domestic science in school. Maisie had had two full years of it and should have learned enough. Rose had written to the authorities for an exemption for her daughter. She had a heart condition and no husband, she told them, and her daughter would be leaving school in twelve months anyway. The exemption was granted.

Chapter 16

Forced labour

Maisie was miserable at home. She missed her lessons and she missed her sport, but mostly she missed her friends. Many of her new high school buddies lived in the north of the city. This was only a distance of some three and a half miles, but there was a distinct separation between North and South Broken Hill – and not just by the spine of mines that divided the population geographically.

Living 'out the south' stamped people with a specific socio-economic brand and not all parents approved their young mixing with 'southies', let alone a German southie. Public transport between the suburbs was difficult, home telephones were uncommon enough that only three digit numbers were needed to cover all home and business connections, and certainly there was not one to be found in the Schuster home.

Sometimes girlfriends living in the neighbourhood called to visit on their way home from school – Joyce and Pauline Morrow, Margaret Mayne, Velma Denham, June Jenkins, and Delcie and Dorothy – but Rose wasn't tolerant of idle pastimes. The girls would chat at the front gate for only a short time before Rose found an excuse to call her daughter in.

'Maisie! Come on, you've got to set the table for tea. The boys'll be home soon.'

The best friendships wither without conversation and John Dougherty soon found someone else to sit with in the quadrangle. Maisie felt lonely – isolated – and crushed each day by a monotonous and rigid cycle of housework.

Monday was washday. Early in the morning she used vinegar and salt to clean the 20-gallon 'copper'. This was a round-bottomed cauldron of copper sheeting that sat in the backyard above an iron fire-grate. After filling it with cold water from the hose, she set a fire beneath to bring the water to the boil and began to scrub the whites, including sheets, with soap on a corrugated washboard. These she added to the boiling water, stirring them occasionally with a wooden pole, while she worked on the coloureds in batches of darkness and dirtiness. By the time they had their turn in the copper, the water had cooled enough not to run the colours. She changed the water for rinsing and then prepared the final touch for the whites, a bath in 'blued' water, achieved by swirling a flannel bag containing a one-ounce cylindrical block of Reckitts' blue iron powder.

The clothesline ran almost the full length of the backyard and was composed of two T-shaped wooden poles, with cross beams drilled to take several strands of galvanised wire stretched between them. It was a clever contraption. The beams tilted on a fulcrum to progressively lower lines for pegging and were held back in horizontal position by tying ropes dangling from each end to a hook screwed into the mid-point of the poles. On 'a big wash', the weight of the clothes dragged down the long wires so another pole was used as a prop in the middle. Maisie struggled with the clothesline. She (like her mother) was not tall, so she needed to jump a little to reach the middle lines and, occasionally, the tail of a sheet dragged in the dirt before she could get it in place. Maisie speculated the abnormal height of the clothesline was not, as Rose said, 'to catch the breeze' but rather to show off the whiteness of the whites above the tall back fence.

Tuesday began with dampening and rolling clothes into tight sausages and repacking them, encased in a table cloth, into the washing basket ready for the day's ironing. Wednesdays were occupied with baking and Thursdays saw all the carpets dragged out of the house and hung on the line for a savage beating. Finally, the last day of the working week meant a clean-through of the house from top to bottom, including washing and polishing the linoleum floors. Polishing was a hands-and-knees job, the polish applied with one cloth and buffed with another. Sometimes Rose would allow Maisie to replace the polishing with a substantial slosh of kerosene to the wash water. But *nothing* changed Rose's housekeeping routine – except dust storms.

Rose's health improved to the point where she shared in the housework and on weekends Maisie had some freedom when her mother went to watch the boys in their various sports. Maxie was now doing very well at school-based cricket, football and swimming (as well as the boxing) and Jackie was now into everything – representing the Zinc Corporation in cycling, athletics and cricket, while playing soccer for the Napredak Club and swimming for the Silver City League Club. He was also playing Aussie Rules for Souths and Rose began taking herself up to the Alma Oval to watch him play. She didn't know it then, but Rose would become a fixture of the South Football Club, sharing Saturday afternoons all her life with a wooden bench, a tartan blanket over her knees and a thermos of tea at her feet. The line of Schuster South footy stars extended well beyond her life – through Maxie's son Reinhold and Jackie's grandson and great-grandsons.

Occasionally Maisie went to the footy too, but part of her begrudged the boys their sports and another part enjoyed the peace at home without Rose. She began to make new friendships – though not those usual for a 14-year-old girl.

These mostly involved the shopkeepers along Patton Street when she went 'to do the messages' listed by Rose. Shopping was an almost daily occurrence because of the lack of suitable refrigeration at home and she brightened the day of Italian and Yugoslav shop owners and staff as much as they brightened hers. Mostly the conversations were upbeat. The 'Aussie spirit' was alive and well in these migrants thought not entitled to it. But they shared an understanding of what it was like to be branded an enemy alien and there was also always a story to tell of how one person or another had been victimised due to their heritage.

The Schinellas attracted more than their fair share of attention for a while. Twenty-two-year-old Pasquale Schinella was three times before the court for having driven a van to deliver fruit and vegetables from his family's greengrocer store in Oxide Street. The fines increased each time to reach £5 (with eight shillings costs) and a threat of internment if he persisted. Pasquale explained he'd been doing all the deliveries by bicycle, but found one order too big for the bike, so borrowed his brother's utility.

'Don't you know that as an enemy alien you are not allowed to do this?' the judge asked him. 'If you appear again in court on this charge you will go to gaol.'

Pasquale's brother was then slapped with a ten shilling fine for not having surrendered the vehicle's number plates. Another brother, Fransisca, came to visit from Melbourne and was found during a raid on the Schinella's Crystal Street house. He was sent packing back to Melbourne with a 21-day gaol sentence (with hard labour) because he hadn't sought permission from police to be there.

Yet the Schinellas remained a community-minded family who sponsored many local sporting teams; supported local competitions; sent their daughters to sing and entertain at the old folks' home; and used their shop as a collection point for paper recycling to support the war effort.

There's an argument to be made that 'the aliens' (of any background) knew the rules and only needed to abide by them to stay out of trouble. But this had now gone on for more than five years – there were livelihoods at play – and the rules were applied so inconsistently. Michael Schinella was fined £3 (with 14 shillings costs) for not having renewed his radio licence for six months. He was joined in the dock that day by 117 local British people who likewise had not paid their fees, but his fine was no different to theirs. Nothing was made of the fact he was not allowed to own a radio, licenced or not.

So rules were rules and everyone knew them, but enforcement of those rules was arbitrary. The inconsistency not only caused confusion, but fear and resentment. It was impossible to predict what might happen next. There was a continuum of indignities for families that had roots in a now enemy nation. Where a specific family sat on that continuum seemed determined by who that family knew, rather than what individual members did. At one end sat long term internment and, at the other, court fines and confiscation of property. A cruel midpoint was men being ordered from their homes and their businesses and their families to work in distant labour camps building roads, mending railways, chopping wood, and shovelling salt to support the war effort.

The German, Yugoslav and Italian communities in Broken Hill knew of the mandatory labour camps (the camps had been progressively established following a February 1942 war cabinet resolution 'to enforce compulsory civilian labour service for enemy aliens') but it was not until 1943 that Broken Hill was directly touched by them.

Sixty aliens between the ages of 18 and 60 were ordered to report to the Central Police Station on 15 April. Here, with little explanation, they were subjected to medicals by local doctors Funder and Richards and 40 passed on for interview by officers of the Allied Works Council (AWC).

Barrier Miner Saturday 15 April 1943 (excerpts)

ENEMY ALIENS INTERVIEWED
BY MANPOWER

Enemy aliens were interviewed by manpower officers at the Police Station today, and the result of the interviews will determine whether some will go to the Allied Works Council projects, or whether they will better serve the country in their present work ...

If men were selected for Works Council jobs they would be directed to work at any place the Government might decide.

Most enemy aliens were used in labor camps on work associated with State or Commonwealth projects. Most of the aliens in South Australia were engaged in wood cutting.

Mr. Marshall explained that for Army purposes, Broken Hill came within the South Australian Lines of Communication Command.

Messrs. Marshall and Argus hope to complete their interviews today. Men selected for work would be notified by the police where to proceed to.

There was no choice in participation. Neither was there a choice in where the work would be performed nor what type of work they would do. The Army Minister Mr Forde explained it by saying that the men had 'enjoyed the security of economic benefits of living in Australia in peace time and must now give national service as other sections of the community'.

His reference was to the fact conscription was then in place across Australia to feed into the Citizen Military Forces (charged with defending Australia in the event of invasion). But these people weren't treated like 'other sections of the community' at any other time. They couldn't drive; they couldn't own a house (or even negotiate a long-term lease on a rental); they couldn't travel to visit family without permission; they were forbidden to speak their birth language; they couldn't own a camera to take family snaps or listen to a radio – but they were expected to make huge sacrifices to support a country that inflicted all these controls on them – to sleep on a concrete floor in a tin hut and work seven days a week. Left at home were wives who tried to keep their shops open and raise their children.

On 3 May 1943, the labour camps were formalised to become the

Civil Aliens Corps. That night, 11 enemy aliens – mostly Italians – left Broken Hill on the train for Adelaide. The next day the *Barrier Miner* reported, 'Those who left last night will be allotted to various works under the control of the AWC.'

More than 18 months later, these men were still away from their families. They were allowed days off – and even leave after a period – but the travel time between rural South Australian camps, Adelaide, then Broken Hill meant those who attempted it often returned overdue for their work and were punished for it. As Maisie's friendships with the shopkeepers developed, she was careful to ask after those still 'away'.

She saw the injustice in all this, and had come to think unfairness an unremitting part of life. She saw it between boys and girls, between mineworkers and town workers, between South and North people and certainly between those born in Australia and those who chose it. The tales from her shopkeeper friends shamed her, because it was an injustice so much greater than her being forced to stay at home with her mother.

A tentative companionship began to develop between Maisie and Rose. Each day, when the mid-morning radio serials came on Dulcie's radio, they stopped work to sit and listen together to favourites such as *Dad and Dave from Snake Gully*, as they shared a piece of fruit and a cup of freshly brewed tea.

It was a Dad and Dave episode that brought about change. Dave kicked his toe against the leg of a kitchen table, bringing raucous noise from the radio, but Maisie was instantly listening to her father's gentle voice as they sat on the white rocks in the backyard.

'When you stub your toe against a rock, *kleine Tochter*, you only need find a man with a broken leg to measure the true strength of your pain. But that does not mean you should not tend the toe. It still hurts. So dry your tears now, but do go to your *Mutter* for a bandage.'

Maisie decided she needed a bandage for her life – so she went and found herself a job.

Chapter 17

Bells and whistles

Maisie's need for 'a bandage on her life' was a godsend for Methodios (Mick) Evangelidis. He had arrived in Australia from Greece in 1937 and in Broken Hill two years later to run the busy South Dry Cleaners at 194 Patton Street. Two years into the war, he tried to purchase Wilson's Dry Cleaners further along Patton Street (at 178) to expand his business but, as an enemy alien, had to seek special permission. His application was buried for months and finally he withdrew it because the shop had been sold to someone else.

Mick was also a tailor and, at the time a 14-year-old Maisie came asking for work in the Christmas of 1944, he'd been struggling for months to juggle the cleaning and pressing of clothes; the store cleaning; counter service; and a huge demand for repairs and alterations (because clothing rations meant old clothes needed to last). Finding staff had been difficult. Hundreds of young girls were working at the Munitions Annexe on wages he couldn't hope to match. They weren't meant to be there.

Broken Hill's clamour for a munitions plant in the early war years had been not so much about patriotism (who knew the war would develop as it did?) but to provide jobs for men turned out of work by the cancellation of export contracts and the closure of the Central Mine. When the factory was finally ready to open in late 1942, there was no need for it on that front. The mines were under pressure to continually escalate production; thousands of men had enlisted; hundreds had left town with travel and accommodation support to work in Adelaide factories; and the men left unemployed were mostly enemy aliens – who certainly couldn't be trusted for this type of work! So the women did it – and by this time the patriotism was fierce.

This gender exchange was a relief to the government, who had been in a stand-off with the BIC over wages. The unions wanted local award pay for their members; the government wanted to pay what was paid in munitions factories around the country. The BIC won, but bringing women into the equation lowered the overall cost because of their lesser wages.

Of the 384 jobs created, only 80 were filled by men. They were employed to 'set' the automated equipment – and then operation of it was suitable as 'women's work'.

'There is practically nothing for the women to do but watch the machine and see that it is in running order and check the measurements of the finished part with a gauge,' Factory Manager J.L. Mayson assured the community through the pages of the *Barrier Miner*. He also promised potential applicants there was 'no strain attached to the work' and that it was 'quite within the reach of an average girl'. Those average girls produced in three years almost 650,000 nose cone assemblies for 25 pound shells, each with 26 separately machined and intricately fitted parts.

Mick Evangelidis thought there was nothing average about Maisie. She was a hard worker, quick and eager to learn, and got on well with the customers at the front counter. Whenever Rose called in, forced now to do most of her own messages, Mick would tell her, 'This is a good girl you have. She is the best girl I ever have work here! There should be more of her along this street'.

Maisie thrived on the praise. Although Mick didn't look like her father and, at 35, was certainly much younger, there was a gentleness and kindness about him that was remarkably similar. She was again feeling a little 'special'.

Her first chore of the day was to run down the street with a billy-can to buy the day's supply of fresh milk. To this, Mick added a surprisingly generous helping of sugar (enough, Maisie thought, to consume all his ration coupons). Maisie was to sip this mixture continuously throughout the day, he warned her.

'The milk will line your stomach against the fumes from the white spirits. The sugar will replace your energy. It is hot work.' And it was.

Initially she just did the menial tasks – sort the clothes, turn the pockets out, brush the seams with a stiff brush to loosen fluff and tobacco and sweep the floor. Within a short time, Mick trusted her to spread the jackets and dresses on a big table and use the white spirits to spot the stains before they went into the big cylindrical machine. When the timer sounded, she mostly beat him to the machine to remove each garment, give it a good shake and hang it over the airer on the back veranda. They almost always shared a companionable lunch and Maisie learned to love Greek food, while Mick remained ambivalent about the home-made German mettwurst Maisie brought. (It was no longer sold in shops, so Rose made her own – albeit with more goat than pork.)

After lunch Maisie brought the clothes in, righted the pockets and folded trousers legs with the seams perfectly together ready for Mick to press. It was a busy day, but she enjoyed it. As the months went by Mick taught her to use the cash register and write up dockets, clean the big machine and even to add white spirits to exactly the right level so the clothes were cleaned without getting wet. The work gave little mental stimulation for a bright young girl, but Maisie was accustomed to mundane tasks and she enjoyed the social contact with regular customers and the friendship with Mick. She felt useful and valued. It wasn't to last.

On Thursday 12 April 1945 US President Roosevelt died and a little piece of Maisie died too. She and Mick were listening to the news on the shop radio when Maxie came rushing in. Rose had had another turn. The doctor had been called and Maisie was needed at home.

Maisie ran all the way, leaving Maxie well behind – although, to be fair, he had already run to the shop. She wasn't sure what she expected to find at the house, but certainly it wasn't her mother sitting at the kitchen table sharing a pot of tea with the doctor. Relief that a loved one is okay when feared otherwise is often quickly replaced by anger. So it was with Maisie. The anger turned to burning resentment when she heard Rose didn't only need her home today, but every day.

She knew it was her responsibility to care for her mother when ill. Topsy was now in Adelaide, Eve in Murray Bridge, and Dulcie was married with twin girls – Dawn and Joyce – so there was no one else. But as the weeks progressed she didn't believe her mother was sick enough for full-time care. The doctor diagnosed 'hardening of the arteries', but Maisie thought her mother was just plain hard. Rose flatly refused for her to go back to work. The few shillings Maisie had been earning weren't enough to make a real difference to the household budget, but having her daughter in the house was enough to settle Rose's fears of being alone. Bickering between the two intensified over the next weeks, with neither prepared to give way. A truce may never have settled on the Schuster household, but for surrender overseas.

On Monday 7 May 1945 the *Barrier Miner* blared across its front page:

COMPLETE NAZI SURRENDER SOON

Allied Headquarters Now Expect End In Few Hours; King George To Broadcast

Speculation the end of the war in Europe was imminent had been around since the beginning of the year. With each successive defeat of German troops, the end had seemed closer, but then people remembered how hopeful they'd been the previous year – until Germany had unleashed its fury at Ardennes in a barrage of artillery fire longer than had been seen before, later to become known as the Battle of the Bulge. So, even with this headline, people were nervous to believe it.

The next day it was real. The mines blew their whistles repetitively, the churches rang their bells continuously and the people of Broken Hill thronged in Argent Street. Coincidentally, the first ball of the dancing season, the Convent Ball, was held that night for 30 debutantes in the Palais de Danse, but it was now packed with such carnival spirit, the dancing was allowed to continue past its midnight schedule to 2 am.

More specific and formal celebrations were held on the Wednesday – with a public holiday for the mines and schools and a surprising forced closure of the city's hotels. Thousands met on the corner of Argent and Chloride streets for a concert and community singalong out the front of the Grand Hotel. On the Thursday, the masses headed for Sturt Park for multi-denominational thanks-giving prayer services and on the Friday people gathered on street corners to blame the Germans for tearing down more than 80 Union Jack flags and V-E Day (Victory in Europe) bunting from shop fronts in the main street. Later it was found to be high-spirited revellers who had taken the flags along to their own celebrations and most were returned. Although the battle with Japan in the Pacific was not yet over, Broken Hill was wild with joy.

The Schusters stayed home during all this. It wasn't that they weren't happy the war was over and that the Allies had won. Of course they were. But each time there had been a milestone in the war – Italy's revolt against Germany; the recapture of Rome; the Allied invasion of Normandy; the German failed assassination of Hitler; the landing in the South of France and the liberation of Paris; the Allies' entry into Yugoslavia and the liberation of Belgrade; Russia's capture of Warsaw and entry into Berlin; and Hitler's suicide – the hatred of all things German had erupted again like an overripe abscess. They were afraid to go out on the streets where there were crowds. They were afraid to gather with other members of the German community. So they stayed home together.

The following week Maxie went back to Alma School and Jackie went back to work, but Rose and Maisie remained secluded a while longer. They hid from the jubilation in the streets as reports came in of 250,000 Germans (sometimes claimed to be 500,000) taken as prisoners, because they thought they would be exposed for not sharing it. It was difficult not to wonder whether Jack's brothers and nephews were among them, though they didn't know whether they had even fought in the war. This led them to talk about the near-destruction of Dresden in February, not far from the Schuster clan base at Lausitz. As Rose spoke with concern about the German people and what she knew of Jack's German friends, Maisie felt a new bond with her. She felt united in the love of their gentle German and she understood her mother's grief in a way she had not been able to when Jack died. She was growing up.

On Rose's birthday in June, Maisie 'set' her mother's hair, painstakingly rolling strands around various size curlers and pinning these in place with a U-shaped prong. The two chatted as Rose sat by the fire for her hair to dry and after lunch Maisie spent some time combing out the curls to form quite an elaborate coiffure. With soft waves around her face, rouge on her cheeks and some lipstick scraped from an empty tube with a bobby pin, Maisie could see signs of a once pretty girl. She would have been a baby once, she thought, and babies aren't born with a hard heart. Things happen to them.

Rose went off to her afternoon tea birthday celebrations with her Housewives' friends and later came home to proudly tell Maisie about the reaction from the other women to her new 'do'. They had loved it! Most wouldn't believe that 'young Maisie' had been able to replicate the new style seen in newspaper advertisements. Rose had promised them Maisie would do theirs too. It was a promise she would come to regret.

Maisie was at first resentful that her mother had so generously committed her time but, as she made the rounds of the women one after another over the next weeks, she found she really enjoyed it. It got her out of the house (though not away from Rose, because she came too) and she enjoyed the challenge as she struggled to reproduce the styles women clipped from the paper. Her tenacity paid off. In early July, neighbour Gloria Sinclair joined the queue of women seeking free hairdos. Gloria owned a Patton Street hairdressing salon and offered Maisie an apprenticeship.

She was so excited. This wasn't just a job – this was a career! Her father had given her a sense she could achieve much in life, her mother had given her a drive that had previously worked well for sports competitions. Now she would combine the two. Rose could hardly refuse her, given the circumstance of the job offer, so Maisie started work the next day.

The senior apprentice at the salon was Valmae Hill, who was not much older than Maisie, but an outstanding hairdresser and excellent teacher and mentor. She would later become renowned in Broken Hill as Val Kelly – as much for her hairdressing as for the fact she produced 12 children in 15 years, yet retained the beauteous youth of a 21-year-old.

Maisie thrived working with Val. Even giving her five shillings weekly pay packet straight to Rose for 'board and lodging' did little to dampen her enthusiasm. Within a couple of months, she was promoted and the pay packet swelled to seven shillings and sixpence. All the praise she received for her work had restored some self-confidence and she refused to hand over the extra to Rose. Maisie now had two shillings and sixpence to spend on herself and felt quite grown-up to be able to purchase her own choice of clothing with the money she saved. Her first three purchases were bras.

Chapter 18

The horrors of war
August 1945

At 9.15 am on 6 August 1945 the United States dropped an atomic bomb on Hiroshima. There had been huge American and Australian losses fighting the Japanese, island upon island, across the Pacific. Japan was in retreat, but refusing to surrender, and this terrible secret weapon was unleashed as a means of changing their minds. It didn't. On 9 August another atomic bomb decimated Nagasaki.

The real mortality of the bombs cannot be known, such was the devastation and chaos. Thousands of people took some weeks to die, having initially been well enough to travel some distance, and this added to the confusion. But it is generally accepted as around 225,000 civilians. In between the two bombs, the Soviets declared war on Japan and began to advance on Manchuria. There is some debate today whether it was the bombs or the Soviet declaration that forced the hand of Emperor Hirohito, but on 15 August he announced Japan's almost unconditional surrender. It would take until 2 September for the surrender to be formalised.

Broken Hill erupted. The mine whistles and sirens again competed with church bells and the streets flooded with people called out of their homes (dressed in red, white and blue) by a need to share their joy widely. This time there was a two-day holiday.

Maisie was initially unable to give herself fully to the celebrations. The announced surrender had come just one day after the fifth anniversary of Jack's death, but it wasn't her personal 'sore toe' that tore at her. She wondered what her father would have thought if he'd read the terrible and graphic descriptions of what happened to those Japanese men, women and children.

The newspapers seemed to delight in detailing it, but it was obvious most commentators didn't yet understand this previously unknown weapon. Perhaps they felt the need to create such explicit imagery because, for everyone, the gruesome consequences of atomic warfare were beyond comprehension. Or perhaps it was that awful human trait that keeps us watching or reading beyond horror.

Maisie decided her father would have told her to find the good in among the bad and that she should rejoice, along with the rest of Broken Hill, that there would be no more killing.

On Thursday morning she went with Dorothy and Delcie and some other girls to watch the V-P Day (Victory in the Pacific – sometimes later labelled V-J Day) procession. It was organised by the BIC and local ALP branch and included about 300 unionists marching along with the BIU Band and the Scotch Pipers Band. The crowds packed into the Town Hall for a thanksgiving service led by the Ministerial Association and Maisie finally had her chance to marvel at the interior of a building that had beguiled her for more than seven years. She found nothing marvellous.

The only thing majestic about the great hall was its size. The paintwork was dingy all over and peeling in many places. Patches of plaster had fallen away to expose the walls beneath and much of the timberwork had been refused paint for so long it was now bare. The high ceiling, once ornate she supposed, was now dirty and red dust clung to long thick spider webs that even her best attempt couldn't imagine to be 'lacy'. The magnificent exterior of the town hall and its deceptive staircase inside led only to a tired old lady that had long given up any pretence of beauty. 'Much like Mum,' was her first thought. But then she realised she, too, was tired and uncared for on the inside and she was not yet 15! She was happy to leave at the end of the service.

In the afternoon the whole family went to a Zinc Corporation picnic on the Zinc Oval. Jackie starred in the bicycle races and other sporting events and the celebrations continued into the night with a spectacular fireworks display. The South and North Mine picnics were held the next day and elsewhere there was a golf competition and a gymkhana.

These celebrations were well planned. On the day *before* the announced surrender, the Mine Picnic Committees had brought into town on the Adelaide train 800 dozen ice creams, 400 dozen cartons of milk (850 gallons), 30 cases of oranges, 20 crates of bananas, and 500 pounds of sausages. The consignment had been warehoused patiently in the cold storage chambers of numerous shops and now came out for distribution accompanied by lollies and nuts for the children.

There were poignant moments in among the revelry. Every gathering included a one-minute silence for those who had died and the RSL led a march to the Fallen Soldier's Memorial. Here bugler Joseph Keenan sounded the 'Stand To' and 'Last Post' and, finally, 'Reveille'.

Of the 4000 Broken Hill people who had left the city to play their part in the war for Australia, more than 2800 young men had been in the thick of the fight. Most of them (2132) served in the Army, but there were 664 in the Air Force and just 25 who found their way into the Navy [*Author's aside: among them, my then future father-in-law Ronald Edward Ellis at 18 years old*]. More than 100 of these people would never come home.

Their bodies lie in 32 war cemeteries in 14 countries. For a few, there is no grave – just a name on a memorial in some distant place. About one-quarter of those from Broken Hill killed in action are in the cemeteries of Papua New Guinea, but battles in Borneo also proved costly for the town and there are more than a few in Germany, at El Alamein in Egypt, at Tobruk in Libya; some in Lebanon, Indonesia, Singapore and England; and solitary Broken Hill graves in France, Greece, China and Myanmar. Broken Hill boys served in all spheres of the war. Fifteen injured made it back to Australian soil only to be buried in it at various locations and just four made it all the way home to Broken Hill to be laid to rest in the Rakow Street cemetery.

Hundreds more came home with debilitating physical injuries and others brought back to their families mental conditions that would be diagnosed today as Post Traumatic Stress Disorder. More than 30 Broken Hill people were recognised for bravery – one Military Cross, nine Distinguished Flying Crosses, two Distinguished Conduct Medals, four Military Medals, three Distinguished Flying Medals, three citations or commendations and ten people Mentioned in Despatches.

One of those Mentioned in Despatches posthumously was Sister Irene Drummond. While there were more than 100 families grieving individually in Broken Hill, the report of this death united the community in sorrow.

Sister Drummond had been dead eight months before the October 1942 news report that she was missing – and years before Maisie stopped collecting school reports and test results for her. The snippets of news that speculated she had been on a ship that was sunk escaping Singapore were largely ignored. There was 'nothing definite' and Broken Hill had an example of the Denton family, who grieved for a son reported dead by telegram only to find he was alive and well. So people chose to believe 'their' Sister Drummond would come home too. Instead, it was Japan's prisoners from Changi and other brutal camps who came home, bringing with them the true horror of this beloved woman's murder.

Irene Melville Drummond had grown up in Broken Hill. Her father Cedric was manager of the Vacuum Oil Company and Irene went to local Catholic schools before the family moved to Adelaide. She returned to Broken Hill as a 28-year-old trained nurse and spent the next seven years winning over the Broken Hill people with her compassion and nursing skills – first as a surgical sister and then assistant (sometimes acting) matron, which she was when Maisie met her.

After leaving Broken Hill in October 1940 to enlist in the Australian Army Nursing Service, Irene left Australia three months later, in January 1941. She was placed in charge of a Casualty Clearing Station at Port Dickson in Malaysia and quickly promoted to matron (with a rank of major) at the Australian General Hospital of Johore Bahru. The rapidly advancing Japanese forced evacuation of this hospital to the bastion of Singapore, where records speak of Matron Drummond's 'quiet efficiency' in setting up a hospital within 48 hours in the St Patrick's School. She 'kept her cool' even as the Japanese made their relentless path southward and managed a well-functioning hospital despite increasing chaos around her, spasmodic air raids and rapidly mounting battle casualties.

As the relentless Japanese march became more menacing, half the 130 Australian nurses at the hospital were evacuated. Matron Drummond and 65 nurses refused to leave and remained to care for the ill and wounded. Among Matron Drummond's charges was Lieutenant (later Captain) Vivian Bullwinkel who had grown up in Broken Hill and returned to train at the Broken Hill Hospital, although she was living and working in Victoria at the time of her enlistment.

By 12 February, Singapore was under constant air attack and surrender was imminent, so finally the remaining nurses boarded an ill-equipped coastal freighter, the *Vyner Brooke*, accompanied by wounded servicemen, civilian women and children in a flotilla of ships preparing for the perilous journey to Australia.

On the sunny morning of 14 February the freighter was anchored in calm waters near an island off the coast of Sumatra when a Japanese plane flew overhead. It circled to machine-gun the boat. When it left, the freighter steamed down the coast. But it had been seen.

At 2 pm, six Japanese bombers came to finish the job and those on board scrambled for life boats as the freighter sank. Matron Drummond was seen to scoop up a small Chinese boy into her boat.

Not everyone made it to Radji Beach on Bangka Island. Some

died on the steamer; others drowned during their many hours in the water as they attempted to swim to shore; others floated past the beach in their life boat to Muntok Bay to live a different story as prisoners-of-war. The group that made it to the beach included civilian women and children, wounded servicemen, some of the ship's crew, and nurses, including Irene Drummond and Vivian Bullwinkel.

The group was divided about the best course of action. Bangka Island was already in the hands of the Japanese and everyone knew there would be no help from the local population, so surrender won out. The ship's Captain, the civilian children and all but one of the civilian women began the ten-mile trek inland to the settlement at Muntok, accompanied by the fittest of the wounded servicemen. Twenty-one nurses, one civilian woman and some of the ship's crew remained with the wounded men on the beach and the next day were joined by some British servicemen who had also been shipwrecked. The following day, they were found by a Japanese officer and 20 soldiers.

Heedless of the group's claim they were surrendering, the soldiers herded the women into a huddled group and left a few soldiers to guard them. The other soldiers marched, goaded and dragged wounded men around a bluff at the end of the beach. The women heard the shots. They knew their men were dead. The soldiers emphasised the fact by coming back into view with bayonets dripping blood.

Some of the women must have held hopes they were to be saved – or why would the soldiers have taken the men out of view to kill them? It was false hope. Or something changed. The officer ordered the women to line up with their backs to his soldiers and walk into the water. Some of the young nurses looked toward Matron Drummond.

'Girls, we have run from the wounded once, we are not going to do it again,' she called out to them.

As she led the nurses into the water she called out again, 'Chin up girls! I'm proud of you and I love you all!'

The officer gave the order and the women were riddled with machine-gun bullets. Irene Drummond was one of the first to fall.

The only survivor of this massacre was Vivian Bullwinkel. She was shot in the side, but the bullet passed through her body. She pretended she was dead by floating among the corpses, even as the Japanese soldiers moved among them, bayonetting any that were not yet dead.

Vivian stayed in the water for hours, only scrambling for cover in the foliage at the back of the beach when she was sure the soldiers had left. There she met up with a British private who had likewise been wounded and feigned death beyond the bluff. They hid together for 12 days, with Vivian tending his wounds, but eventually surrendered at Muntok. The private died soon after, but Vivian remained a prisoner-of-war for three and half years. As the only survivor of the massacre, she testified at a Tokyo war crimes tribunal in 1947. Her diaries provided intimate and damning evidence of the slaughter.

Vivian Bullwinkel died in July 2000 at the age of 84. She left a long list of wonderful post-war achievements – including rescuing Vietnamese war orphans from Saigon, establishing scholarships for Malaysian nurses and ensuring there was a fitting memorial to her colleagues who died on Radji Beach. Her nursing achievements and her time as a prisoner-of-war are well documented in books and film.

Irene Drummond's legacy is less tangible, but her touch on others outlived her. Her nurses who survived the horrors of imprisonment at Muntok would always remember her compassion, leadership, heroism and indomitable spirit. Many wrote of it. Broken Hill people who knew her would always remember her kindness and skills.

Maisie was 15 when she was confronted by the details of 'Sister' Drummond's death. She shed many tears for her. She had met this

Broken Hill's much-loved 'Sister Drummond'.

woman only once, as a child naïve enough to believe women weren't killed in war. She was old enough when she learned of her death to understand the personal plans she had made with her that day would never have become reality – but she was still young enough to believe this wonderful nurse now really was an angel. She thought Jack and Irene would really like each other.

As a 19-year-old, Maisie would stand among the thousands of people that turned out to honour their favourite nurse with the consecration of a landscaped park and playground on the corner of the hospital grounds. It was constructed with almost £700 raised by the community and a plaque reads:

To recall the heroic sacrifice of a former sister of this hospital

SFX10594 MAJOR IRENE MELVILLE DRUMMOND.

One of 21 Australian Army nurses massacred by the Japanese
Army at Bangka Island on Feb. 16th 1942.

This park is fondly dedicated.

Lest We Forget

Vivian Bullwinkel and Irene's father were guests of honour at the dedication and the crowd was hushed as Cedric Drummond spoke of his daughter.

Barrier Miner Monday 10 October 1949 (excerpt)

High Tribute Paid to Heroic Nursing Sister

Impressive Opening Of Memorial Playground

"It is certainly a trying time but one which will live in our memory. The love and affection that has been bestowed upon my daughter by Broken Hill and its people is no greater than the love she held for the people of Broken Hill. I shall always remember this garden and I hope that it will give great pleasure to the people of Broken Hill always. My daughter's love for children was second only to her love for tending the sick and the suffering."

Neither Cedric nor his daughter ever knew how much that love for children impacted on a ten-year-old girl who needed a plan for her life, at a time when the most important thing in it was gone.

Chapter 19
Changes and chances
1946

The Bangka Island massacre was one of many horror stories involving Broken Hill people to emerge at the end of World War II, in a town already frustrated because surviving loved ones had yet to come home. Australia still had a significant role as part of the British Commonwealth Occupation Forces in Japan, so army discharges were taking some time. As information filtered back and people began to learn of incredible atrocities, the joy they had felt in Japan's surrender was replaced by anger and racial hatred.

This was a time Maisie didn't feel victimised for her heritage. It seemed the boiling hatred had a clear focus on Japanese people rather than Germans. Perhaps it was images of skeletal Australians forced to build a ridiculous Thailand-Burma railway that directed the hatred, but those images should have been countered by the horrendous photographs also emerging from Auschwitz. Instead there was only the occasional unkind goad.

'See your cousins got done like a dog's dinner!'

Maisie shrugged it off and sailed through the end of 1945 and early 1946. She loved her job, her 'pin money' and her freedom. She now had a lovely circle of friends – Helen and Barbara Battnich, Olga Cetinich, Nera and Doris Separovich, and Hilda Ravlich – and the girls often went dancing at the Town Hall or the Palais de Danse, where they also had fun rollerskating. Jackie Davey (one of the boys Maisie had invited to rescue Jackie's 14th birthday party) was now her regular boyfriend, although she dated the gentle Milton Lavers for a time and would always remember him with great affection. It was a heady time for a girl not yet 16.

It wasn't 'heady' for Rose – more alarming. She felt her daughter had 'got a little uppity' because of the praise she received at the salon; was powerless over how Maisie dressed because she had no control over how she spent the balance of her wage; and now there was a social whirl that kept her away on weekends, in addition to the weekdays at work. She didn't *know* about the dating, but suspected it. Maisie would later regret she didn't see the warning signs.

By the middle of the year most of the returning servicemen and women had arrived and thousands of people turned out to cheer them as they trooped in a Victory Parade on 10 June. Many had been away for several years – young men grown old in battle – and they marched in a streetscape significantly changed. Buildings had been torn down while others had gone up or been extended. The munitions factory had been constructed and was now handed to the Technical College for the training of apprentices; there was a Woolworth's store; the hospital had opened and had a 100-foot chimney stack that hadn't been there before; the RSL Club now occupied the Palace Hotel – the list is long. But the changes weren't just to infrastructure. Women had been working, not only in the munitions factory, but on the mines. It was a shock to find them out of the cafeteria, working as typists, tracers and laboratory assistants. They didn't go back.

More welcome changes included a new industrial agreement that gave better pay, increased overtime rates, extra paid holidays – and a new method of calculating lead bonus payments that was bulking out pay packets. Workers would have been even more pleased if they'd known this new system would result five years later in the lead bonus being worth almost double their basic wages. And there was no shortage of jobs. Broken Hill was booming. Civilian industry had a ravenous need of metal having been denied it for six years, and even the pastoralists were thriving, with the same insatiable demand for their wool. Life, for almost all, was good. Only those left with depleted families grieved in this brave new world.

This time it was Delcie Baum who came rushing to Patton Street

Victory Day Celebrations, 10 June 1946.

to bring Maisie home from work because Rose had 'had a turn' and, this time, Maisie found Rose in bed.

'The doctor's gone, girlie,' she declared. 'He said I have to stay here for four weeks.'

At first, Maisie wasn't alarmed. She'd been at the salon for almost twelve months and Mrs Sinclair agreed she could take holidays to care for her mother. Then she called the next day to visit Rose and things changed. The salon was just too busy to wait for Maisie to come back and she couldn't really afford a second-year apprentice anyway. Maisie's place was home with her mother who needed her.

Maisie spent the rest of that day crying on her bed. It was fortunate there was a big pot of pea and ham soup sitting on the back of the kitchen stove (a constant in winter) or the family would have had no dinner. Eventually she took a bowl and some toast to her mother, but when the boys sat expectantly at the long wooden table she yelled at them to get their own.

Maisie (15) with Dulcie's twins Dawn, left, and Joyce on holiday in Semaphore.

'Why does it have to be me?' she stormed. 'Yes, you've got a job Jackie, but so did I! So you're still at school Maxie, but so was I!'

She knew it wasn't the boys' fault. Jackie's income was several times hers and much needed. Maxie was not yet 14. Later, she felt guilty about the explosion but, if she was honest, the guilt was more that her mother would have heard her. It had felt good to yell at her brothers.

Rose was now 55 – the same age Jack had been when he died. There had been several scares before her father had finally succumbed to the 'dust on the lungs' that killed him. Maisie remembered her father had been told his illness was like trying to climb a sand dune, that every step up would be followed by a little slide downward as the sand gave way beneath his feet. She worried that her mother's footing on life might be similarly tenuous and she resolved to be kinder. This resolve had a little hiccup when Rose, who had missed the Housewives' Association meeting on the Wednesday, decided 'a walk in fresh air' would do her some good and went to watch Jackie play football on Saturday.

The outing proved to be a godsend. Though Rose still refused to be left alone full-time, it signified she was able to cope for some hours, so Maisie formed an escape plan. She dragged the boys' old bike from behind the sleep-out, gave it a quick spruce up, wired a new basket to the handlebars, and it was ready for action. She was now a mobile hairdresser!

It took little time to build a substantial clientele – both from Rose's friends and neighbours who were willing to pay for what they previously had had for free and from clients who liked Maisie from the salon. The guilt at poaching was fleeting.

She soon had a regular route for each weekday. On the morning run, she did cuts, shampoos and 'sets'. The sets for older women meant meticulously and tightly rolling the hair on orderly rows of curlers – a strip through the middle first, then two equal sections on each side of the head, rollers decreasing in size from top to bottom. Hollywood starlet Rita Hayworth was the style guide for the younger women, so Maisie bought her own supplies of butterfly clamps and setting lotions. Wave-sets were achieved by pinching the hair horizontally between the index and middle fingers and holding this in place by a metal spring clamp in successive rows following the same pattern as the rollers, or more ornately positioned to one side.

She repeated the route in the afternoon when the sets had had a chance to dry, but this round was shorter because some women managed their own comb-out. She soon became adept at creating glorious 'Victory Rolls' (bouffant backswept coils at the front and sides, so named because they were meant to replicate the victory roll manoeuvres of war-time pilots). After the drabness of the war years, her clients were grateful for a little glamour.

The business quickly became quite lucrative. She charged one shilling for a cut, two shillings for a shampoo and set, and an extra shilling if she had to go back for the styling. It was much more than she had been earning as an apprentice. Even when Rose increased her board, she still had plenty of cash left after purchasing her products to save a nice little nest egg.

The social whirl, however, had stopped. Even had there been time and Rose's approval, the constant pedalling between house-calls and the chores at home made her too weary for it. But she was less lonely than she had been on previous home confinements because her life had new purpose: she was creating a garden in tribute to her father.

Jack's beautiful vegetable gardens had long gone. Six years of drought and Maisie's lack of heart to battle against the elements to sustain them now had the backyard a barren waste. Even the fruit trees had withered. The only memorial to what had once been lush and bountiful were the circles of rocks, once whitewashed, but now red with dirt. These she moved one by one to the front yard to form a layered rockery and, in between, she planted cuttings and succulent pups she begged from clients on her hairdressing round.

Most gardens in the town were now bare or consisted only of drought-tolerant species. From August 1943 to January 1946, Broken Hill only survived because of water trains that rolled into town with supplies pumped from the Darling River at Menindee. The Stephens Creek Reservoir, 10 miles from Broken Hill, was dry and there was little in the huge Umberumberka Reservoir (built 22 miles north-west of the city to hold almost three million gallons) – certainly not enough to supply residences and mines. Between four and eight trains a day supplied the mines (up to five million gallons weekly) so what was left in Umberumberka could be saved for the town. A small crowd usually watched as the trains took more than an hour to disgorge their water into troughs to then flow to a receiving tank and on to huge tanks on Water Works Hill.

In May 1946, the first sod was turned in an ambitious project funded by the mining companies and the New South Wales

Government to build a 72-mile pipeline to carry water from the Darling River at Menindee to the Stephens Creek Reservoir and then in to Broken Hill. The 24-inch concrete-lined pipe was to carry five million gallons of water daily. Ultimately it would take six years for the mammoth pipeline to be built – and another eight to harness the Darling River and construct the Menindee Lakes Storage Scheme to guarantee Broken Hill 'a permanent water supply'. [*Author's aside: It didn't. Although it stood the test of time for more than 60 years, Broken Hill is again battling with water and, at the time of writing, the New South Wales Government has announced a $500 million project to build a 270 kilometre pipeline from the Murray River to provide water security for the city and surrounds.*]

The 1940–1946 drought had broken on 17 January with a three-day deluge that saw Umberumberka rise eight foot five inches in a few hours as its catchment area drained. The trains had stopped, but Broken Hill gardeners had learned lessons from the heavens they'd refused to learn from Albert and Margaret Morris.

Maisie would later wonder if she had understood more of the conversations between Uncle Bert and her father than she'd thought, for her rockery garden flourished beyond all expectations. Everyone could grow cactus and succulents, but no one could coax the kaleidoscope of colours Maisie achieved in massed flowerings. It became a stopping point for those walking to the Patton Street shops and she basked in the praise. Gardening would remain a passion all her life and she created many showpieces, but this first garden of scavenged bits and pieces remained the one of which she was most proud.

So this most recent period of 'home detention' had some benefits, but it was nonetheless frustrating. Maisie had enjoyed a significant period of responsibility at work, some financial independence and success as an entrepreneur, but was now returned to the status of child. She felt suffocated. As she progressively resisted being under

Rose's direction, the tenuous armistice began to crumble. Rose didn't feel Maisie too grown for a good slapping when needed and only an extraordinary opportunity defused a looming explosion.

The new owner of the South Rosette Hairdressing Salon on the corner of Patton and Bonanza streets was not a hairdresser and was looking for someone to manage the salon, supported by a young apprentice. It was the manager's position she offered Maisie.

'But I'm not even qualified,' Maisie protested. She wasn't keen to return to an apprenticeship, but she felt any other offer was a mistake. 'I can't do that!'

All manner of things can be made to happen in a town like Broken Hill. First, there was a visit to the Trades Hall, where her old bosses Gloria Sinclair and Valmae Kelly helped to convince the new Town Employees Union Secretary Jack Davey that Maisie was talented and clever enough for the job. He arranged for an examiner to come from Sydney. It was standard practice for all women who completed their four-year apprenticeship to sit both a theoretical examination and a practical demonstration prior to certification. This was fast-tracked for the end of 1946, with Maisie in the mix. She passed with flying colours.

She was just 16 years old. Not only was she a registered hairdresser and beauty operator, but managing a busy salon at the intersection of South Broken Hill's two main streets. Her base salary of four pounds two shillings and nine pence was already a princely sum for the day, but quarterly bonuses for attracting new clients meant she, and her friends, thought she earned a fortune!

Maisie's apprentice was 15-year-old Lorna Harris, who proved to be a quick learner under the tutelage of a boss just one year older, as Maisie had done with Val. Lorna also became a renowned Broken Hill hairdresser, but as a young girl just didn't quite manage to wash the towels to Maisie's satisfaction, so she took them home and washed them herself – to Rose's mortification.

'If you're going to be a manager, girlie, best you act like one!'

Maisie ignored her. She was proud of herself and with pride comes confidence.

This was a time of contentment but, as usual when life was either very good or very bad, her happiness only underlined the fact her father wasn't there to share in it. She knew he would have been proud and imagined him looking down and nodding in approval. It didn't occur to her that all this would not have happened if Jack were alive. He would never have allowed her to be forced from school and would not have had her cycling around town to support herself while maintaining a full household at home – and it is difficult to imagine what Jack would have thought of Dukey Butcher.

Maisie was in love. Charlie (Dukey) Butcher was a handsome young man, with a cheeky grin and manner to match. They met at a dance and were instantly smitten with each other. He was a little older than her, but Maisie had become a true beauty – shoulder length dark curling hair, deep brown eyes and – though she pined for long slender legs – a nipped waist, curvy hips and full breasts. Dukey would not have changed a thing about Maisie. She would always remember him leaning in close to croon the chorus of Perry Como's 'Sweet Sixteen' when they danced:

> *I love you as I never loved before,*
> *Since first I met you on the village green.*
> *Come to me or my dream of love is o'r,*
> *I love you as I loved you, when you were sweet,*
> *When you were sweet sixteen.*

Maisie wasn't ready to come to Dukey as he may have liked. There's no love like the first, but though she was old enough for the fever of it, she wasn't old enough to know how to manage it. Despite this, the pair became inseparable and the months that ensued were magical.

Chapter 20
Escape to the city
1947

The early months of 1947 were calm in the Schuster household, but tense across the city. Rumours of an uncontrollable fire in old workings underground at the North Mine had everyone on edge. Fire is feared in any underground mine, more for the products of combustion than the flames. Colourless, odourless, carbon monoxide from charred timbers is lethal. Spontaneous combustion was relatively common in the Broken Hill field – old stopes had old timber props buried under mullock left rich in highly flammable zinc powder. As the rumours spread, miners became increasingly nervous and company reassurances did nothing to settle them. On 25 March smoke entered stopes where men were working. Again, it was played down.

'It's just an old hot spot,' Manager A.R. West told them. 'We've known about it for 15 years. It waxes and wanes and it's just doing a bit of waxing at the moment. It'll only take a few days to deal with it.'

It took a week to even find the seat of the hot spot near the old No 1 shaft, and much longer to put it out.

They pumped slime and water from the mill to a point above the fire – the slime meant to fill fissures in surrounding rock, thereby starving it of air and stemming fume leakage into other levels of the mine. Three weeks later, they were still pumping. On Anzac Day, the men poured out of the mine as water poured down on them. The water from the sludge had found its way down and across to the No 2 shaft, so they were drenched as they entered and exited their work stations. Mr West acknowledged this was inconvenient for the miners at the start of a shift because they then had to stay in wet clothes all day, but noted getting wet at knock-off was okay, because they could 'quickly and easily dry off'.

Teams of men were already working around the clock to attempt to seal the hot spot, now a new team was sent in to build a dam to capture the run off water and redirect old skimp passes to carry it. Ultimately, it would take seven years before the company could claim it had fully extinguished the hot spot that it thought it could manage in a few days.

Dealing with the fire was expensive, but that year the North had money to burn – extraordinary post-war world metal prices almost doubled the annual profit to £1,137,456, even after accounting for the associated massive increase in lead bonus payments to employees. These payments were now extreme enough that half of it was compulsorily transferred into bank accounts rather than included in bulging pay packets. It was a forced savings plan popular with housewives – and, for some, it was their only guarantee of having cash left after the Friday night game at the two-up school.

This illegal gambling den was mostly ignored by the local police, but occasionally the constabulary were prompted to spring a lightning raid and dozens of men would be dragged off to court. At the end of March, 53 men were caught in the police net and it took a list of their names in the newspaper before Rose was fully convinced Tommy and Jimmy weren't among them. 'The game' wasn't only patronised by miners. The congested semi-circles of defendants who stood as a group before Magistrate H. Isles' bench three weeks later comprised miners, labourers, engineers and businessmen. They all found justice benign.

Barrier Miner Thursday 17 April 1947 (excerpts)

Two Up School Raid Has Sequel In Court

When police officers paid an unannounced call at premises situated at 413 Argent Street on the night of March 28, they surprised a number of men who, it was alleged, were engaged playing 'two-up' ...

Most of the men appeared, but in cases where some were working, friends represented them, pleaded guilty and paid the fines. The defendants were represented by Mr. M.A. Brown ...

Sergt. Costello said that ... the defendants present were around a padded ring and were playing 'two-up'. The police seized £6/10/.

'WELL CONDUCTED'

To Mr Brown: [*In answer to Mr Brown, Sergeant Costello said*] The place was well conducted. There was no suggestion of a nuisance. The place was conducted so well that one would hardly know a two-up school was in existence.

Mr. Brown said that the men were of good repute and were playing a "national" game. He wished to stress that because of our isolation the men had to find some outlet for their leisure. They did not have the amenities of city people. The police regarded the game as a sort of safety valve and a defence against crime. He pleaded for leniency.

Fifty-two defendants were fined £1, in default 48 hours' imprisonment; while William Burke with a previous conviction was fined £1/10/, in default three days' imprisonment.

The money seized by the police was confiscated.

The town was abuzz – not about the arrests, nor even about some of the juicier names listed, but about what could have prompted the police to raid it this time. The game was on every Friday night and everybody knew it. A raid usually meant the proprietors had done – or not done – something to cause offence.

The two-up game, however, was not dominating the kitchen table in the Schuster household. Here, the North Mine hot spot was the hot topic and the conversation was heated because Jackie had announced he intended to go underground at the Zinc Corporation when he turned 18 in June. Rose wanted him in his safe gardening job, Jackie wanted the money. Maisie agreed with Rose's view, but didn't say it. She was delighted that, for once, the yelling wasn't about her. That wasn't to last.

Rose had had enough of Dukey Butcher. She had assumed him a dalliance, but it had now been some months and she feared he would take her daughter away. She began to state her case plainly. It was time for Maisie to end the courtship and stay home more. Her gallivanting was making her mother unwell.

Rose should have had more patience. Cracks had begun in the romance and, without her mother's interference, Maisie may well have just let them open wide. Dukey's best mate was Freddie Betro. Today the relationship would be called a 'bromance' – they did everything together. Maisie liked Freddie and thought him 'good fun', but resented his influence on her boyfriend. When she first met Freddie he was courting two girls – one of whom he later married, and Bubby (Avis) Carroll. Maisie wasn't experienced enough to deal with Freddie's impact on her relationship and was ready to end it about the same time Rose started interfering. Instead, she found she really liked Bubby and now it became a foursome. Bubby's older sister, Iris, was going with Clem James the butcher (whom she later married) and this couple often joined the group.

Perhaps Maisie, too, would have married her childhood sweetheart, if Bubby and Iris hadn't been going on holiday. They were off to Adelaide to visit their brother and invited Maisie to go too. Rose objected. The argument between the two escalated until an enraged Rose flew at Maisie and knocked her to the ground. Maisie boarded the train with Bubby and Iris two days later – but with scratches on her face, a black eye and a resolve not to come back. She had decided to stay at Topsy's and look for a job.

Topsy was shocked to see her young half-sister, but not as shocked at her face as Maisie had expected. She had lived it. Topsy had left home very young to marry Clarrie Martin, but after their divorce had married Bill Treagus. Topsy and Bill now had their own family issues to deal with and harbouring Maisie would be a problem for more reasons than just Rose's fury. But Topsy understood. The solution was to find the almost-17-year-old country girl a job that came with accommodation.

Despite having had three jobs (and a profitable little business) Maisie had no experience with job applications and interviews. With Topsy's coaching, however, she scored the first job for which she applied – on the cashier's desk in the cafeteria at the Adelaide Railway Station. The job came with a shared room upstairs and she was thrilled to find her roommates were Broken Hill girls, Betty Hebbard and Betty Maxton. They were older than her, and only casual acquaintances, but it seemed a good omen.

Freedom was exhilarating! She should have been at least a little daunted by the hustle and bustle of the city, but she wasn't. She had fond memories of the time as an eight-year-old when the family had lived for a while on the Esplanade at Semaphore and she had gone weekly to the Adelaide Central Market with her father. When she went there now, the smells of the market made her remember the smell of him. It saddened her, but filled her with confidence. She could do anything! Even the smart clothes of the Adelaide women couldn't undermine her confidence when she fronted for her first day of work – although it wobbled a little as she encountered the great hall.

The centrepiece of the beautiful old Adelaide Railway Station was a grand marble hall, originally the passenger waiting area. Topped by a 36-foot dome, it was supported by eight giant Corinthian columns and finished with imported European marble. The cafeteria was in the underground floor, just off to the right of the station platforms where trains arrived to disgorge their passengers, all with somewhere important to go. Maisie stood in the centre of it. She felt like a rock in the middle of a stream with life opening and closing around her. Then she took a deep breath and went in.

Maisie and Phoebe, Adelaide, 1947.

Her new job wasn't difficult – or interesting. She sat on a stool with a cash register in front of her at the end of a long self-service race of sandwiches, pies, small cakes and buns. But interesting times were ahead. A tea and coffee urn sat to the right of her and this was tended by a bright and bubbly Phoebe Beasley. The girls quickly became friends.

Phoebe and Maisie made a striking pair that was the undoing of many an Adelaide boy. Requests for dates were constant – to each girl. If the suitor was appealing, the response was always the same, 'Sure, if you've got a mate so we can double-date with my friend'. If agreed, a rendezvous was arranged at a specific location within the station building. Very often, the girls both made arrangements for the same time on the same night using different locations. They hid, giggling, while they checked out which male pair had the best mutual prospects. The other hapless pair would be 'blue-ducked' and told the next day, 'Oh sorry, we waited for you, but you didn't show. We're a bit booked up now'. A little heartless maybe, but

Maisie was footloose and fancy-free and having an absolute ball with her new young friend.

The pair did everything together, including travelling to Phoebe's home at Old Noarlunga on weekends. There were tinges of sadness in the early visits as Maisie watched the easy relationship between Phoebe and her mother with envy. Over time, Mrs Beasley mothered her too and the sadness was gone.

She was also getting more than her fair share of attention at work. The cafeteria chef made up little cardboard boxes of goodies for her to collect after work and the station manager began to linger by her end of the counter for a chat. He was a gruff man and most staff were afraid of him, but there are advantages to being brought up in a tough mining town. Gruff men are common. Maisie also had Jack's lesson that 'all men are equal – they just do different jobs' to bolster her confidence, so she chatted along with him as though he were a ticket collector. He found this refreshing and when his secretary resigned, offered Maisie the job.

'I can't type!' she exclaimed in astonishment.

'That's okay – I don't have many letters!' he countered. She protested further about a general lack of secretarial skills (and a lack of appropriate clothes) but soon found herself working in the office.

From the first day, she knew she wasn't suited. She found the work difficult, yet dreary, and yearned for the social contact of the cafeteria. She also missed working with Phoebe. After a few weeks, she begged to be allowed to return. That would be seen as a demotion by the other staff, he told her, but he readily agreed that office work didn't appear to be the right career choice for her. Still fond of Maisie, he arranged instead a move to the more prestigious dining room cashier's position. She accepted this, but was a little resentful because the new job had her on different shifts to Phoebe.

It was during this time Maisie took up smoking. Tobacco was in short supply and still strictly rationed despite the end of the war but, as government employees, the railway station staff could arrange to receive an allocation of cigarettes or other tobacco products as part of their weekly wage. Maisie took up the option to send cigarettes home to Jackie and Maxie, who were struggling to find adequate supplies in Broken Hill. Here they had to be registered with a grocer who knew them to be smokers, but still only allowed them to buy one packet of tobacco or two packets of 20 cigarettes each week. The boys were delighted Maisie could access additional supplies and, initially, reimbursed her for their spoils as agreed. As time went on, the payments became less regular. Maisie began to stockpile the cigarettes and told them she would send no more until the debts were paid. The money never came – the cigarettes were there – so she decided she would smoke them herself! It was a habit she never overcame.

Phoebe also sometimes smoked, but neither girl let on to their families, so during the weekend visits to the Beasley home, the two girls spent much time perched on the broad stone windowsill of Phoebe's bedroom, fanning the smoke to the outside with folded sheets of paper.

One late afternoon about a month after her 17th birthday (which was celebrated with a surprise decorated cake from the chef) Maisie sat smoking in the corner of her room above the station, crouched over a little heater. There was a knock on the door, but before she could rise to open it, Topsy and Eve walked in.

She quickly pushed her hand, still holding the cigarette, up under her dress and greeted the two women with a weak smile. It was not usual for her sisters to visit her there, but they began to offer pleasantries as though it were. Smoke began to curl out from under Maisie's skirts. All three chose to ignore it for a time but, finally, Topsy could stand it no longer.

'Girlie, you're either going to have to smoke that cigarette or put it out. You're going to burn your fanny off in a minute!'

After a frozen moment, Maisie jumped up and put the cigarette out. She still couldn't bring herself to smoke in front of them, despite having been well-sprung. Amid the laughter that followed, the three reminisced about happier times when Jack had been alive and had equally sprung Topsy and Eve in a similar situation when they had been hiding in the toilet at the bottom of the backyard. Jack had disgorged a hose through gaps at the top of the wooden door, calling out in mock alarm, '*Mutter! Mutter!* Come quick! Come quick! Your shithouse is on fire!' as he drenched the girls. There were other similar yarns, such as when he hid slivers of matches down inside individual cigarettes so the sulphur burst into flame as the girls smoked.

Maisie was having such a good time sharing stories with her sisters in that little cold room she forgot to wonder why they were there.

And then it came. Rose was again unwell and the family had decided it was Maisie who should go home to look after her.

Chapter 21
Pretty in pink
1947–1948

The first few weeks were the worst. Rose was indeed unwell but, while helpless physically, she had an active and bitter tongue for the daughter who had deserted her. The barbs were sharper when she realised Maisie had nothing to show for it. Wages at the Railway Station had been reasonable – but not generous – and she had easily spent the little left after deductions for accommodation and cigarettes. Rose reluctantly agreed housework could be an exchange for board and Maxie gave her small amounts for pocket money. At 15, he had now left school and was labouring for a builder.

Maisie's spirit was crushed. After years of paying her own way, she was reliant on her little brother for handouts and she could hardly retaliate against Rose's rancour when her mother was so ill. Her throat clamped around words that ached to get out. She felt guilt at her resentment at being there, but eventually forgave herself because she reasoned she wouldn't feel that way if their relationship was anything like Phoebe had with her mother.

A rekindled friendship with Bubby was the light among the gloom. There was no such rekindling with Dukey. They tried for awhile, but the fire had gone out. Letters of misery back to Adelaide brought Phoebe for a Christmas visit and much excitement, but this didn't play out as expected either. This was a very different Maisie to the carefree young lass who had left hopeful lads waiting on railway station steps. This girl had responsibilities beyond her years – and another best friend to boot. Phoebe and Bubby were jealous of each other and the visit became more uncomfortable as it progressed. Phoebe returned to Adelaide and there was token correspondence for awhile, but it dribbled out. A fair-weather friendship, by its nature, is always lost at the time of greatest need. Maisie's pall deepened.

Soon there was someone else to care for. Her grandmother was ill and came to stay with Rose. It was a strange arrangement. The constant friction between Rose and Maisie was only an inheritance of the tension between Rose and her own mother. Rose's father had died when she was five and Mary married Edward James two years later, produced a son within a year and another two children quickly. Mary's focus was on her new young family and Rose felt unloved and unwanted. She may have been right. Granny James left nothing to Rose in her will, with her assets shared among Rose's younger brother Bill and the surviving half-siblings. Yet it was Rose's house she chose – from among a large extended family – in which to die.

Barrier Miner Thursday 12 February 1948 (in total)

DEATH OF MRS. M. E. JAMES

Mrs. Mary Evelyn James died last night at the residence of her daughter, Mrs. R. Schuster, 25 South Street. Born at Wentworth 75 years ago, Mrs. James was educated at Wilcannia.

She is survived by two sons, Messrs. W. Seward and E. James, two daughters, Mesdames R. Schuster and J. H. Harding, a sister, Mrs. A. Baum, 21 grandchildren, 24 great-grandchildren, and one great-great grandchild. One son, Elias, and two daughters, Mary and Elizabeth pre-deceased her.

The funeral was arranged for this afternoon, the cortege to leave the residence of her daughter at 4 o'clock for the Methodist Cemetery, where her remains were to be interred in the same grave as those of her husband, Mr. Edward James, who died in 1938.

Rev. R. C. Gutherberlet was to conduct the service at the graveside. Norman Woodman had charge of the funeral.

Granny James's death united her daughter and granddaughter for awhile. Maisie felt for Rose in her grief and pondered on the depth of her mother's sorrow for the loss of a relationship that had not been loving. She feared that grief one day.

Meanwhile, there was another relationship beginning to cause concern. Maisie had come home to find Rose had a boyfriend! Dick Summers was a retired widower who dabbled in art. In the months Maisie had been in Adelaide, Dick had become a regular visitor at the Schuster house, enjoying Rose's cooking and companionable evenings in the front lounge room. Maisie was stunned. It's a rare child who sees a mother as a person and Rose was 57 years old, with every year showing.

'Why didn't you tell me?' Maisie demanded of the boys the first time Dick turned up at the door.

'We were hoping he'd go away,' Jackie explained.

But Dick didn't. Maisie found she liked him well enough (and the boys did too) but, for all three, it was strange to think of Rose with anyone other than their father. As Rose's health improved, she began going out to the cinema with Dick and Maisie was again surprised. Dressed in a fashionable pinstripe suit, with a straight skirt and fitted jacket with padded shoulders, Rose was attractive. She had buried two husbands and three children, had eight children living and several grandchildren from the oldest of her offspring, but when she stepped out with Dick she looked none of those things. She just looked like a smart woman out on a date with a smart man.

It's difficult to understand why Jackie, Maisie and Maxie were so unhappy about this new phase in Rose's life. Jack had been dead for more than seven years and all three were intent on making their own lives. Maisie's only explanation in later years was they thought it disrespectful to him. She at least felt liberated by the relationship and set about finding work. The lure of attached accommodation took her to the Grand Hotel as a waitress.

The Grand at this time lived up to its name. An imposing two-storey brick and stone building with cast iron railings around

The Grand Hotel, c. 1949.

the upper balcony, it dominated the main street by occupying the entire southern corner of Argent and Chloride streets. It had been built just five years after the birth of Broken Hill and was such a prestigious structure it had served as the Town Hall for many years, with most early important meetings and receptions for visiting dignitaries held within its walls.

As with all Broken Hill hotels, the Grand bar stayed open well past the mandated 6 pm closing time. Forced early closing had been in place across Australia since the early years of World War I, when it was introduced partly as an austerity measure and partly to 'improve the morals' of Australian men. The only thing it really improved was the speed at which men could down their beers as the clock counted down to 6 pm, leading to the term 'six o'clock swill'. There was no need to guzzle in Broken Hill – the city simply ignored the regulation and bars stayed open until 11 pm, or later, as they pleased.

In February 1947 (before Maisie went to Adelaide) the NSW State Government yielded to lobbyists and held a referendum to determine the voting public's preference for a 6 pm, 9 pm or 10 pm closing time. A continuation of 6 pm closing won easily. Sturt

(Broken Hill) was one of few electorates to vote for 10 pm closing, but it didn't really matter – pubs in Broken Hill continued to set their own times. [*Author's aside: Broken Hill claims it was responsible for the end of early closing. In 1953* NSW *Premier Joseph Cahill sent a division of policemen to deal with the recalcitrant city, but they eventually gave up – the Silver City miners would drink as long as they liked and hotels that wanted their business would serve them. A state-wide referendum the next year narrowly won 10 pm closing – but in Broken Hill the result warranted less than a shrug.*]

At the time of Maisie's employment, the Grand was a popular late-night drinking venue, but still very upmarket. She arrived for her first day on the job trying to emulate the waitresses she had seen at the Adelaide Railway Station, with pad in hand and a pencil tucked for easy access behind one ear.

'Oh, no, Miss Schuster,' she was told. 'That is *not* the way we wait on diners at the Grand. You will have four tables to serve and will do our guests the courtesy of remembering what they have selected from our menu.'

It was a new world for Maisie, but she was eager to embrace it.

She quickly made friends with another waitress, Aileen Tomsley, and Eva Stevens who worked behind the bar. Bubby fitted well into this little group and a new social scene began to unfold. The young constables based at the Central Police Station across the road called in to the Grand to collect meals for prisoners held in cells out the back of the station. Flirting was cheerful and constant. Neither the young policemen nor the Grand staff were ever short of dates or dance partners at the Palais.

In May the ball season opened, again with the Convent Ball, and Maisie was excited. Her date was a nice young policeman and she had made a pretty gown from fabric bought on sale. At the last minute, her date was sent out of town on prisoner escort duty. She had two choices; miss the ball or go alone.

Deciding to go wasn't especially brave – she knew more than half

The centre of Broken Hill's night life, the Palais de Danse.

the people on the Palais floor would be single – but, once there, it took all her courage to go in through the doors. Swirling past her in time to Bill Denley's Orchestra were the most magnificent ball gowns she had ever seen.

Broken Hill had had enough of austerity. The hall was a spectacle of colour – and shine. Off-the-shoulder bodices were decorated with diamantes, sequins and glittery fabric flowers; full and flowing skirts flaunted satin, silk, shantung, and tulle; extra glamour came from silver lame, gold lame, intricate lace and tinselled embroidery. The social editor of the *Barrier Miner* was loquacious in her descriptions the next day. Blue wasn't 'blue' – it was azure blue, lagoon blue, delphinium blue, powder blue, or heaven blue. But there must have been something about Maisie that impressed – in among the descriptions of the ornate gowns worn by 'the belles of the ball' was, 'Miss Maisie Schuster had triple frillings forming a peplum on her frock of coral pink crepe'.

She scored another mention three weeks later when she wore the same dress to the Church of England Debutante Ball – only this time the fashion editor thought the dress was 'powder pink'. Maisie's home-made dress was reported again at the 1949 Convent Ball, but as 'pearl pink', and there was special mention of the 'square net yoke' she had inserted to update it.

Maisie's self-made ball gown.

Feeling under-dressed at the start of her first ball was reminiscent of her first school social in more ways than one – she danced every dance, and the last few were with someone special. 'P.C.W.C.' ('Police Constable William Clarence' Johnson) was one of the regulars to the Grand for prisoner meals. Clarrie, as he was known, apart from Maisie's playful P.C.W.C. tag, had a long record with the ladies. He was handsome, his lovely face was accentuated by a terrific smile, and his looks were backed by a personality that made him great fun to be with. All the girls were envious when he and Maisie began to date seriously.

An early vow to only give her virginity 'to the man who has his name on my marriage certificate' nearly came undone with Clarrie. Good girls didn't have sex before marriage and bad girls were known and remembered for it. The vow had yet to be seriously challenged, but there was something about Clarrie that wanted her to change that way of thinking. It was only a set of circumstances that prevented it.

The manager at the Grand was Lionel Turner, an amiable man who was well-liked by most of his staff. His wife spent most of her time in the bar, keeping an eye on him. She thought her husband far too friendly with some of the hired help, particularly Eva. Tension erupted one night in the bar, with a dreadful argument between Mrs Turner and Eva – surpassed only by the row that followed between Lionel and his wife in the managers' living quarters.

'I want her gone!' was clearly heard through the walls more than once.

Maisie headed out at the end of her shift to visit Rose and the boys. If Eva were sacked, work at the hotel would lose much of its charm. She was already tense, but she found greater tension in the Schuster kitchen. Rose had told Jackie and Maxie that Dick had proposed and she wanted to know how they felt about that. The boys felt strongly – but not in the way Rose would have liked. Maisie sided with her brothers. After they went out, Rose turned on her.

'You put them up to this. You're a nasty, spiteful girl. They liked Dick well enough until you came home!'

She threw a teacup at Maisie. The cup missed and shattered against the sink, but its contents had sailed onto Maisie's white work blouse as it passed.

The next morning Eva came in to ask for her pay to be made up. She was heading to Sydney.

'Why don't you come with me?' she asked Maisie. 'I hear tell there's plenty of work and it'll get your mum off your back,' she ventured.

To be fair, Rose wasn't much on Maisie's back. She thought her daughter's social life far too frivolous and had the usual chastisements about the clothes Maisie wore, but her complaints about Clarrie Johnson were only that he was 'a ladies' man'. As much as she ever approved of Maisie's choices, she approved of Clarrie. And she had been much more amiable since the relationship with Dick had escalated. Nonetheless, the idea was tempting. She thought of the tea stain she was having trouble removing from her blouse and she thought of the fun she had shared with Phoebe in Adelaide. Change and new adventure were appealing.

'Let's do it!' she said – and left to tell her mother the news.

Rose didn't marry Dick Summers – and she never raised the topic again with her sons and daughter. She refused him on her children's say-so, because they refused the concept of a replacement for Jack. But the spirit in the daughter was well present in the mother – she simply lived with him in semi de facto style at a time when convention decreed it a sin. Maisie eventually grew very fond of Dick. She kept a painting he did for her of a wilted poinsettia in a vase all her life and it remains in the family today.

Chapter 22
Upstairs downstairs
1948–1949

Maisie trembled with excitement when she boarded the train. By the time she arrived at Sydney's Central Railway Station the next day, the trembling was from cold and exhaustion – and because every part of her body had become locked in perpetual motion.

The first nine hours were relatively comfortable. The 422 miles between Broken Hill and Parkes were aboard the Silver City Comet, which had the prestige of being the first air-conditioned train to run in Australia. At its launch in September 1937 it was also the first all-diesel air-conditioned train to operate anywhere in the British Empire – and one of the fastest, with its dual engines capable of speeds up to 80 miles an hour on the flat. The New South Wales Government and Broken Hill were immensely proud of it.

The Comet was now more than a decade old and its original plush blue leather seats were worn, but the ride was still somewhat cushioned and it was at least warm. They left at 9 am and arrived in Parkes at 6 pm, having shared a single meal in the buffet car to save money. The next leg on the old steam Central West Express was horrendous. No air conditioning here – and rattly sash windows that let in the freezing air as they clattered overnight through the Blue Mountains. Maisie and Eva were so cold, they took turns lying full-length face-down on the tin foot-warmers on the floor, unbuttoning their coats so the warmth could stop the pain in their nipples. They had little sleep.

Two steaming mugs of coffee each in a station café warmed them enough to move on. They rented a locker to store the heavier of their two suitcases apiece and took the others with them to hunt down a job and accommodation, having no plans for either. A taxi driver was full of information and drove them directly to the Capstan cigarette factory at Kensington. The tobacco industry in Australia was still trying to catch up to demand after the war, which had left three-quarters of Australian adult males as smokers and a continuing shortage in all popular brands. (Maybe 'the war' shouldn't be blamed – maybe it was just that anything in short supply is attractive.)

'You'll have no trouble getting jobs there,' the cabbie told them. 'They're crying out!' And he was right.

They were hired on the spot and told to return the next day with birth certificates. Now this was a problem. Along with the popularity in smoking had come controversial research into side effects of the habit (World War I claims that tobacco could cure asthma had long gone) and the girls needed to be 18 to work in the factory. Maisie was months short.

Naïve country girls in a big city often bring out the best in people. When this situation was explained to him, the kindly manager said they could not work at Capstan, but sent them with a note to a nearby employment office – which, in turn, sent them with papers for work and accommodation in the Earl's Court residential hotel overlooking Manly Cove. Within hours Maisie and Eva had collected their suitcases and were on a ferry to a new life.

Earl's Court was an imposing four storey building, set on a slight hill which gave residents an excellent view of the water and Manly Wharf. Big black block letters proclaimed its name along the full length of the façade and an Australian flag flying from a tall mast gave it an air of importance among the surrounding buildings. Mostly, it was constructed of huge blocks of sandstone, but the balconies on each of the above-ground floors were surrounded by timber railings connected to the floor by wooden slats in geometric patterns and the street-level veranda was enclosed with wooden framed windows to provide sunrooms for the mostly older clientele, so the overall effect was a little higgledy-piggledy.

One of the two proprietors, spinster sisters called Misses Steyne, actually clapped her hands with glee during the interview – 'The Grand Hotel' generated a certain image – and Maisie and Eva were quickly shown to tiny rooms in the basement staff quarters. Their jobs were in the dining room, working split shifts and serving three meals a day, but the work wasn't hard and the tenants had a genteel air that impressed the mining town girls.

Refinement of character, however, was entirely restricted to the upstairs inhabitants of Earl's Court. Below stairs lived an assortment of people who may have stepped straight from an old English soap drama.

The cook was openly gay in a time when it was illegal and certainly not admitted, while the chef was crazy, wildly waving his meat cleaver during bouts of rage, which occurred with remarkable regularity. The yardman was a drunkard and had a regular morning round collecting almost-empty bottles left behind by male visitors to the staff rooms. He tipped the dregs into one bottle and kept it close throughout the day so he could sustain his half-tipsy state. Some of the giggling from the basement rooms at night was at the poor yardman's expense, because male visitors had added other liquid to their 'empties'. Two other waitresses, Sandra and Del, often let their wharfie boyfriends Ken and Dave into their rooms at night, which astounded the two young Broken Hill girls – by its fact alone, but also because of the noises that escaped through big gaps under the doors.

Eva's room had a history. The little bedroom had previously been occupied by 'Nancy' and the girls knew this because, from the first night, Eva was regularly woken by knocking at the door and a range of male voices calling, 'Nancy, are you there?'. Explaining Nancy no longer slept there did little to stem the flow of visitors so, on the third night, Eva pulled her mattress into Maisie's room and the two girls shared cramped quarters. Nancy later returned to live in her old room and she surprised the girls by more than her nightly visitors. She functioned only on copious amounts of alcohol and Bex powders.

Bex was one of two analgesics regularly consumed by many women as a pick-me-up to 'get through the day'. Vincent's was the other. They both contained aspirin, phenacetin and caffeine (therefore known as APCs) and few homes of the time were without a box in their cupboards. Rose was a regular consumer – almost always with a cup of tea for an extra dash of caffeine – and Jackie, Maisie and Maxie were regularly dosed with the powder mixed in a teaspoon of honey. Australia led the world in APC consumption in the years after World War II and it was not until the 1970s that the powders were linked to the irreparable kidney damage they caused. By then, addictions were widespread.

Nancy regularly borrowed a box of powders from one of the girls in the morning, returned later in the day with a replacement box and one for herself – and then knocked on the door again before the night was out to re-borrow again.

Maisie and Eva were gobsmacked by it all, but their naïveté was on a crash course. They went to dances at the nearby Memorial Hall and, as new girls on the block, were rushed with attention. In progressive dances, each new partner would say something like, 'You're new. Here on holiday?'. When the girls' responses were, 'No, working at Earl's Court', the very next question would be, 'Can I take you home?'. It became obvious Earl's Court had a reputation for gentility upstairs and impiety downstairs.

The girls made a pact to always stay together and thought this would save them – until one night they accepted an invitation from a couple of lads to 'go for a drink' and this turned out to be in the vacant block next to the dance hall where a bottle of wine and some empty anchovy paste jars lay waiting under a bush. The girls then resolved to lie about where they worked and never accept an escort home – even as a foursome.

Maisie (17) working at Earl's Court in Sydney, 1948.

This was one of the reasons Maisie resisted strong pressure from the waitresses, Sandra and Del, for an introduction to Jock Cameron. The other was that she thought any mate of their wharfie boyfriends would be a bit loose for her. She almost missed the love of her life.

Maisie and Eva had grown to like the other girls, even Nancy. Behaviour only shocks when it's first encountered and they were good workmates. One night Sandra and Del and the boys took Maisie and Eva with them for a drive around Manly in Ken's car and they pulled up on the Corso to chat to a man walking. Jock Cameron. Maisie took no notice of him, so the following week when a young man asked her to dance at the Memorial and introduced himself as Arnold, Maisie didn't recognise him. She only saw a nice young man with blonde curly hair, intense blue-green eyes and a ready smile. He was well-spoken, with lovely manners, and he danced well. They enjoyed several dances. It wasn't until they met up with Eva out the front of the hall that the truth came out. Eva remembered him.

Arnold (Jock) Cameron had been equally pressured by his mates to meet Maisie, but had not been interested due to the Earl's Court reputation until they'd met that night on the Corso. He'd been impressed by her looks, but also by the fact she hadn't laughed at one of Dave's coarse jokes. He'd gone to the dance because he'd been told she'd be there.

By now a little smitten, Maisie accepted a date for the pictures the next night. Eva liked him too and convinced Maisie to borrow her clothes so she could dress appropriately for a city man and a city date. Maisie waited out the front for Arnold and saw him walking up the hill – a nice sports coat, open-neck shirt, long shorts and knee-high white socks. She'd been into her room and changed into her own clothes by the time he reached the corner. This wasn't the big city – this was a beach resort town, and this was a man she could be comfortable with, just as she was. They fell in love quickly.

Arnold had missed her 18th birthday by a few weeks. Rose hadn't; she'd sent a gold watch with a note to say she was giving it to Maisie now, because she wouldn't be alive by her 21st. But Arnold showered her with small gifts. They danced and laughed and went to the cinema and walked along the beach and ate hot chips while they watched sunsets together. She loved the way he left her to sit out the dancing every now and then while he crossed the room to ask a plain 'wallflower' for a couple of dances; the way he took off his jacket to put it around her shoulders if their walks turned chilly; and the time he took off his shoe and filled it with water for a panting stray dog that was too frightened to drink from his cupped hands.

Arnold was almost six years older than Maisie. At the time she was collecting her sixth class school reports for Sister Drummond, he was already in the Army, having lied about his age to get there. Arnold was just one month past 17 when he enlisted, but gave his date of birth as two years earlier. His father, James Gerald Cameron, was a World War I hero in France, awarded a Distinguished Conduct Medal, and perhaps Arnold had thought to emulate him. Or it could have been, like many young men of the day, that he saw it as an opportunity for adventure. There are 66 so-called 'boy soldiers' on the WWII Honour Roll.

Whatever his motivation, Arnold was just 17 years and nine months when he landed with the 2/5th Australian Infantry Battalion at Milne Bay in Papua and spent three months battling the oppressive combination of extreme humidity, voracious insects and tropical disease before he first battled the Japanese just one month after his 18th birthday. This was a bloody and desperate fight to defend the mining town of Wau in New Guinea, a crucial access point for the Japanese to the Australian base at Port Moresby. He spent most of his service in the jungles of New Guinea and three years with the Occupation Forces in Japan at the end of the war.

Arnold had been home only nine months when Maisie met him and he wouldn't talk to her about the war. She didn't press him. There was so much about him that was reminiscent of her father and she didn't want to contrast this with thoughts of him killing people. Perhaps she should have pushed.

For at least part of his service, Arnold was a stretcher bearer. His service records show he had a tough time of it. He had bouts of malaria and dysentery and chronic hayfever caused by the jungle moulds that left puffy slits where his eyes should have been. Much later she would see horrible scars left by acne rampant across his back and chest that became weeping purulent sores.

Others have written of the mental scars that came from being a stretcher bearer in war, not so much from gruesome cargos, but from guilt – deaths caused because their fatigue stopped them

*Stretcher bearers of D Company 2/5th Battalion, New Guinea, July 1943.
Arnold Cameron, right, with the jaunty helmet, was 18.*

crossing a thousand yards of knee-deep mud quickly enough to
reach medical help in time; screams that came when they slipped
in the mud and the rocking of the stretcher grated shattered bones
together; or times when they went back for a soldier after delivering
his mate only to find the first had drowned in new mud he couldn't
escape – these memories stayed long after the image of wounds
inflicted by others disappeared. But Arnold never spoke of these
things, and certainly not to Maisie. He also didn't tell her how
many times he see-sawed between the rank of private and corporal,
demoted when he failed to return to the base on time after leave or

was drunk on site. Arnold's war record is dotted with more than a dozen annotations of him being absent without leave or returning to base drunk and disorderly, mostly in Japan, but they began just two months after his enlistment. Sometimes he was fined a few shillings, sometimes a few days' pay, and more than once he was gaoled. Maisie really should have pushed.

The first time he turned up for a date 'with too much drink in' Maisie was upset and told him so. He struck a little boy pout, looked up under thick lashes and cajoled, 'Awww ... Poor Arnie ...'. She forgave him. The next time, he was hours late for a date but was repentant.

'Max is in town,' Arnold said. 'He's my big brother and I couldn't let him down. It won't happen again, I promise.'

It did.

There was always an excuse.

'It's Christmas! I couldn't let my mates down. We all had to have a shout.'

'Ronnie lost his job and his girl. He needed me and I couldn't just leave him there.'

It was never Arnold's fault.

Life became a roller-coaster – the high points were wonderful, but there too many nights filled with a sinking feeling while she waited for him. Eventually, she told him it was over. Bad timing.

'Oh, not tonight, darling. Please. We're going to Mum's for dinner and she's been cooking all day ...'

Maisie loved the kind and gentle Jesse May Cameron. Like Rose, Jesse had had a hard life. While her husband had been a war hero, he'd also been a drinker and she'd been largely left to rear their brood of three daughters and three sons. The sons included Max, who was always in trouble (some of it serious) and Arnold with his heart of gold, though he'd learnt well from his father and brother. But Jesse was very different to Rose. Jesse's only flaw as a mother was maybe that she was too soft. She adored her children and each of them knew it – even the troublemakers. She'd been widowed two years when Maisie met Arnold. Maisie went to dinner.

'You're the best thing that ever happened to Arnold,' Jesse told her as they did the dishes. 'It's been really hard for him since the war. But you're so good for him. He's really settled down. I think he's really going to make it'.

Maisie thought she'd sooner have a boyfriend that was the best thing that ever happened to *her*, but being 'a best thing' was not a bad thing to be. There was also Rose. She'd written pages to her mother about Arnold and how much she loved him – and Rose had written back to tell her not to waste the paper.

'He won't last. They never do.' One more chance for Arnold.

In between slip-ups, he was a loving and attentive boyfriend – and great fun. Encouraged by Jesse, Maisie thought her love would be enough to change him. If she could just stick by him, he wouldn't need to drink so much. Then he was sacked from his job. He'd been working with Max as a bricklayer and one day they came back from lunch very late and inebriated. They were ordered off the site and told not to come back. An opportunity arose for a six-month contract on a major construction site in Melbourne and Arnold wanted Maisie to marry him and go too. She had the good sense to refuse him, but not enough to give up on him.

'You go, Arnold,' she said. 'Take the job. If you come back to me sober and steady after the six months, I'll marry you.'

Arnold lasted only two months.

'I've done it! I've stopped drinking. I can't live without you. I could only do it because I love you so much.'

Maisie believed him because she wanted to. Weeks later they were on the same old merry-go-round.

'I can't do this anymore, Arnold,' she eventually told him. 'I'm going home to Broken Hill.' She wasn't about to be persuaded this time – she'd already bought her ticket.

'I'll come too! Please just give me one last chance?' he begged.

They spent a long time talking and at the end of it she was convinced. Without the influence of Max or his mates at the pub, Arnold may very well become the man she wanted for her future.

She bought his ticket, because he had no money.

Chapter 23
Home fires burning
1949

Rose was pleased to see them. She didn't like Arnold and let them both know it, but sensed he was the reason her daughter was home and was grateful for it. Even without knowing their problems, she was convinced it wouldn't last and let them both know that, too.

Dulcie liked him very much. She loved the light in Maisie when she was with him and was equally charmed by him. She lent them money. Rose handed over the housekeeping in exchange for their accommodation, but kept a running tab for food and 'extras'. Maisie fixed the old sleep-out for Arnold, scrubbing, painting and making curtains, while he looked for work. She slept with her mother again and was washed with the memories of the time they had shared a bed after her father died.

Finding work proved more difficult than they expected. The mines desperately needed labour, particularly for expansion of the New Broken Hill Consolidated mine, but Arnold couldn't work on the mines.

Broken Hill took the term 'closed shop' to an extraordinary level. No one could work *anywhere* in the city without union membership – and this was closely monitored. 'Badge Show Day' was held quarterly and every employee in the city was compelled to wear a badge distributed by the respective union to show their membership was current. The badges changed each quarter and there were different colours for each shift, so there was no possibility of borrowing someone else's badge. If a worker didn't wear a badge on Badge Show Day, he or she was exposed – and couldn't work again until union clearance was obtained.

Arnold was happy to join a union, but union membership to work on the mines was restricted to locals. This rule had been in place since 1932. It stopped men coming into town to take local jobs, earn 'the big bucks' and then take the money home to spend. 'Locals' were clearly identified as those who had been born or educated in Broken Hill, or been resident for the preceding eight years.

In 1950, the rules changed. The eight-year residency expanded to encompass anywhere within a 300-mile radius of Broken Hill, although this still excluded any major population centre such as Adelaide. Men who married local girls were also accepted; and sons of locals or former locals could work on the mines as long as their fathers met (or had met) the residency rule. Under pressure from the mining companies, another clause was added to allow in anyone already on Broken Hill's electoral roll on 3 July 1950. It took a stop-work day, one-week strike and two mass meeting ballots before the unionists agreed to the concessions.

The new union membership classification rapidly attracted an influx of 500 jobseekers to Broken Hill and new bachelor quarters were constructed to accommodate them. The set of amendments created a 'B Group' eligibility status. Only true locals were in the 'A Group'. Some today think Broken Hill's 'A Grouper' and 'B Grouper' nomenclature is part of a mythological social snobbery. It was fact.

Arnold's arrival in Broken Hill was too early for the broadened eligibility, but it wouldn't have made any difference – without marriage to Maisie, he was way down the alphabet.

Eventually, he found work at the Broken Hill and Suburban Gas Company. Anyone could find a job at the gasworks because no one wanted to work there. It was hard, hot, smelly work on three shifts and low pay. The Town Employees Union kept pushing for better conditions but, every time they did, the company said it would have to raise gas prices and then the town was in an uproar.

Gasworks all over the country were struggling to compete with the electricity that now lit people's homes. They sometimes struggled with the supply of coal, too. In Broken Hill, there were enough gas refrigerators and gas stoves remaining to sustain demand, but the manufacturing plant was old and could only work with good quality coal. If the wharfies delayed shipment from Maitland, the plant had no capacity to use lower grade resources. But the biggest issue locally was labour. The company took on new employees, trained them up – and then they left.

When the gasworks didn't have enough men on a shift to keep the furnaces fed and stoked, homes, restaurants and hotels received gas at low pressure. Chefs, cooks and housewives learned to use electric grills, or reverted to their woodstoves, and found bottled kerosene in heaters more effective than unreliable gas. Sales decreased, issues escalated, work conditions worsened and it was even more difficult to recruit labour. Sometimes there were so few men on a shift, the gas was rationed and pumped into the city only at meal times, and it was often turned off at 7 pm.

Arnold hated the work. He came home at the end of his shift dirty, sweaty and exhausted, but Maisie was proud of her man and met him with a kiss at the front gate. True to his word, he stayed away from the pubs. With no money to spend, it may well have been more by necessity than conviction.

Mostly they stayed home with Rose and Dick, but occasionally Dulcie slipped Maisie the cost of tickets and they went to the pictures with Jackie and a lovely blonde girl he was dating, Yvonne Black. As soon as Arnold had a weekend shift off, they walked up to the new Zinc Corporation Twin Lakes for a picnic. It was almost as good as their beach picnics at Manly.

The lakes were man-made by the company on the mine site (but with an entrance off the Mildura road) as a public recreation facility and had opened just before Christmas. The joined lakes were 600 yards long and Maisie and Arnold's hand-in-hand stroll around the perimeter covered three-quarters of a mile. The water was treated effluent used for the mine orchards and wasn't suitable for swimming, but they rowed in a supplied canoe and sat on a blanket watching children with toy sailing boats. Maisie began to dream of her own children.

The next Thursday Arnold was hurt at work. Another employee knocked a heavy red-hot rod used to stoke the furnace and it fell across his arm, leaving a deep burn that would later turn into an unsightly scar. Years later, Arnold would regularly tell an entertaining story to blokes in a bar about how he was scarred in the war.

The gasworks manager drove him to a doctor and then home once it was dressed. He was in a lot of pain and even Rose was sympathetic when she saw the ooze on the bandage. The next afternoon he went to work to collect his fortnight's pay and didn't come home.

Dulcie and Ken drove Maisie to the gasworks, the hospital and the police station. That sinking feeling was back. They drove past a number of hotels in case he was standing with groups of men outside and Ken went in to the most likely. Eventually they went home and Maisie crawled into bed next to Rose, fully expecting to find him passed out in the sleep-out the next morning. He wasn't. Late in the morning a telegram arrived from Parkes: SORRY I BLEW IT STOP I LOVE YOU STOP ARNIE.

She cried. But she didn't just cry for herself; she cried for him too. She knew he would be hungover, in pain, and ashamed. She cried for the loss of him, but also for his loss of her.

The first letter took a week to arrive. Harry, the co-worker who had caused the accident, had wanted to buy Arnold a drink to say sorry. Arnold agreed to just one at the adjacent Gasworks Hotel. But the one had been one too many. He hadn't been able to stop and had spent too much of his pay. He knew this pay was meant to reduce their debts to Dulcie and Rose, so when Harry suggested 'the game' to win back what he'd spent, Arnold thought it a great idea. He would win enough at the two-up to clear the slate with her family and buy her something nice as well. In his words, he 'blew it' – the whole pay. He couldn't come home because he couldn't face her. He couldn't face Dulcie because she'd been so good to him and was dependent on the partial repayment he'd promised. And he certainly couldn't face Rose. Harry took him to catch the night train and paid for his seat.

The letter tugged at Maisie – but not enough. She replied to this one, but ignored all the others that followed. She burnt them in the kitchen stove, but kept the love poems he included in the envelope. Twice he sent her money for Dulcie and Rose, but when a third package was accompanied by a note that told her to put it aside toward her ticket back to him, she sent the money back instead.

Slowly she rebuilt a life without him. Her new job was at Greene's Exclusive Frock Salon, which was very upmarket – black and white uniforms, silver name badges and bouffant hairdos for the staff; and a clientele drawn only from the upper levels of Broken Hill society. Rose rebuked her for 'talking with a bloody plum in your bloody mouth' and chided her for working in a store in which none of her family could afford to shop. The salon lifted more than Maisie's elocution. She began to date again, although not more than twice with the same young man – until Eric.

Eric came from Melbourne with a sophistication Rose found pretentious and Maisie found appealing. They became quite close until Eric came for tea one night and Rose told him about Arnold while Maisie made the coffee. Later as she sat in the car with him to say goodnight, Eric asked her whether she was still in love with Arnold. Maisie acknowledged to him – and herself – that indeed she was. Eric went back to Melbourne and Maisie began to keep Arnold's letters as well as his poems. She began to sometimes write back.

Jackie and Yvonne married and Maisie was caught up in the romance of it. She clipped the article from the newspaper on the Monday and read it several times. At 18, she was still young enough to read it with her name and Arnold's in the appropriate places.

Barrier Miner Monday 4 July 1949 (excerpts)

BRIDE MARRIED IN MARINE BLUE CREPE

A posy of pastel flowers was carried by Yvonne Joyce Black, eldest daughter of Mrs. D. Howse, of Beech Avenue, Mildura, and the late Mr W. Black, formerly of Broken Hill, when she married Alwyn John, eldest son of Mrs R. and the late Mr. R. Schuster of 25 South Street, at the Central Street Methodist Church at 4.30 on Saturday. Rev. A. Simpson officiated.

Mesdames Dalziel and Lamb and Miss Maisie Schuster decorated the church with pastel flowers.

Given away by her stepfather (Mr. Howse, of Mildura), the bride wore a ballerina length frock of marine blue crepe, with a V-neckline edged with a collar and an inset of ecru lace which had blue piping tying into a bow. A self sash was tied at the front. Her crownless chip straw halo hat had matching veiling and a bandeau of blue hyacinths. Her accessories were black and she wore a locket loaned by her mother.

THE BRIDESMAID

The groom's sister, Miss Maisie Schuster, attended as bridesmaid. She wore a mustard crepe frock, with a pleated white lace inset. The side darted bodice had a peaked, piped waistline and a flared skirt. Her halo hat of mustard straw matched the bride's. She wore black accessories and the groom's gift of pendant and matching earrings ...

Horseshoes were placed by Mrs. D. Howse, Dawn and Joyce Dalziel and slippers by Phillip and Barry Vale. About 100 guests attended the reception at the Mechanics Institute ...

The couple have made their home at 25 South Street.

It was a beautiful wedding – a very pretty, blue-eyed, blonde-haired bride and a tall dark and handsome groom. Every girl there wanted a wedding like that. Maisie wanted a wedding like that. But she only wanted it with Arnold. She resolved to try one last time.

Telling Rose took some courage, but she steadfastly bore the brunt of her mother's fury.

'You'll be back, my girl. And with your bloody tail between your bloody legs. You mark my words!'

Maisie vowed to prove her wrong and gave two weeks' notice to Lorna Greene, gratefully accepting a glowing reference to help her find work in Sydney. Then she was on her way to Arnold. They both cried when he met her at the station.

And so began the happiest time of their lives together. Jesse May persuaded Maisie to live with them rather than look for live-in work.

'He's been trying really hard to pull himself together, love,' Jesse explained. 'With both of us to come home to every night, he'll come home sober.' He did.

Maisie found work in the clothing section of a major department store and was promoted to assistant manager within the first month. The Greenes had trained her well. Her first purchase on staff discount was a dressing gown and slippers for Jesse. She loved sweet Jesse May and was well loved in return. Jesse hugged her for no other reason than she was walking past.

Arnold was bricklaying in Manly. Every afternoon he had a couple of beers after work, but then was waiting when Maisie finished work to walk home with her to 49 Pine Street. After the first few weeks, she stopped holding her breath on her way to the front doors and expected him to be there. They began to save for a wedding, so there was not much dancing in those gentle days, but walks along the Corso window shopping, warm nights on the beach and weekly 'special' outings when they took Jesse May to the pictures. She loved how much he loved his mum.

Then Max came home.

Max wasn't happy to find Maisie living there – and even less happy to find her in his room, so that he had to share with Arnold. He became more petulant when Arnold wouldn't stay with him at

Maisie and Arnold, Manly Corso, 1951.

the pub after work, preferring to keep his eye on the clock and walk up on time for Maisie.

'Just lookin' for the bald spot,' he'd say, grabbing Arnold on both sides of his face to bend his head. 'That pretty thumb is sure to have left a mark by now!' It proved a popular joke with the other drinkers, and Arnold tried to laugh with them. But he started to get fidgety.

Both Maisie and Jesse were nervous. Maisie tried to talk to Max about it and Jesse suggested Max might like to find somewhere else to live since the little house was so crowded. Arnold was now a 'Mumma's boy' as well as henpecked. Max started bringing beer and whiskey home to drink at night in front of Arnold, even though neither of the boys had drunk in front of Jesse May previously. He goaded Arnold when he stood strong against offered drinks. One night, he pulled Arnold's head down to check his 'bald spot' and Arnold hit him.

The violence that erupted was startling. They smashed furniture and smashed each other. Jesse cried and Maisie screamed at them, but long pent up fury takes more than a little while to spend. Eventually, when she feared only one would emerge alive, Maisie was able to drag Arnold away from Max and push him through the front door.

They walked the streets of Manly. He wouldn't look at her, much less talk to her, but she stayed with him. They reached a boarding house and he disappeared inside. She stood stunned, and then he was out again, with a bottle in a brown paper bag. Then he looked at her – as he lifted the bottle to drink from it. He kept swigging as they walked and finally she thought him calm enough to go home. Max would be in bed by now. Neither had brought keys with them, so they knocked at the door. Max opened it, and lent close to whisper in Arnold's ear, who rocked on unsteady legs. Arnold took a feeble and misaimed swing with the empty bottle. Two policemen stepped out from behind Max and arrested him.

He spent the rest of the night sleeping it off in a cell behind the Manly Police Station. Still she didn't leave him. She had tea and biscuits with the constables at the front counter and asked for a blanket to cover him.

The next day everyone was repentant – including sweet Jesse May, who asked Max again to leave, but didn't have it in her to kick him out. Maisie took the day off work because she had had no sleep, but sleep didn't come now either. Her mind was a jumble. Arnold's rage and violence frightened her. She remembered other hints of it, like the time in their early dating when he had thought another man a bit too attentive to her at a dance. He had pushed the man away and held Maisie's upper arm too tightly as he led her from the hall. She had had bruising the next day, but passed it off as an accident. She had no idea what she should do now. Everything had been wonderful until Max came home. She looked to her father's moral compass for guidance, but he didn't talk to her.

When Arnold awoke later in the afternoon, he had a solution. A mate of his, Bluey, was heading to Queensland for work and he thought they should go with him. She didn't see this as running away from a problem. Again, she chose to see it as running toward a new life.

Chapter 24

Queensland's princess

The train ride north was exciting, but two years with Arnold had taught her any bated breath of anticipation should be accompanied by deep gulps of caution. She had agreed to go to Queensland on the premise she would find live-in work. References from the Adelaide Railway Station, the Grand in Broken Hill and Earl's Court in Sydney made this feasible, but Arnold's mother had again asked her to consider living with him. Jesse May was a highly principled woman – prudish by some measures – but protecting Arnold was paramount to morals.

Maisie spent much of the journey in thought about the right thing to do. This time she well knew what her father would say, so she didn't invite him into the conversation. A 20-year-old girl more often lives in dreams than places, so by the time they arrived she had decided on a compromise. She would live with Arnold, but not share his bed. Bluey would live with them to save money – and save her from herself.

Those first weeks in Brisbane were full of fun, love and happiness – and poverty. Even as a trio, they could afford little, but found a single room with use of a bathroom down the hall. The only furniture was a double bed (which Arnold and Bluey shared) and a stretcher on the balcony shielded from the street by a curtain for Maisie. Their kitchen was an electric jug on the floor connected to a metered power outlet and their dining table was a suitcase on top of the bed. They pooled meagre cash to buy eggs, bread and tea – and shared a single meal in a café so they could comb supplied customer newspapers for jobs (and steal the salt and pepper shakers). Each shilling gobbled by the electricity meter was precious, so the eggs were washed in the bathroom sink, boiled in the jug – and the same water used to make tea.

Bluey found work on the wharves, Arnold in a nearby bakery and Maisie in a men's boarding house, serving breakfast and cleaning rooms. While they waited for their first pays they lived on eggs, day-old pies Arnold brought home, and a little package the cook at the boarding house made up for Maisie each afternoon – sometimes bread and butter pudding, sometimes squishy tomatoes and almost always a slice or two of cooked meat or some fruit.

Bluey was nowhere near the chaperone Rose and Jesse had been. After a month and two pays, Maisie and Arnold were ready for their own private space. They found a room in a share house with three other couples. Each bedroom was large enough for a double bed, small sofa, and table and chairs, and they all shared the bathroom, kitchen and laundry. Arnold worked at the Brisbane Fruit and Produce Exchange in Turbot Street and Maisie found work at a swanky hotel on the dawn shift serving breakfast to businessmen with early flights. The tips were fantastic, but the job caused the other tenants to ask Maisie and Arnold to leave; their sleep was disturbed by the 4 am taxi the hotel sent to collect her for work.

They moved to New Farm, which was still close to Arnold's job at the markets. Maisie found work in Penney's Department Store, first on a side-entrance delicatessen, but with a quick promotion to supervisor of the cake island in the centre of the store. A couple of years later, the Penney's chain was acquired by Coles and became that company's introduction to large-scale food retailing.

Their new accommodation was with the Carr family in a lovely big house adjacent to the New Farm Ferry Wharf – a small room, but opening through French doors onto a long balcony from which they overlooked the meandering Brisbane River and the Carrs' yacht moored at their personal jetty. There was quite a little community here, with the Carrs' daughter Nellie living in an extended unit downstairs with her husband and two children, and two other couples also renting rooms upstairs near Maisie and Arnold.

To an outsider, they were a happily married couple – so when she finally agreed to marry him, it had to be in secret. No dream wedding for Maisie. One of Arnold's workmates and his wife stood as witnesses and 'the reception' for a few of Arnold's friends was at the workmate's home, with a wedding cake purchased on discount from Penney's cake island and party food from the delicatessen (supposedly for someone else because everyone at work thought she was married).

A subsequent article in the *Barrier Daily Truth* had less column inches than comment elsewhere in the paper about how well Jackie and Maxie had run in the South Football Club Picnic's 100 yard race.

Barrier Daily Truth Thursday 4 December 1952 (in total)

BRISBANE WEDDING

At the Presbyterian Church, Linnerfield, Brisbane on November 19, the marriage was solemnised of Miss Maisie Elaine Schuster, youngest daughter of Mrs. R. and the late Mr. R. Schuster of 25 South Street, Broken Hill, to Arnold Cameron, second son of Mrs. J. G. and the late Mr. Cameron of 49 Pine Street, Manly.

So, no pretty dresses or bridesmaids described in intricate detail, no 100 friends and family at the reception and no young girls sighing at the romance of it – but two weeks later they honeymooned on South Molle Island. Arnold had won at the races. It was typical of their roller-coaster lives.

Soon, however, the dips in the couple's ride reached new depths. During alcoholic binges, the violence Arnold had shown toward Max that night in Manly was turned on Maisie. There is much writing today about why women stay in abusive relationships. We know some women misguidedly feel it is their fault. Maisie didn't feel it was her fault. The problem was, she didn't think it was Arnold's fault either. It was 'the drink'.

Maisie and Arnold's wedding, November 1952.

So they cycled through happy times, wonderful times, drunken times, a recovery period, back to happy times ... Arnold didn't remember what he did to her when drunk. He was appalled when he saw her face the next morning and wept. Sometimes she comforted him; sometimes she forgave him but withheld affection; other times she remained so angry that, when he refused to leave for work without a kiss goodbye from her, she gave it with revulsion simply so he would go away from her.

She was ashamed to go to work with a bruised eye or a split lip, but went anyway because they needed the money for the next time he came home with a full pay spent. Her colleagues didn't believe her explanatory stories of course and she felt pitied and judged. The bruises looked far worse on a pregnant woman.

Two months after her wedding Maisie knew she was carrying Arnold's child. She should have feared this as a chain to him, but instead she thought it would be the making of him. Sober, Arnold was still kind, loving, generous and fun. He was helpful to old people on the street, often gave the last coins in his pocket to the homeless and made children laugh in delight at his antics. She just knew becoming a father would ensure this side of Arnold – the Robert Louis Stevenson equivalent of Dr Jekyll – would win out over the evil Mr Hyde. She wrote home excitedly to tell Rose.

'No news to me,' came the reply. 'I knew you were pregnant when you got married!'

Protestations it wasn't so had no effect on Rose and she and Dick turned up in Brisbane at the end of July to await the birth of a new grandchild. Christine Anne Cameron was born on 9 September 1953 at the Women's Intermediate Hospital in Brisbane, weighing 7lb 7ozs and measuring 21½ inches long. Rose was grumpy she had had to wait so long and Dick had gone back to Broken Hill weeks earlier for a scheduled rope quoits competition.

Much had changed in the lead-up to Christine's birth. Maisie and Arnold had left the Carrs for accommodation more appropriate to a growing family, despite Mr Carr's offer to turn part of the balcony into a nursery. For the first time, they didn't have to share their space. Their little house in Red Hill had two bedrooms, kitchen, dining room, bathroom and toilet, with a small sunroom at the front and a laundry beneath stairs at the back. They bought good quality laurel maple furniture on time payment and Maisie created a beautiful garden in the backyard. They made friends with the neighbours, had young couples over for dinner, played cards inside

*Rose and a pregnant Maisie at Brisbane's
Lone Pine Koala Sanctuary, 1953.*

and shuttlecock outside. They also bought their first car. It was a
Whippet Tourer, branded for the small swift dog, but was more than
20 years old! Maisie wasn't sure whether she worried more about
Arnold driving it (he hadn't had a licence for many years) or the
car rattling into pieces. However, their neighbour was a mechanic
in the Air Force and repaired the car for them, using parts he stole
from work. It turned out that the Whippet's motor was remarkably
like the Jeeps of World War II. It soon hummed in perfect tune.

For those five or six months Maisie was blissfully happy. The
progressing pregnancy did indeed have the effect on Arnold she

had hoped for – he drank very little after handing over most of his pay for furniture payments and nest-building for the child. Without 'the drink', there was no violence.

Both Maisie and Arnold adored Christine and called her 'little princess'. She had her daddy's blonde curls and blue-green eyes and dimpled chin. Jesse May came to visit when Rose went home, but Maisie didn't really need any help. The baby was easy to care for and Arnold doted on both of them.

This time there was no trigger for the change. Arnold simply started drinking a little more, staying out a little later and becoming a little rougher with Maisie when she reproached him. She learned that if he hadn't come home by 9 pm, she shouldn't be there when he did. The owner of a nearby delicatessen had become her friend and the two fixed a little space at the back of the shop with a stretcher and basic supplies for the baby so Maisie could use a key to let herself in and spend the night. Arnold never knew where she went and sometimes her escape from one beating only led into another, because the next night she wouldn't say where she'd been.

If we allow even momentarily Maisie's view that 'the drink' was an entity and capable of actions, then it was a cruel creature. One night when it was raining so hard she didn't want to take Christine out in her stroller, she feigned sleep instead and 'the drink' burnt her with a cigarette to waken her. And still she stayed.

Not long after this, she awoke on another rainy night to hear a ruckus in the kitchen. She ran for her child only to find she was not in the cot. She found her in the kitchen with Arnold and two dirty drunks, one bouncing Christine on his knee to give her a 'horsey ride'. Arnold had brought them home to see the beautiful little daughter about whom he was constantly boasting. This finally gave her the strength to leave him. Maxie wired her money for the airfare and she left the next day.

Rose was happy to have her home and delighted in her youngest granddaughter. Jackie and Yvonne now had two daughters, Janet and Kayleen, and Maisie thought she had never seen her mother so happy as when she was watching over the three little girls together. Jackie and Yvonne now had their own home at 62 Morish Street, so Maisie and Christine moved into the sleep-out she had once renovated for Arnold. This adjoined Maxie's bedroom but, rather than being annoyed at a baby in the house, he was enchanted by her. Maisie often woke in the morning to find Christine chortling away on Maxie's bed, because he had come in from night shift (he was now at the Zinc Corporation) to find her awake.

Yvonne was her confidante, and the only one in the family to know the true cruelty of the Cameron home. Dulcie and Ken were her saviours, regularly calling to take her out to housie.

This wasn't the benign fund-raising past-time for senior citizens it has (mostly) become today – it was a significant gambling alternative to horse and greyhound racing. Cash housie-housie (bingo) could prove quite lucrative for those with quick hand-eye coordination, and thousands of young people and couples turned out across the country most evenings to packed halls. Only three years later, poker machines would be legalised in NSW clubs, but at the end of 1953 housie-housie was considered a national gambling problem serious enough to warrant legislated amendments to the Lotteries and Art Unions Act, to restrict the price of housie cards to threepence each and limit any cash prizes to £6. However, Broken Hill played equally by its own rules for housie as it did for two-up. The card prices – and therefore potential winnings – remained much higher than that.

Housie-housie at that time was the city's main entertainment for those without the energy or inclination for dancing, because the BIC had placed another boycott on the picture theatres. More than 8000 unionists were banned from movie-going until the cinemas abandoned a bid to increase prices – or renovated their premises sufficiently to warrant the increase.

The BIC demanded all wooden seats be removed, deck chairs installed in outside cinemas and 'the ugly and obvious conveniences' be replaced by 'decent retiring rooms, particularly for the ladies'. The dispute didn't include the Tivoli, because it had burnt to the ground in December 1952. The fire was labelled Broken Hill's 'most spectacular blaze' – for the intensity of the fire, but also perhaps for the circumstances. The Tivoli had been purchased by Ozone Theatres for an undisclosed amount, but insured for £5000. When Ozone tried to on-sell the building, it passed in at auction when the highest bid reached only £2000 and the fire destroyed it weeks later. Police found no evidence it was deliberately lit. The 1954 picture theatre dispute lasted three months and was only resolved when the Department of Labour and Industry stepped in to declare the three shillings and nine pence cost of back stalls and two shillings and threepence for front stalls were fair prices.

So at the time Maisie arrived back in Broken Hill with a young baby, Broken Hill's housie halls were full. Good door takings meant big prizes and Maisie had learnt from Arnold that returns came in proportion to investment. There should also have been lessons about big losses following big wins, but for some reason they didn't come.

Dulcie and Ken provided her initial stakes, but then she was on her own. She played the maximum six cards at a time – which meant every number to come from the caller would be on at least one of her cards (and often several) – and bought the more expensive cards at three shillings and sixpence each. One night she won a bullseye jackpot (a full card on exactly 50 numbers called) which was worth an extraordinary £85! There were numerous smaller wins – full house, lines, four corners and double bubble (calling housie on 11, 22, 33, 44, and so on). Before long, she had paid Maxie back for the airfare; paid Rose for board; and bought Christine a little pink fluffy jacket and beret with matching shoes to go to town to see the Queen.

Queen Elizabeth II and His Royal Highness the Duke of Edinburgh visited 57 centres across Australia during their 58-day tour of Australia in the year following her coronation, but Broken

Queen Elizabeth beneath a protective parasol in Argent Street,
March 1954.

Sir Norman Mighell escorting the Queen after a comfort stop
at the Zinc Corporation's Directors' Cottage.

Hill tarted up for its turn on 18 March 1954 as though it were the only destination. A decorations committee had formed months earlier and more than £3000 was raised in the community to ensure the city would be appropriately decked in red, white and blue to welcome its royal visitors. More than two tons of bunting, garlands and banners was brought into town by train from Adelaide, the last of it requiring a 183-mile mad dash by car to Terowie to collect mistakenly off-loaded boxes.

The full length of the eight-mile royal progress route was decorated with draped strips of bunting; businesses hung gold banners or silhouettes of the Queen; and each new section of the city sported a 40-foot by 3-foot welcome banner. The Town Hall displayed a four-foot by five-foot portrait of the Queen and garish blue paint – which made Maisie gasp in horror as she joined the thousands of people in Argent Street hoping for a glimpse of their new young Queen.

Maisie thought of her father and the love they had shared for this beautiful old building that had now lost its majesty in honour of a majestic visitor. She had equal disdain for the gaudy bunting that hid the true colour of her glorious home town. After having lived in three capital cities, she now appreciated the romance of Broken Hill and she was certain Queen Elizabeth must be tired of the sameness of these decorations in every Australian town and being forced to look beyond the clutter to find the natural beauty of her sojourns. She may have been right.

Barrier Miner Friday 19 March 1954 (excerpt)

QUEEN AMAZED AT BROKEN HILL; COURAGE PRAISED

Her Majesty, Queen Elizabeth, in her reply to the address of welcome presented by the Mayor (Ald. W. Riddiford) yesterday paid a tribute to the resolute courage of the pioneers of the industry. Her Majesty said: "The citizens of Broken Hill have given us a welcome we shall always remember, and I thank all for it. I thank you also for your kind words of loyalty. I do not think that anyone could fly, as I have done today, across the vast stretches of the Australian outback and come to this modern city, built upon the barren reaches of the Barrier

Range, without a sense of amazement at the achievement which its existence represents.

'The story of how this great mining centre, which has become one of the main springs of Australia's industrial strength, has been built, and equipped for every need of modern life, in the face of every difficulty which nature could devise, is surely one of the most remarkable and romantic in Australian history.'

It's doubtful whether Queen Elizabeth and Prince Philip did long remember their visit to the Silver City as she promised, but Broken Hill certainly still remembers it. However – true to the city's character – this is much less for the pageantry of the occasion than for the fact the Royal bottom sat on a toilet seat during a comfort stop in Zinc Corporation accommodation that later became a mine manager's home. Even today, any mention of the visit brings forth mention of the seat.

Despite her aversion for the decorations, Maisie did enjoy the parade. She had gone in with Rose and Dick and was surprised by the camaraderie that developed between the three during the long hours of waiting and the brief drive-by. Christine was not happy sitting in her stroller with her only view the backs of people's legs, so Maisie had her on her hip. The six-month-old found the fluttering flags entirely entertaining and continually bounced and jiggled as she reached for them. Maisie's back was hurting.

All mothers know that ache, but Maisie had also sustained several back injuries at the hands of Arnold, so she was filled with gratitude and surprise when Rose held out her arms for the baby. What surprised her more was the look of sympathy on Rose's face. In that fleeting expression, they bonded as they never had before. When Dick later held out his arms to relieve Rose, Maisie linked her arm through her mother's and they smiled at each other. She was struck by the thought that Rose must once have felt the same overwhelming love for her as she now felt for her own daughter.

After the Royal procession headed back to the aerodrome, the crowds began to prepare for the planned massive street party. Now Maisie's ache was not for her back, but for Arnold.

Each member of her family had played a part in trying to cushion her from the grief of leaving Arnold, but it hadn't been enough. People assume the loss is less for the one who leaves than the one who is left, but it isn't so. Maisie knew Arnold would be suffering without her and Christine – and this time she somehow rationalised his pain was her fault.

He had written almost daily and, while she hadn't read his letters, she hadn't burnt them either. She had noticed the writing becoming more spidery on the envelopes – to the point where now she felt the postie was only able to decipher them because of their regularity. The night of the Queen's visit, she minded Jackie and Yvonne's sleeping girls while they joined Rose and Dick at the street party. She sat alone in the house and read every letter.

The last told her he was ill (he had recurrent bouts of malaria throughout his lifetime) and had broken his leg taking some laundry down the back steps of their house.

When she told the family she was going back to Brisbane only to care for him until he was well, no one believed her. She wasn't sure she believed it herself, but she knew she had to go.

Chapter 25
Cracks in the castle
1954–1955

Maisie was shocked when she saw him. She had expected the plaster cast on his leg and the crutches, but he was so thin! His skin was sallow, the acne had returned on his chest and climbed his neck, his hair was long and looked dirty, his clothes were filthy and even with the anti-malarial tablets he sweated profusely and shook with tremors. At his worst, Arnold had always been well-groomed. This person looked like a homeless drunk, although she could smell no drink on him. She cared for him tenderly over the next weeks and he was tender with her and their child. Maisie went down to the markets to explain his absence and his boss promised to keep his job open.

'Jock's a top bloke,' he told her. 'He's a hard worker and all the blokes like him. You just have to do something about his drinking.' If only she could.

After her visit to the markets, his mates started to call at the house, bringing boxes of vegetables. She took them gratefully and made him nutritious soups and tasty stews, but she wished they wouldn't come. She feared they would start bringing booze as soon as he was well. They didn't, but they brought a different pressure.

'Jock's a mess when you're not here,' each told her. But they also told her he drank too much. They were kind to her and began to bring large punnets of beautiful juicy strawberries just for her, gifts from the growers.

Slowly he recovered and went back to work. Now she feared he wouldn't come home each afternoon. But he did – and sober. She wrote to Rose that she wouldn't be coming back to Broken Hill for a while. Rose replied she hadn't expected her yet, but the sleep-out was there when eventually she needed it.

Maisie, Christine at eight months and Arnold,
May 1954.

They made friends with a young Chinese family across the road. Young Norma King Koi was just a couple of months older than Christine and the two little girls played happily together. Maisie regularly took Christine by bus and ferry to visit the Carrs and Nellie gave her boxes of beautiful-quality clothing that her children had outgrown. Now Christine really did look like a little princess. Arnold came punctually to pick them up in the car at the end of these visits and gradually she came to feel confident he would be there.

They went to the races together often, but turned it into family picnics on the lawn rather than Arnold in the bar. Sometimes he went without her if Christine wasn't well, but came home relatively sober and demanded a kiss from Maisie for each pound note he peeled off from his wad of winnings, until she had almost all of it. On one of these happy events he brought home enough for her to pay cash for a new electric refrigerator and she delighted in its gleam in the kitchen. She spent hours polishing their beautiful old dining table and even the wooden slats that lined the walls. She was happy in her castle.

Christine walked and talked early and delighted them both with antics such as regularly toddling in with a pot plant from the sunroom – a chubby fist around its neck to show them it was, 'Hmmm, pretty'. Eventually the plant became quite loose in its pot and, on most occasions, the pot and the dirt would end up on the floor with the greenery still clasped in a little hand. They laughed together at the shocked look on her face as she bent to look at the mess at her feet – and she laughed at their laughter. They planned evenings at the pictures and Maisie dressed Christine in her beautiful gifted outfits, walking down to the corner to 'wait for Daddy'. She was filled with joy when her daughter clapped her little hands in excitement as she saw the old car coming up the hill. It was too good to last. Not long after Christine's first birthday, Arnold came home smelling of beer and Maisie froze.

'It's okay. It's under control. I've only had one,' he reassured her.

The next night it was more, but he was cocky.

'I've got this! It's under control … I promise not to spoil things.' But he did. The next night it was after 10 pm before he came home and Christine was asleep with tear-stained cheeks because they'd had to turn around on the corner and walk back up the hill when Daddy didn't come.

Maisie was on edge waiting for the beatings to start again. For a while they didn't. But, when they did, she still stayed. If alcohol

Maisie and Christine, 13 months, October 1954.

was Arnold's weakness, then he was surely hers. She was addicted to the life they had when he was sober and was always waiting for it to come back.

Then she was pregnant again. This time she wasn't quite as delighted. She wanted the baby – very much – but she no longer had the belief a baby would magically rid Arnold of his demons. Arnold was overjoyed. He surprised Maisie by saying he wanted another little girl.

'I want another little princess like Christine, but this time with big brown eyes and chocolate curls like yours!'

When he shoved her to the floor one night for yelling at him about coming home 'with too much drink in', she was stunned when the pain in her abdomen was stronger than the pain in her back. He thought she was exaggerating and left her there to go back to the pub. Maisie called for Mrs Merritt, a neighbour, who came in and left again quickly to call Dr Goldberg, who had delivered Christine the year before. Dr Goldberg examined Maisie and sent Mrs Merritt to call for an ambulance. While they waited, Arnold came home.

'Aw, she's just having you on,' he told the doctor. 'She just doesn't want to get up and cook my tea!'

Maisie lost the baby in hospital the next morning. Arnold was distraught and ashamed, but Maisie had hardened.

'I'm going home, Arnold. Nothing will stop me.'

She did go home, but Arnold went with her. He managed to convince her he should drive her in the Whippet, telling her he knew he was no good for her or their daughter, so he would take her home to her family where she would be safe. Maisie thought of the last plane trip home with Christine – a crying, vomiting baby. They had had a three-hour stopover in Sydney and long flights either side of it that made Christine scream with pain on landings and take-offs. Maisie agreed, on the condition Arnold understood they were no longer husband and wife.

That lasted only as long as it took to reach the New South Wales border. Then she extracted a different promise. She would give them a chance in Broken Hill to be a stable family, only if he promised to leave if he failed. He promised.

They had a wonderful trip over the two weeks that followed. They stayed in tiny towns along the way, had picnics by the roadside and took delight in Christine's reaction to the animals she saw along the way. They sang 'Old MacDonald Had a Farm' at the top of their voices and giggled at Christine's attempts to make the animal sounds. They giggled too, when the old Whippet (packed to the hilt) smoothly chugged up the heights of the Blue Mountains watched by open-mouthed drivers of modern cars with their bonnets up and steam billowing from over-heated engines. Their secret Air

Force parts worked a treat. By the time they arrived in Broken Hill, Maisie's belief was restored. Surely it would work this time.

Rose was welcoming and Jackie, Maxie, Dulcie and Ken were excited. They had missed their sister, adored Christine and liked Arnold. Only Yvonne was hesitant. There was much back-slapping from the boys about Arnold's car. They couldn't believe the old Whippet had travelled more than a thousand miles of rough terrain (including outback roads) without a hiccup. Maxie, especially, delighted in it and thought Arnold 'a good bloke' when he agreed to swap cars for awhile with his new Ford Zephyr. Broken Hill claims it had a higher number of cars per head of population during the 1950s than any other city in the world, except Detroit. The beautiful old wood-framed Whippet stood out in all the shine, and handsome Maxie had no problem enticing the local girls to go for a ride in it.

This time Arnold found work quickly – as a barman at the Alma Sporting Club right next door to Rose's house, but facing Boughtman Street. Maisie shuddered at the thought, but Arnold was adamant the job was a godsend.

'It's perfect, Maisie. This way I can have a chat with the blokes without having to have a drink to do it.' Maisie was sceptical and reminded him of his promise.

'If it doesn't work, Arnold, you said you would go …'

'There's no need to worry about that,' he cajoled. 'I won't let you down this time.' It's likely Arnold truly believed it when he said it, but they both should have known.

The Alma Sporting Club was known as 'the Billies', apparently after a sporting team trip interstate where members were told they had behaved 'like a pack of billygoats'. At the time Arnold worked there, the club had a large membership, but was still operating out of old Army drill buildings that had been moved from the north of the city in 1924. There had been various renovations over the years and a liquor licence acquired in 1931, but the modern building that became a South Broken Hill icon was not opened until 1958. The 1954 membership was set at two pounds two shillings, with ten shillings of this directed toward the building fund.

Even without a purpose-built facility, the Billies had a membership larger than the RSL Club or the Barrier Social Democratic Club (the Demo) because the South had a larger proportion of young working-class families. The club ran billiards, euchre and darts tournaments with more than 100 members competing in each, entered teams into local cricket and soccer competitions and had 'mixed nights' when members brought their wives along for film shorts, dancing, bands, or special performances by the Billies Club Orchestra. But, essentially, it was a men's club, with all the associated conveniences that that connotes – including on-site bookmakers.

For the first few weeks working at the Billies, Arnold was on his best behaviour. He came home promptly after work, handed most of his pay to Maisie and only occasionally smelled of beer (which he said came from working with it). His tax refund cheque arrived and he cashed it and gave her that too. They began saving to buy their own place and Maisie started working part-time at the dry cleaners to add to the kitty. Her father was back in her head, 'When you grow up and you have some money, *kleine Tochter*, you buy property. Always you have money in the land, and the land will always be there. It is important, *Liebchen*, and you must remember what I say'. She remembered.

Then he began to 'pop next door for a minute' after tea or call in on his days off 'to collect my winnings on the horses'. Maisie warned him to 'take care', but he again reassured her.

'I'm off it. Don't worry. I'm the family man you wanted.' What she wanted was to believe him.

One night she was due to go to housie with Rose and Ken and Dulcie. Arnold had 'popped in next door' and wasn't home on time. Ken went in to get him. Arnold came, but stumbled as he came into the house and Maisie promptly told the others she wasn't going.

'Don't be silly,' Ken told her. 'He was fine in the Billies. He's just doing that to make you stay home.'

Eventually, she was persuaded and left with the others. They were part-way into town when she realised she couldn't do it. Ken dropped off Rose and Dulcie and returned to the South. When Maisie tried to open the back door, it wouldn't move. She looked in through the bathroom window and saw Arnold slumped on the floor, with his shoulder against the door. Christine was there too, crying and trying to pull her father up by the hand.

'Up Daddy. Up now. Daddy get up.' Arnold only lifted his head and waved a hand toward her.

'In a minni darling. In a minni. Just give Daddy a minute.' Maisie noticed with horror the hand he gestured toward Christine held a flask. She ran around to the front door and was grateful to see Ken had waited to see she was alright. They went in together and bundled up Christine.

'That's it, Arnold! That's the last chance gone!' she yelled at him. Ken took the rotor button from the car as they left so he couldn't follow her.

She intended to spend the night at Dulcie and Ken's, but Christine went to sleep almost immediately in the car, so Ken persuaded her to still go into housie and he would wait with Christine out the front. She won no cash that night.

At 10.30 pm they all went back to the house, with Ken intending to stay until Maxie came home from afternoon shift. As she had suspected, Arnold wasn't there. Ken went home and Rose and Maisie went to their beds.

In the early hours of the morning Maisie suddenly awoke with a weight on top of her and unable to breathe. Arnold was kneeling on her chest and had a pillow held down tight over her face. She struggled, but couldn't shift him. She banged her fist on the wall behind the bed and at last Maxie rushed in and dragged him off her. Maxie threw Arnold out of the house and a short time later they could hear him trying to start the car. They heard the bonnet of the car slam. Maisie remembered the rotor button and feared he would come back – but he didn't. He still wasn't there in the morning.

Maisie was due to go to work, but before she left she packed all Arnold's things into the car, added a pillow and two blankets, set a box of food on the front seat and put the rotor button back in the distributor. She put half the tax refund money into an envelope and taped it to the steering wheel with a note. It was short and to the point:

'You really blew it this time. Remember your promise. There's nothing left for us, Arnold. Go home to Manly. Christine is inside with Mum so you can say goodbye to her, but we have nothing left to say to each other so don't contact me. There's no one more sorry than me that it can't work for us, but we really have come to the end of the road. Please make this one promise to me that you actually keep. Goodbye my love, Maisie.'

When she came home from work, he was gone. He hadn't gone inside to say goodbye to Christine or Rose, but had left her a note in the letterbox.

'I am so, so sorry. I will keep my promise to you, but please try to forgive me. I will love you forever, but I will wait for you in Manly only one month. We can go back to Red Hill together. Your loving Arnie.'

There were telegrams from various places along the route to Sydney asking for money – the car had broken down; he had a petrol leak so was spending more than he should on fuel; he was sick and had no money for a doctor; he was hungry and had no money for food. She wired him money each time he asked for it. Finally she sent £100, which was the last of the tax refund. The telegram that went with it said only, 'THAT IS IT STOP I AM OUT STOP'.

He reached Manly and then the letters started to come – long eloquent letters that told her he was sober and repentant and had

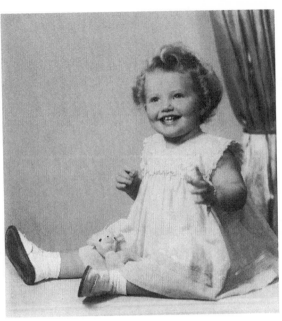

Christine at two years old in Broken Hill, 1955.

learned his lesson; then romantic letters that expressed undying love for her and included beautiful love poems; then piteous letters that described how he had run up to a little blonde curly-haired child on the beach because he thought it was Christine. This time, she read them all as they came and immediately dropped each into the wood stove. Even the poems.

She never saw Arnold again – and it would be a decade before Arnold saw Christine. Though Maisie recalled happy memories of him many times as she aged, her final memories of him also remained – of her two-year-old daughter trying to pull him up from the floor and her brother pulling him off her as he tried to suffocate her. During the month Arnold spent at Manly waiting for her, Maisie spent time in a solicitor's office attempting to file for divorce.

Buckworth and Buckworth became an iconic law firm in Broken

Hill (and remains today as Buckworth Keady Lawyers) but in 1955, the practice was very new and Maisie was George Buckworth's first divorce case. He was about the same age as Arnold, but had led a remarkable life.

George Grainger Buckworth lied about his age to enlist at 17 and later became the RAAF's youngest squadron leader. At 18, his plane was shot down over Belgium and he spent almost two years as a prisoner-of-war, before escaping back behind Allied lines and being sent to England to fight on. He was awarded the Croix de Guerre for his heroism, including bravely withholding information about the Belgian Resistance. During his imprisonment, he endured long forced marches under horrific conditions in which thousands of prisoners died, and his Mention in Despatches notes, 'The unquenchable optimism and unselfish support of Flight Lieutenant G.G. Buckworth for his fellow prisoners of war during a long march in appalling winter conditions undoubtedly contributed to their survival'.

After the war, George completed his law degree at the University of Sydney, met and married Patricia (Pattie) Oldfield, also a solicitor, in 1950, became a barrister and re-enlisted in the RAAF to work in legal and security roles. For a time, he worked for ASIO – under its founder Colonel Charles Spry – and even had a role to play in the infamous Petrov Affair, surreptitiously accompanying KGB agent Evdokia Petrov on her plane to Darwin as she struggled (under KGB escort) with her decision to join her husband in defecting to Australia.

George only resigned from the RAAF and his more secret work so he and Pattie could establish the Buckworth and Buckworth practice in Broken Hill. So George should have had no trouble in managing a naïve local girl setting up her divorce petition, but he did.

Maisie was adamant she didn't want to say bad things about Arnold, much less say them in court. She wanted no alimony for herself, she wanted no child maintenance for Christine. She didn't want any distribution of their assets (the Red Hill house had been sub-let furnished). She just wanted Arnold out of her life. But she did want full custody of their child. George was impatient with her.

'Understand the law, Mrs Cameron. People before the divorce court are either blameworthy or blameless. If you intend to be so kind to your husband, then he's not likely to be thought the blameworthy.'

He was right. There was no such thing as a no-fault divorce in those days. It was not until the Family Law Act of 1975 that irretrievable breakdown could be used as the sole reason for dissolution of a marriage.

'You have three choices only – adultery, cruelty or desertion. The first two are difficult to prove and the third will mean you need to wait at least two years before we can start.'

Adultery was immediately dismissed as an option. She'd never suspected Arnold had been with another woman. George thought maybe an investigator might prove otherwise. Now she became impatient with him.

'But it doesn't have to have happened while you were living together,' he explained. 'I'm sure we could prove it now.'

He didn't even get to describe the difficulties of obtaining that proof. She hotly dismissed it. The conversation would likely have been much more heated if George had dared tell her that, in Victoria, a female petitioner needed to prove her husband had engaged in 'a repeated act of adultery', while once was enough for a husband to divorce his wife!

Desertion was unfair. Arnold had left her, but only because she insisted on it. She told George she felt she was the deserter and that she had been in the process of doing that for more than three years.

'Even a brief reconciliation means the separation period must start again, Mrs Cameron. And if you are the deserter, you are not entitled to custody of your child.'

'Cruelty' was the remaining option – but Maisie thought it cruel to brand Arnold with that. Sober, he had always been a kind and loving husband and father. It was the drink that was cruel.

George was by now more than exasperated.

'Take these papers to read and come back when you really want my help. I can help you, but you must also help yourself.'

She resolved to put the divorce on hold for now and focus on helping herself in other ways.

Chapter 26

Planning for peace
1955–1956

Maisie's plan to help herself included her own hairdressing salon. She needed a stake in the ground on which to grow a new stable life and reasoned that should be an income dependent only on her. First, she needed to build some capital.

An advertisement in the *Barrier Miner* caught her eye – an imposing promotion for the Freemasons Hotel. Phrases leapt from the page; 'Headquarters for the Discerning Traveller', 'Appointments are the Most Modern in the Hill', 'Excellent Cuisine – Maximum of Comfort'. It sounded like Earl's Court.

On the same page, but some distance from the display advert, a small classified announced vacancies at the hotel for a laundress to do private washing and ironing for guests, a waitress in the dining room and an experienced barmaid for the front bar. Maisie made an appointment with the manager.

At that time the Freemasons *did* have the most modern appointments of Broken Hill's accommodation houses, but it was also the city's oldest operating hotel. It had been built in 1886 as the Broken Hill Hotel and underwent a transformation and name change in 1891 to become the Freemasons. It was owned by the South Australian Brewing Company in 1940, when the NSW Tooth & Co brewery bought it and spent more than £20,000 in six months to revamp it into a grandiose establishment across the entire north-eastern corner of Argent and Oxide streets. Included in the refurbishment was the 'Blonde Lounge and Ballroom' upstairs, named not for the ladies but for the beautiful light timber used for the furniture and fittings.

The change of ownership caused a ruckus about more than the

change of furnishings and beer. Miss Marie Isobel O'Keeffe took to the NSW Full Court to challenge a law forbidding single women to hold publican licenses (married women and even widows were allowed). Miss O'Keeffe asked for a writ of mandamus to compel the Broken Hill licensing magistrate and the Broken Hill District licensing inspector to hear her application – but gave it up in frustration months later. A nominal male licensee was brought in to satisfy the legislation, but Miss O'Keeffe ran the establishment in all but name. She should have held out – a few weeks later, Miss Ann Veronica Furling was given leave by the Full Court to have her late mother's licence for the Oaks Hotel at Neutral Bay in Sydney transferred into her name, and became the first single female publican in NSW.

By the time Maisie returned to Broken Hill with Christine in late 1955, the Freemasons had changed hands again (for £45,000) and was still upmarket, but had developed a regular clientele of travelling salesmen who occupied smaller budget rooms. It was also favoured by outlying pastoralists who booked it out when they came to town for the annual Pastoralists' Ball.

'Squatters Week', as it was known colloquially, almost always left a mark on the Freemasons, but the honourable landowners always paid for the damage before returning to the isolation of the outback. A favourite Broken Hill story tells of a night when these visitors took umbrage with the tunes (or the tuning) of the Blonde Lounge piano and picked it up in unison, leaving behind a gobsmacked but still seated pianist. They marched it out through the open French doors to throw it over the balcony. The story has it the piano smashed on an old Holden being driven through the intersection and 'the silvertails' were so repentant the next morning they took the owner down the street to Argent Motors and bought him a new Vauxhall for more than £1000.

Apart from the flying piano, the Freemasons was renowned for its wonderful ornate dining room that hosted Broken Hill's elite

The Freemasons Hotel (eventually to become the West Darling).

The Freemasons Hotel bedecked for the Queen's visit, March 1954.

for dinner parties, wedding receptions, engagement celebrations, birthday parties and official functions. Maisie had been there only once, but knew it would be a good place to work. She wasn't ready to face drunks propped at the bar or unwelcome advances from men 'in their cups', so during her interview she put her own proposal to the manager – an employment package she told him would suit them both – and walked out with it as a done deal.

From 6 am to 8 am she prepared early breakfasts for the salesmen who needed to be out and about before normal shop hours – porridge, toast and tea or coffee, with the option to call on the cook if there were too many orders for bacon and eggs. She was home from this job in time to get Christine's breakfast before the pair walked the four blocks from South Street to the Patton Street kindergarten. Then she caught the bus back into town for her lunchtime waitressing job in the dining room. Lunch was mostly only for hotel guests but, for this meal, the diners were a little more posh and Maisie's skills from Earl's Court stood her in good stead, both with the guests and the boss. By 3 pm, she was back out the South again to collect Christine from kindy, prepare her an early tea, bathe her and leave her ready in pyjamas for Rose to put to bed later. Then she was back into town again for a shift as a drinks waitress in the dining room from 5.30 pm to 11 pm.

The routine was hectic and punishing. Maisie felt she deserved punishment for what the separation was doing to Arnold. What her imagination didn't tell her, he did – in long, detailed letters. Jesse May wrote too. Maisie replied to tell them both she was going to divorce him and that she was moving on with her life.

She had no time for 'proper' dating in those early months at the Freemasons, but had no inclination for it anyway. She became good friends with June Connors who worked in the front bar. June was from Orange in western New South Wales and had only come to Broken Hill to meet a new baby nephew whose father was under-manager at the hotel. [*Author's aside: Like many who visit the Silver City for a short time, June never escaped. At the time of writing, she lives there still as June McMahon.*] Maisie and June occasionally went on picnic dates with a couple of guests from the hotel, but Christine went too. She also went on platonic outings with her mother and a jewellery salesman, who gave Maisie a beautiful set of gold filigree and marcasite earrings before he returned to Melbourne, and sometimes with Beau Francisco. Beau was a teetotal shearer (a rare combination) who lived at the hotel between sheds. He was happy enough with the family dates for awhile, but when he wanted the relationship to become more romantic, she quickly called a halt. She never wanted to love a man again.

The first time Gil Carlin asked her out, she refused him. Danger was written all over Gil. He was tall and strikingly handsome, with glossy black hair in thick waves on top and blue-grey eyes that reminded Maisie of her father. He sat half-way along the bar every night after work nursing a few scotches on ice. She never saw him drunk – or rowdy – but he drank consistently. He smiled at her often when she brought her drinks tray into the small 'Employees Only' area at the end of the bar for June to fill the order. She was happy enough to smile back. He always looked sad and she was charmed by the fact his smile was slightly crooked in what she thought was an otherwise perfect face. She knew he was building to ask her out because, for more than a week, he'd been taking his position at the bar one stool closer to the end. So, when he finally built the courage to ask her 'to the pictures one night', her response was harsh.

'No thanks,' she told him. 'I've just rid myself of one drinker.'

When she came in with her next order, he was gone. The next night, he tried a different approach.

'If you let me give you a ride home so we can talk and get to know each other, I won't touch another drink all night.'

She laughed.

'Ha! I'd like to see that!'

True to his word, he drank lemonade for the rest of the night and, at the end of it, he asked again to drive her home.

'No thanks,' she said again. 'But you've done well. Perhaps I'll take a raincheck on the offer.'

After a long and sober night, Maisie's response didn't go down well.

'I don't give rainchecks. Next time you'll have to ask me.'

But he did ask again. And again. Finally one night when the dining room had been packed for a function and her sore feet baulked at the idea of a bus ride home and a walk at the end of it, she said 'Yes, please'. Their friendship developed slowly.

Gil was a widower with a little girl called Jenny. From the outset, he was a gentleman. They chatted comfortably when she came into the bar with her drinks tray and drifted into a routine where he gave her a ride home to the South most nights, despite the fact he lived in the north-west of the city. The more she learned about him, the more she liked him. He was nothing like Arnold.

Gilbert Wallace Carlin (born 7 November 1924) was almost six years older than her, but had really only worked one job in his life. He became an apprentice fitter and turner at the North Mine straight after school and then moved to the Zinc Corporation with his qualification, where he was a star player on the company's baseball team and earned the nickname of Dasher. He married his high school sweetheart, Patricia Mary Marks, but in a steady and orderly process. They became engaged in July 1947 when he was 22, married in May of the following year and celebrated the birth of Jennifer Ann on 1 October 1949.

Gil and Pat had steady plans and worked toward them. They rented at 503 Beryl Street while they were building their own home at 32 Jamieson Street 'out the South' and moved in before it was quite finished to save on rent – but their happy times in this home were heartbreakingly short. Gil's blonde and beautiful wife was struck down by leukaemia. Treatment in the 1940s and 1950s was limited, but primitive blood transfusions supported by experimental use of medication (including arsenic) was available in Melbourne. Pat died there on 18 October 1953, just after Jenny turned four. She was brought home to be buried in the same grave as her father (Thomas Henry Marks) who had died in 1939.

The first time Gil brought Jenny along on an outing, Maisie thought she might be making a mistake. Jenny was obviously not happy about this new woman in her father's life, but it was more than that. Jenny was a tall, thin little girl with pale skin, not yet freckled, and a tight pony tail of white-blonde hair. She was very quiet, but extraordinarily well-mannered, and politely but briefly answered all Maisie's attempts at conversation. Christine, by contrast, was short, chubby and loud. She bounced all over the back seat of the car (and Jenny) and clambered happily all over Gil when they stopped. Maisie doubted the girls would 'get on'.

That first outing as a foursome was to see the wildflowers at Red Hill about ten miles along the road to Menindee. The year of 1955 was the wettest on record for the Broken Hill district, and came after four years of punishing drought. Parched land has a forgiving heart after rain and the countryside erupted in colour – purples and blues of wild lilac and Salvation Jane (Paterson's curse); reds of wild hops and pinks of pussypaws; white and yellow everlasting daisies; and white Darling lilies along creek beds. Sturt's Desert Pea was everywhere among the other splotches of colour, but it draped Red Hill alone to form a glorious red and black carpet. This flower is South Australia's floral emblem, but Broken Hill claims it as its own. The blood-red leaf-like petals are contrasted with a glossy black bulbous centre (sometimes very dark red) and it grows in clusters of six to eight flowers on short thick stalks with grey-green leaves. Occasionally clusters deliver an 'albino' plant, with ghostly blooms in among the vibrancy. A single plant can cover more than six foot of sandy soil and, that year, the spreading plants were interwoven to wrap Red Hill entirely.

There were other family groups there to see it that day and Maisie and Gil had trouble chasing down an exuberant Christine who ran and stumbled between groups, chatting in her own language to strange children and picking blooms from scattered clumps at the base of the hill. Jenny, however, stood still and silent.

'Don't you want to pick some flowers too, Jenny?' Maisie ventured. Jenny eyed her steadily.

'I've got my good clothes on, thank you.'

Later, when they all went back to Gil's parents' house for afternoon tea, Maisie began to understand this quiet politeness in a six-year-old. It was a loving home, but full of sadness and proper behaviour. Jenny was 'Jennifer' here.

Maisie was embarrassed by so many things on that afternoon visit, but the first was the disappointed look Edith Willard Carlin gave Jenny when she saw the red-brown marks on her white skirt. Maisie knew these were from Christine's shoes as she scrabbled around in the car, rather than any lack of care of Jenny's part, and she apologised for it. She found herself apologising often in the next few hours. Christine had no manners when it came to eating orange cake with a dessert fork, seemed incapable of holding a glass of milk, and clearly had no understanding of the concept that 'children should be seen and not heard' when in the company of adults. Jenny understood remarkably well. Edith was polite, and kind, but her shoulders were held well-back and her smile was firmly fixed.

There was more awkwardness when discussion turned to Maisie's work at the Freemasons. Gil had only told his mother he had met Maisie there and Edith had assumed it had been at a social function. During the part of the conversation that exposed Christine's father was still living and Maisie not yet divorced, Edith needed to excuse herself from the room for a moment to compose herself. Maisie sensed her status would have been no more improved even if she were a divorcée.

Gus Carlin (Augustus Lesley) was Grandmaster of the Manchester Unity Independent Order of Oddfellows; Edith was President of the Wesleyan Methodist Church Ladies Guild; Gil's older brother Colin was Superintendent of the district's Methodist Sunday School Teachers Association; and his wife Nadine was an active member in the Ladies Guild with her mother-in-law.

In contrast, Maisie was half-German, which was still considered an affliction a decade after the end of the war, and a practicing

Lutheran. She had a mother born in Wilcannia and two brothers who were as well known for having a good time as their sporting achievements. And poor Edith was yet to learn of the shenanigans of Rose and Dick!

Later, Maisie would be well-loved by the Carlins – and love them well in return – but that first meeting was farcical. Maisie's tension overflowed in the car on the way home.

'So, you're ashamed of me, then. You didn't tell them anything about me!' Gil maintained the half-crooked smile with which he'd viewed the afternoon's exchanges.

'They know I love you, Maisie. I told them that. And the only consent I need to marry you is yours.'

It stopped her for a moment, but he didn't get off that lightly. She had much more to say on that ride out the South, but Gil took it in his stride. It transpired he *had* told *Gus* all about Maisie – they just thought things might go more smoothly if Edith could meet her before she heard much about her.

That day was the first mention of marriage between them, but it had been obvious for some time it was Gil's intention. He was candidly romantic toward her and she revelled in how 'special' he made her feel, but she felt incapable of returning his love in the way she knew she should.

She felt for both Gil and Jenny at the loss of Pat – at Gil's loneliness and six-year-old Jenny's life as a little adult. She *wanted* to be in love with him and she knew she should, but even when she tried to convince herself she was, there was always something to prove it wasn't so – like the day she saw he still kept a photo of Pat in his wallet, and she felt no jealousy at that.

Gil, on the other hand, showed open jealousy if he saw a man make moves on her at the Freemasons. He still drank there every night, but had switched from whiskey to beer for her approval, even though the head often became flat because he didn't like it much and consequently drank slowly.

She wondered whether she was being fair to him and contemplated ending it, just so she wouldn't hurt him. He was a good, kind and gentle man and offered her all the stability and security she had yearned for with Arnold. She did love him, just not with the heady excitement she'd once felt for an entirely different man. She convinced herself maybe her loving friendship would be enough, because he made her feel that her friendship was a truly valuable thing.

Before she came to a decision about Gil, she was distracted. Rose offered to loan her the money to open a salon. There was a vacant shop in a group of four in Picton Street, just off the corner of Boughtman. It was perfect – just a little more than a three-block walk from home and only half a block from Dulcie and Ken's house at 76 Boughtman Street. The shops had only been built in 1950 and included Whitelums' delicatessen on the corner, a butcher and a greengrocer. The middle shop was tiny and needed refurbishment to create a beauty salon, but she had learned how to handle a paintbrush and Gil came every night after work to help her. On weekends Gus came too. He was a carpenter by trade, although he worked underground at the South Mine, and the two men built benches and framed mirrors while she decorated in white and mauve.

Maisie was very proud of the little salon and renamed it the Christine. It took very little time to build a substantial clientele. While it had been eight years since Maisie had shown Broken Hill women her hairdressing skills, they weren't forgotten. The Christine was a convenience for those in 'the south of the South', cutting blocks from the walk to Patton Street, but Maisie was thrilled when women began to travel from town, too. One of those was Edith Carlin, ostensibly to look at the work Gus and Gil had done on the shop, but also looking for a new blue tint for her light grey hair. Maisie nervously persuaded her into a new cut as well and Edith became an ardent ambassador for the salon among her church fellowship.

Maisie relaxed into life. She enjoyed her work, was home every night to put her child to bed, and spent more time with her during the day, too. Christine was now almost three and less of a handful for Rose, so she went to kindergarten only on alternate mornings, spent the others with Maisie at the shop and afternoons at home with Rose so she could nap in her own little bed. Christine brought Maisie and Rose closer than they'd ever been and underneath Maisie's satisfaction with her new life was a deep sense of gratitude to Rose that she had made it possible through her loan and childminding. Part of her satisfaction came from being able to repay that loan in regular weekly payments in addition to the contribution she made to the household for board.

Gil was now a big part of her warm peaceful life. She could no longer envisage life without him, but had yet to fully commit to a future with him. The turmoil of life with Arnold began to blur. He kept writing to her, though not as often, and she kept reading them, through not replying. She did write to Jesse May though – newsy letters about Christine's little milestones. She told Jesse about the hairdressing salon and was astonished at the reply.

Jesse May wrote she loved her as a daughter and was therefore delighted at the new life Maisie was building for herself and encouraged her to go ahead with divorcing Arnold. The letter enclosed a separate statement outlining what she knew of the cruelty and violence in her son's marriage. Maisie gasped when she read the extent of Jesse's knowledge. Arnold must have told her, because she hadn't.

'Arnold regrets everything, dear Maisie, deeply,' she wrote in the letter, 'But I see now he will never change. He is an alcoholic. Use my statement to help get your divorce. You need to do it for you and Christine. Please don't let Arnold know I have done this, if you can help it. He's my boy and he needs me.'

Gil had asked about her divorce, more than once. She had tried to explain how she felt about describing what her husband had done, but she couldn't do that properly without describing how breath-taking he had been when sober – and he didn't need to hear that. Jesse's permission – encouragement – to tell what needed to be told, made it right.

George Buckworth was pleased to see her. He was gentler once he had her full story. He even seemed to understand when she told him the reason she was not seeking financial support from Arnold was that she knew he would be unable to sustain it. There would be many times when he would simply have no money. She didn't want him to 'get into trouble'.

The content of Jesse's letter wasn't used in the proceedings, but the fact it existed was. Arnold threatened to contest the divorce, but didn't. The decree nisi was issued on 10 July 1956 and, since there was no appeal, the decree absolute was granted 24 January 1957. This document granted sole and permanent custody of Christine to Maisie.

Chapter 27
Nestling and nesting
1956–1957

Peace at 25 South Street was a beautiful thing, but everyone knew it was tenuous with Rose and Maisie living there together. It lasted a year and the family had stopped waiting for the explosion when it came. Such a little thing ignited it – but who knows how lives would have been different if it hadn't happened?

Rose and Maisie had worked together for days baking and preparing for Christine's third birthday on Sunday 9 September, which was celebrated with a party for more than 20 children on the side sleep-out. The next morning Maisie was making a packed lunch for her and Christine to take to the salon when Rose came into the kitchen.

'Don't use that ham, Maisie. It's for Maxie's crib.'

Maisie argued the ham was left over from the party for which she'd paid entirely – even to the extent of replacing the flour Rose used in the cakes.

Rose argued Maxie was a man who needed meat in his sandwich and Maisie was bloody selfish for thinking to take it from him.

Maisie argued she paid the same board as Maxie, with extra for Christine, and was tired of having to make sure Maxie had 'the best'.

Rose argued she had lent her the money to buy the salon so she wouldn't 'get in' with the uppity Carlins over the hill, but she was still seeing him.

Maisie packed everything belonging to her and Christine and moved into the back of the salon.

It was a tiny little room that contained a two-seater lounge, just big enough for Christine to sleep on, a small fridge with a primus

Christine's third birthday party at 25 South Street –
a catalyst for change, 1956.

stove on top, and a hand basin in which they bathed. There was a toilet out the back. Gil was upset at her staying there and offered his empty house in Jamieson Street, just around the corner from the salon. He was hurt when she explained that would make her feel more committed to him than she was ready for just yet. It didn't stop him from wanting to help her, so he found his own way. He bought a new single mattress for Jenny's bed at his parents' house and brought the replaced perfectly good mattress to the salon so she at least had something soft to sleep on. It stood against the wall during the day and filled the tiny floor space at night.

Life wasn't easy, but the family rallied around her. Dulcie and Ken and Jackie and Yvonne had both offered her a home. When she didn't accept, they invited her often for meals. Yvonne had a new baby (Maxine), but Dulcie's twin daughters (Dawn and Joyce) were young teenagers so she often took Christine home for the afternoon, allowing Maisie to focus on her clients. Maxie came to visit after work and took them for rides in his car to relieve the claustrophobia of their cramped situation and Gil was there every step of the way, quietly providing support, but backing off when Maisie told him to.

Christine charmed the clients and the neighbouring shopkeepers. It was a safe little neighbourhood, but Maisie still worried when Christine escaped through the front door and wandered up and down on the footpath at the front of the shops. She came back chewing on a lolly from the deli, having obtained it from Mrs Whitelum with a stone wrapped in foil paper that Christine fully believed looked like a coin. Or she would be dangling a piece of fritz from the butcher, obtained with a dimpled smile, or munching on a raw onion from the grocer, filched when he wasn't looking.

It had only been a month, but pressure was building. Each week Maisie gave Yvonne the loan repayment to pass on to Rose and she had reached a point where there was only one remaining. The excitement at this caused her to soften toward her mother. Rose had a sharp tongue, but she was always there when the chips were down. Putting the pound notes in the envelope for the final payment brought back the gratitude she'd felt when Rose made it possible for her to own the salon. Now she was using it to remove her granddaughter from her. She began to think about how to effect a reconciliation.

Rose beat her to it. The day of Maisie's 26th birthday (always celebrated on 8 October until her latter years when it was discovered her birthday was actually the 7th) Maxie came into the salon just as she was closing. He had a beautiful marcasite bracelet for her and a soft toy for Christine so she wouldn't feel left out.

'These are from me, but the card's from Mum,' he told Maisie. 'She says you're to keep the last loan payment as your birthday present. She's in the car.'

It was a move halfway. Maisie went out to the car and thanked Rose for the card, and the cash too – although somehow this took a little shine off her pride at repaying the loan so quickly. They chatted amiably for a bit, sticking to safe topics such as Christine, while each tried to think of a way to broach the prospect of Maisie's return to South Street without giving power to the other.

'Come in for a cup of tea, Mum. There's no need for us to talk here in the street.'

'No. I'm not coming in there – even though I helped to pay for it – until you come to your bloody senses and come home where you belong.'

Rose's clumsy effort at inviting her was enough.

'I don't belong there, Mum. I haven't belonged there since I was ten years old. Christine and I are moving into Gil's empty house for a while. Then we're going to get married.' The statement shocked her as much as her mother. Rose regretted her stance instantly, but it couldn't be undone.

Would Maisie have made that decision without the argument with Rose? Probably. She did love Gil (and later Rose would grow to love him too). At that point though, she only knew that he made her feel good about herself. He made her feel special. She was reconnecting with a sense of worth another man had given her more than 15 years ago. Somehow, around Rose, she always felt she was failing.

Gil was delighted at the sudden turn of events, although Maisie didn't tell him yet about the marriage part. She laid down rules.

'I'll pay rent. It has to be a proper business arrangement. You can't just come and go when you please. No just popping in anytime because you own the house. And it'll be a teetotal house. No drink there, Gil.' He agreed to it all.

She was a little surprised when they went to look at the house. Gil had warned her it was unfinished when he first offered it, but she knew he and Pat had lived there with a toddling Jenny and also that another family had rented for awhile, so the extent of the work remaining was a shock. The main bedroom had only a rough concrete floor and the walls and ceiling of this room weren't lined at all. The linoleum in the other bedroom, lounge and kitchen had been left dirty and broken by the previous tenants. One of the front windows was cracked and the foundations at the front of the house were showing because the front veranda had yet to be built. Maisie had immediate flashes of Christine tumbling down the makeshift wooden front steps and disappearing under the house – which clearly showed thick white spider webs and signs of other life that had crossed the road from Albert Morris's bushy regeneration area opposite.

It was not unusual for young families to live in half-finished houses in Broken Hill at the time. At the end of 1948 the Zinc Corporation had launched an innovative scheme to address the city's post-war housing shortage by assisting employees to build their own homes. The scheme included everything needed to build a basic family home with little input from tradesmen. The company arranged for customised plans to be drawn up by the Housing Commission and the Materials Supply Department in Sydney, for a structure that could readily be built by unskilled labour. Prefabricated steel frames were brought from Sydney to be erected by the homeowner with the help of a mate or two, who would in turn be assisted on their own site. The plans allowed for a choice of cladding such as timber, hardboard or asbestos cement sheeting, with Masonite linings. Tradesmen were required only for final touches and certification of plumbing and electrical work. Technical advice, surveying and even submissions for council approval and title searches were handled by the mine.

To put the cost within reach, the company set up a Cooperative Building Society with a float of £300,000. This, it estimated, would build at least 200 homes since most of the labour was free and the subsidised and bulk-purchased materials for each only amounted to £1000 to £1500. Employees repaid their loans with 2% interest at a rate of six shillings and eleven pence per pay for each £100 they borrowed. To top it off, the company introduced an amenities scheme which allowed employees a low-interest loan to fill their dwellings with appliances and other requirements – again, with minimal repayments deducted from pay packets.

The scheme, of course, was a rampant success. For many years weekend and twilight hours in Broken Hill were disturbed by a multitude of hammering and drilling across development sites, but filled with the happy sight of groups of men or husband-and-wife teams cobbling together their new homes. This is the reason an extraordinarily large number of Broken Hill people will say today, 'My father (or grandfather) built his house with his own hands'.

There were two drawbacks to the scheme: there were only a handful of designs, which gave an unsettling uniformity to homes in many areas of the city (which remains even today in some sections of the South) and many couples moved in as soon as one bedroom and the kitchen were completed, which meant many dwellings took years to finish when motivation waned or building help was required elsewhere to get a mate under cover.

Maisie wasn't at all disappointed to see Gil's house in the state she found it. One of her reservations at living there had been that she was moving into Pat's home, but now she saw there was enough work remaining that the house could really belong to her and Gil once they married.

The door to the top bedroom remained closed and she and Christine slept in the other bedroom while she worked on the rest of the house. Dulcie came to help her clean it and polish the linoleum floors. Dulcie and Ken and Jackie and Yvonne gave her bits and pieces of furniture. Gil came to help her dig gardens for the front yard and she planted a hedge to soften the severity of the cyclone wire front fence. There was a built-in wood stove in the kitchen so she invited them all around for a roast dinner and even Rose came to celebrate. Despite his earlier agreement, Gil wouldn't accept the rent money so Maisie bought a cash tin and paid money into it each week. She forced him to write a receipt even though the cash tin stayed at the house.

Maisie felt satisfied, independent and safe. She knew she was going to marry Gil and she knew by now she would be happy with him, but she just wanted a little more time to relish this stage of her life. Then a letter arrived from Nancy (of Earl's Court fame). Arnold was planning to come to Broken Hill and snatch Christine so Maisie would follow. Nancy had details – the date, the accomplice, the kindergarten venue and the circuitous return trip through Victoria so the NSW Police wouldn't find him as he passed through country towns.

As the date approached, Maisie closed the salon for two weeks and Gil drove her and Christine to Adelaide to stay with Topsy. During the visit Topsy's little dog bit Christine on the face near her eye, badly enough to require sutures and close enough for there to be some concern her eyesight might be affected when the wound became infected and the sutures would no longer hold. Maisie blamed Arnold. When Gil came to collect them, she told him she wanted to get married as soon as possible. She never knew for certain whether Arnold attempted to implement his plan, but Dulcie and Ken were adamant they had seen him in Broken Hill that week.

Now, after months of stalling, Maisie felt some urgency for a wedding. Rose was unwell and thought Maisie was determined to marry quickly so she wouldn't have to move home to look after her. Maisie stayed at Jamieson Street but cared for Rose until she went to hospital to have her gall bladder removed. Then Rose decided Maisie must be pregnant. In truth, both Maisie and Gil were just keen to cement their commitment to each other.

They chose the Methodist Church because it was important to Edith. Maisie would like to have been married in the Lutheran Church to honour her father, but she remembered he had never been overly concerned about what denomination marked his milestones. He had married his first wife according to the rites of the Methodist Church and buried her in the Church of England cemetery; married his second in the Church of Christ and left her with the help of a Lutheran pastor, but into a Church of England grave. Maisie thought a Methodist wedding would be just fine by him. Reverend Pitman had difficulty finding a vacant spot for them on short notice and the venue changed three times before it settled at the Methodist Church in Oxide Street. They would have to be on time, he warned them, because there was another wedding immediately after them.

Given it was a second wedding for both they didn't plan an elaborate affair, although Gil would have given her whatever she asked. The Carlins offered their long sleep-out for the reception, Edith and Dulcie shared the catering and Auntie Eva Smith baked and decorated the wedding cake. June Connors from the Freemasons was Maisie's bridesmaid and Gil asked his younger brother Don to be best man. Maxie stood in for their father to give Maisie away.

There were no plans for a honeymoon. The grandmothers would each keep their granddaughter for a week and Maisie and Gil would spend the time at Jamieson Street finishing the main bedroom and painting the rest of the house. She had refused when Gil wanted to buy her an engagement ring.

'No, let's spend that money on the house,' she told him. 'If we put that with the rent money in the cash tin, we can even put the front veranda on.' She should have known he would find another way. On the morning of their wedding Gil gave her a single strand of pearls and matching earrings in a heart-shaped grey velvet box – and a beautiful eternity ring.

'I agree with you,' he said. 'An engagement is a temporary thing and we are forever.'

He had also bought her an elaborate orchid spray to wear. She put it in the fridge 'to keep it fresh', but it froze instead and, when it defrosted, wilted and flapped about in the breeze on her way to the car. They laughed together about it and she replaced it with a gladiolus from the front garden she had established when she first moved into the house. Somehow it seemed more fitting.

Chapter 28
A family of four
April 1957

'**N**ow Gil's my dad-dy! Now Gil's my dad-dy! Now Gil's my dad-dy!'

Christine's sing-song joy bounced around the walls of the church as surely as she bounced around on her new grandmother's knee. Edith was holding her because it was only two weeks since Rose's surgery and the whispered phrase had been meant to provide a sense of solemnity to the occasion. Instead, this thought so excited Christine she chorused it to the world. The congregation erupted in laughter.

The strangers who had crowded into the rear of the church ready for the next wedding must have thought it was 'about time'. Certainly, Dulcie, Jackie and Maxie did; about time their sister settled down with a good man who loved her, respected her and would keep her safe always. But Christine's delight surprisingly wounded Maisie.

'Poor Arnie,' she thought. 'Poor Arnie, to have lost the love of his life for alcohol and now to lose his precious little daughter to another man. And so completely.' Because she knew already Gil would be the only father Christine would ever need. This marriage meant there would never really be a place for Arnold in his child's life.

She smiled toward the blonde curls and hoped it masked what she felt. Gil didn't deserve for her to be thinking of Arnold today. But he sensed her emotion and moved a gentle hand to cup her elbow. It was enough. The touch sent her thoughts tumbling now to her father and his gentle hand always on her shoulder in time of need even when he was long gone from her. Now Gil was in the shadow of yet another man. But when she turned to look at him, she felt the love for him there. Not the adoration she had felt for Jack. Not the passion she had felt for Arnold. But a quiet and strong love.

There would no roller-coaster highs with this man. She knew that. But there would be no plunging depths either. She and Gil and Jenny and Christine would make a solid little family and one day they would add to it – to link them all together, forever. She slid her arm through Gil's and together they took their first steps as husband and wife. Gil moved to take Christine from Edith, shook hands with Gus and reached an arm around Jenny to draw her close. Maisie was left to face her mother awkwardly. She felt a rush of sympathy at Rose's wince as she stood to greet her. But it was soon gone.

'You spoil that child! Maybe now she'll have a firm hand.'

Maisie looked over Rose's shoulder to Jackie and Maxie, who were smiling broadly, and saw her father so clearly present in their faces. Again she felt the ache for Jack Schuster that would resurface all her life in times of joy or sorrow. The boys hugged her tightly and Yvonne slipped a beautiful satin covered horseshoe over her arm. Maisie turned back again to Rose to see whether, now she had delivered her admonishment, there might be a show of love and happiness. Rose stood resolute, hands linked together in front of her stomach so her handbag couldn't escape.

Now, new thoughts. She knew Rose was in pain but, in those few seconds standing before her, she realised how much of her own pain she could lay at her mother's feet. If she hadn't been so desperate to escape her, would she ever have gone to Sydney and met Arnold in the first place? If she hadn't been so fully convinced of her own worthlessness, so inured to violence, would she have been so prepared to accept what he did? If she hadn't been so determined to prove her mother wrong, would she have stayed with him so long?

Left to right: Edith Carlin, Maxie, Rose, Maisie, Gil, Jackie, Bridesmaid June, Don Carlin; Jenny is at front; Dulcie, with Dawn and Joyce at rear. Disruptive Christine is absent.

She saw Gil waiting patiently for her, Christine on one hip, Jenny by his side. And there was Jack again. Not in appearance (for in that they were opposite), but in the gentleness and the quietness and the kindness and in his absolute love for her.

The four made their way together down the aisle collecting more horseshoes and little crocheted shoes strung on satin ribbons among the hugs and kisses. As they emerged on the steps at the front of the church, coloured confetti descended on them from all directions and sat on their shoulders and in their hair as they posed for photographs, hurried, because the next wedding party already waited in cars drawn up to the kerb.

'Let's not take the week on our own,' she whispered to her new husband. 'Let's take the girls home with us tonight.' And he agreed – because that was what she wanted.

A family of four.

Barrier Miner Saturday 20 April 1957

CARLIN – CAMERON

MARRIAGE

On Saturday, April 13, at the Oxide Street Methodist church, Maisie Elaine Cameron, youngest daughter of Mrs. R. Schuster, 25 South Street, was married to Gilbert Wallace Carlin, second son of Mr. and Mrs. G. Carlin, of 283 Garnet Street.

Mr. Max Schuster, the bride's brother, gave the bride away at the ceremony performed by Rev. C. L. H. Pitman.

The bride wore a rose pink paper shantung frock horizontally pin striped in white and a matching bolero, the bolero being edged with guipure lace. Her head-hugging chapeau was of white grosgrain, patterned with an opalescent thread. Her corsage was of gladioli, and her accessories pink, with white gloves.

Miss June Connors attended the bride wearing a dusty pink taffeta under wild rice linen lace. The frock, fashioned on slim lines, was cross-over at the neckline with a side bodice fastening. Miss Connors wore a flamingo pink hat, the pleated frill being surrounded with French flowers.

The groom's brother, Mr. Don Carlin, acted as best man.

For the reception, which was held at 283 Garnet Street, the wedding cake was made by an aunt, Mrs. Eva Smith.

Epilogue

My mother's decision to marry Gil Carlin gave me the best father and big sister a girl could have. Mum and Dad had a stable and loving marriage for 39 years, until his death from emphysema at the age of 71 on 19 June 1996. I miss him still.

In the early years, they renovated and extended 32 Jamieson Street. She planted the quarter-acre block with kikuyu lawn and I have a clear vision of her working in a swimsuit on her hands and knees under a sprinkler, planting rows of runners she had salvaged from other areas. Together, they studded the lawn with fruit trees – lemon, orange, grapefruit, nectarine, peach, almond, apple and a magnificent mulberry that stained our fingers and clothes and grew big enough to cradle a tree-house. The back section of the yard was given over to terraced rows of vegetables, while a cactus rockery close to the house amazed visitors with its exotic flowers. The gardens and fruit trees kept my grandfather with her.

She kept my father with her too. I think we all knew she saved a little place in her heart for Arnold, but he was also in her head. Dinner was on the table at 6 pm sharp in our house, and Heaven help Dad if he came in from the pub at five past! One of the few times I saw him angry with my mother was to tell her, 'You punish me for what Arnold Cameron did, not for what Gil Carlin does!'

I first 'met' my father when I was 12, after having had no contact for a decade. My grandmother Jesse May always sent birthday and Christmas cards, with lots of love and a ten-shilling note, but there had been nothing from him. I forgave him birthdays, but reasoned it was Christmas all over the world and, even drunk, he should have remembered me. Now I think maybe he loved me enough to stay out of my life. The Christmas of 1965 I was delivered to spend a month with him at the home of his older sister Beatrice in Sydney. Aunty Beat replaced my mother as his rescuer and made sure he was on the straight and narrow before I arrived. He tried really hard to stay sober for that four weeks, but couldn't manage it. Two or three letters followed in the weeks after the visit and a beautiful boxed pale blue peignoir set (far too grown-up for a 12-year-old) – then nothing again.

Later, when I was 18 and moved to Sydney to nurse at Prince Henry Hospital, we attempted to build a relationship. He signed into a rehabilitation centre at Morisset, north of Sydney, and I visited him there, sometimes taking his beloved Jesse May along too. Again, he tried to turn his life around for me, but didn't make it. Alcoholism is a relentless disease. I hurt Arnold deeply when I asked Dad to give me away at my wedding. To me, there was no choice. To him, it was rejection of the cruellest kind.

Arnold Cameron died in the RSL Veterans' Nursing Home at Narrabeen on 16 June 1988. He was 63 years old. The last two years of his life had been spent there, sober, but suffering dreadfully from emphysema. I wasn't there for him. My cousins were. He was a favourite uncle, when not 'on the grog' and they sometimes took him out to the football. He remained charismatic until the end, but there was never another relationship for him after my mother. I'm told there are no unknown brothers or sisters for me to discover.

That visit with him in the Christmas of 1965, however, had a surprising outcome. Mum and Dad had long since given up hope their marriage might produce offspring but, with me in Sydney and Jenny old enough to stay home in Broken Hill in her new job at the local council, they finally had their honeymoon nine years after the wedding – touring New South Wales and Victoria in a caravan. Their third daughter, Donna Lesley, arrived on 21 September 1966.

The quiet and proper little Jennifer Ann grew into the most amazing and vibrant young woman. Jenny was the type of sister who almost daily doled me replacement bus money (with only a wry smile) when I claimed to have lost mine at school – and took Donna to the Silver City Show each year because Mum and Dad claimed to be too old for it. Jenny became the type of mum who, when other mothers decried the school holidays, invited all the neighbourhood children in for a Minties hunt in her backyard. Jenny died on 2 August 1989, at the age of 39, from pancreatic cancer. There are no words to adequately describe what this loss meant to her three daughters and those of us privileged to love her.

Rose Schuster, who feared she would not live to see my mother's 21st, lived 19 years past it. She died from a heart attack in the Broken Hill Hospital on 20 April 1970, two months before her 80th birthday. My mother was heartbroken. From the day after her wedding, she had gone to 25 South Street every morning to light the fire, boil the kettle and make her mother's first cup of tea for the day, apart from the times Nanna lived with us when she was unwell. We were not close (I think I remained a spoiled child) but she determinedly taught me to knit. However, it must be acknowledged that children brought up in the same family often have different perspectives on its dynamics and my cousins (those the children of sons) remember Nanna Schuster as generous, kind and fun-loving.

My grandfather's extraordinary impact on my mother remained throughout her life. His lesson to 'always invest in the land' saw Mum and Dad buy a succession of run-down houses and blocks of flats to renovate and 'flip'. She laid carpets and tiles; painted walls and ceilings and rooves; and created gardens for them all – despite enduring back-pain that tormented her. But my grandmother can be seen in these efforts too, and in other ways.

In the 1960s, I played softball in a team called 'the Imps' and Mum went to watch. She decided she'd like to play too, formed a team called the 'Ancient Imps', took on various voluntary roles – and became President of the Softball Association. In the 1970s, Donna was a swimmer. Mum went to watch, took on various voluntary roles – and became President of the Swimming Club. In the 1980s, Mum took leathercraft lessons, sold the beautiful handbags she created, set up her own lessons in the back sleep-out – and her teacher came to learn. In the 1990s, after moving to Adelaide, she volunteered as a court companion, took on the most difficult cases (that frightened others) – and became the nominated mentor to new volunteers. In the 2000s, she went to play canasta, volunteered in various roles – and became President of the Association. In the 2010s, at 77, she went to volunteer in the kiosk at the nursing home where my daughter Nikki worked – and soon had their systems sorted and a new fundraising scheme in place. Then came a succession of illnesses and surgeries from which her recovery was truly astounding. Her spirit remained extraordinary.

My mother died on 20 January 2013 following a heart attack in the Flinders Medical Centre. During an emergency episode the evening before, she asked doctors working to save her to, 'Please move out of the way'. She was watching the Australian Open on television – Roger Federer was playing rookie Bernard Tomic and the youngster was 4–1 up in the second set. In the early hours of the next morning, when they worked on her again she told them, 'Please just let me go'. They did. I miss her every day.

Acknowledgements

My deepest thanks to Michael Bollen and each member of his team at Wakefield Press. It's not only the quality of their work that is remarkable, but the degree of caring that accompanies each step of the publishing process. It has been an absolute pleasure to work with editor extraordinaire Margot Lloyd. Margot meticulously improved my work, while delighting me with her enjoyment of it. My thanks also to Emily Hart and Liz Nicholson for the wonderful cover and Michael Deves for his extra care with images and typesetting.

There are other people to thank: Peter Ellis, for his faith in me to do this and his patience during our daily phone calls as I rabbited on about yet another interesting (to me) little fact I'd discovered; my daughter, Nikki, who is always my inspiration to achieve; my grandchildren Cameron and Ryley Jae, who put joy into my every day; and my young nephew Griffin, who gave special purpose to this book.

My sister Donna I thank for so generously allowing me a free rein. Not once did she question what I was writing about our mother. Likewise, all my wonderful cousins – I appreciate that some parts are their story too and they have had no say in my telling it.

I'm grateful also to the people I asked to dredge up decades-old memories to 'fill the gaps' – in particular my Mum's cousin and friend Dorothy Separovich (nee Baum) who served me high tea and had photo albums ready for our chat, and my mother's bridesmaid June McMahon (nee Connors) who helped with colours for black and white photographs. There were others – people who, in true Broken Hill spirit, were happy to chat with a strange woman on the phone. I thank you all, but particularly Mrs Duggan from Picton

Street and Mrs Quinlivan from Boughtman Street and hairdresser Val Kelly (nee Hill).

My cousin Dennis Richards, who I found through tenacious sleuthing and extraordinary luck, was generous in providing information about my father and photographs I'd never seen – valuable not only for the book, but me personally.

The Lutheran Archives, at Bowden in South Australia, provided a wealth of information and I'm grateful for the assistance provided by Janette Lange and Danna Slessor-Cobb.

Alison Wayman at Outback Archives in the Broken Hill Library went beyond her role to find specific information for me about historical businesses in Broken Hill and the newspaper clipping I so desperately wanted of my mother's second wedding. Alison also helped me find the Broken Hill photographs included in the book, which Outback Archives generously allowed me to reproduce.

References

Primary Research

Many of the Broken Hill stories recounted here have been achieved through primary research – of articles written at the time and published in the two local newspapers, the *Barrier Miner* and *Barrier Daily Truth*. The majority were found on the National Library of Australia's Trove website at www.trove.nla.gov.au. At the time of writing, some relevant publications of the *Barrier Daily Truth* had yet to be digitised and were accessed in hard copy in the Outback Archives of the Broken Hill Library. However, it should be noted I was guided expertly in what to research by R.H.B. Kearns, *Broken Hill 1940–1983*, Broken Hill Historical Society, NSW, Revised Edition November 1987.

Information about German people resident in Broken Hill during World War II, the so-called 'enemy aliens', was sourced through the National Archives at www.naa.gov.au. By searching the collection, I was able to explore security investigation dossiers for 12 people relevant to my story. However, to find more general information about enemy aliens interned or investigated, I also used the National Reference Service.

The Lutheran Archives at Bowden South Australia provided information, not only about the Lutheran Church, but also about the minutiae of daily living in Broken Hill – mostly in diaries, newsletters, and letters pastors wrote to the synod seeking a pay rise.

I was surprised to find I couldn't easily locate accurate data about the number of Broken Hill men and women who died while serving their country in World War II. I had expected a list of names (such as can be found on the local War Memorial for World War I fatalities). When local potential sources were exhausted, I tried the Australian

War Memorial Research Centre and was again surprised to find no such list existed. Eventually, time spent talking with a very helpful person at the Commonwealth War Graves Commission provided tips on how to search the database so that I was able to compile my own list of more than 100 names. Completing and sharing the list is a project for another time.

Secondary Research

Albert and Margaret Morris

Australian National Botanic Gardens, *Albert Morris and His Legacy*, Powerhouse Museum Exhibition notes, 2009

Bird, Louise, Designing with Natives: Rethinking the Role of Australian Native Plants in the Open Spaces of Elizabeth and Golden Grove, *Flinders Journal of History and Politics*, Volume 27, 2011

Jones, David, *Re-greening 'The Hill': Albert Morris and the transformation of the Broken Hill landscape*, Deakin University, 2011

Museum of Applied Arts and Sciences, *Greening the Silver City: Seeds of bush regeneration*, Powerhouse Museum Exhibition, August 2007 to April 2010

Broken Hill

Broken Hill Australia, *Broken Hill Synagogue* at www.brokenhillaustralia.com.au

Broken Hill City Council, *Broken Hill History: Gold storage during World War 2* at www.brokenhill.nsw.gov.au/broken-hill-history

Broken Hill City Council, *Broken Hill History: Six o'clock swill* at www.brokenhill.nsw.gov.au/broken-hill-history

Buckworth, Nicholas with Veitch, Harriet, War Hero, POW, Lawyer, Spook and Businessman, Obituaries, *Sydney Morning Herald*, 21 November 2009

Eklund, Erik, *Mining Towns: Making a living, making a life*, UNSW Press, 2012

Frasier, Daniel, *Behind the Taps: The West Darling Hotel*, ABC Radio Local Stories, February 2010

Mann, Leon, *Broken Hill Synagogue* at www.jewishaustralia.com

National Foundation for Australian Women in conjunction with University of Melbourne, *Housewives' Association of NSW (1918–)*, at www.trove.nla.gov.au

Schulz-Byard, Noah, *History of Broken Hill: The Billy's Club*, episode 21, ABC Radio Local, 7 July 2011

Schulz-Byard, Noah, *History of Broken Hill: Umberumberka Reservoir*, episode 23, ABC Radio Local, 21 July 2011

Sleath, Emma, *March 18th, 1954: Broken Hill welcomes Queen Elizabeth II*, ABC Radio Local Stories, March 2009

Irene Drummond and Vivian Bullwinkle

Australian War Memorial, *Guide to the Papers of Vivian Bullwinkel* www.awm.gov.au/findingaids/private/bullwinkel/

Australian War Memorial Roll of Honour *Irene Melville Drummond* www.awm.gov.au/people/rolls

Australia's War 1939–1945, *Fall of Singapore*, at www.ww2australia.gov.au

Gorrell, Julie, *Drummond, Irene Melville (1905–1942)*, Australian Dictionary of Biography, Volume 14, MUP, 1996

Meacham, Steve, Stoic Nurses Stared Down Atrocious Death, *Sydney Morning Herald*, 25 April 2012

Muntok Peace Museum, Officer's Investigation of Island: Incredible escapes of S.A. nurse and British stoker, as published in *Adelaide Advertiser*, 18 September 1945

Schulz-Byard, Noah, *Two of Broken Hill's Bravest, 70 Years on*, ABC Radio, February 2012

Shaw, Ian W, On Radji Beach, Pan Macmillan 2012 (excerpts only as published *Sydney Morning Herald,* 2012)

Enemy Aliens, Internment, Allied Works Council

Cosmini-Rose, Daniela, Italians in the Civil Alien Corps in South Australia: The 'forgotten' enemy aliens, in *Journal of the Historical Society of South Australia*, number 42, 2014

Glaros, Maria, *'Sometimes a little injustice must be suffered for the public good'*, PhD, University of Western Sydney, 2012

National Archives of Australia, *Civil Aliens Corps Records Held in Perth: Fact sheet 182* at www.naa.gov.au/collection/fact-sheets

National Archives of Australia Research Guides, *Safe Haven: Records of the Jewish experience in Australia, 'enemy aliens' and internment (World War II)* at www.guides.naa.gov.au/safe-haven/chapter5/enemy-aliens

Rando, Gitano, *Italo-Australians during the Second World War: Some perceptions of internment*, University of Wollongong, 2005

Spizzica, Mia, When Ethnicity Counts: Civilian internment in Australia during WW2, in *The Conversation*, 20 September, 2012

Family Life

Australian Bureau of Statistics, *Year Book Australia 1944–45 Clothing and Food Rationing*, updated 22 November 2012

Carrick, Damien (presenter), *1956 and the No Fault Divorce*, audio with retired Family Court judges John Fogarty and Austin Ashe, The Law Report, Radio National, 19 September 2006

Living-Family-History website, *Living in the 1940s* (blogs and unauthorised articles) at www.living-family-history.com/1940s.html

NSW State Archives and Records, *Divorce Records Guide*, at www.records.nsw.gov.au

State Library of Victoria, *Australia and World War II: Food Shortages and Rationing*, ergo.slv.vic.gov.au

Whiteford, P., Stanton, D., Gray, M., Families and Income Security: Changing patterns of social security and related policy issues, in *Family Matters* No. 60, Australian Institute of Family Studies, 2001

World War II

Australian War Memorial, *Conscription* at www.awm.gov.au/encyclopedia

Australian War Memorial, *Conscription during the Second World War, 1939–45* at www.awm.gov.au/encyclopedia

Australian War Memorial, 2/5th Australian Infantry Battalion, from Syd Trigellis-Smith, *All the King's Enemies: A history of the 2/5th Australian Infantry Battalion*, Australian Military History Publications, Sydney 2010

Editors of Legacy Publishers, *Japan Surrenders and World War II Ends: June 1945 to September 1945*, at www.history.howstuffworks.com

National Archives, *The Bombing of Darwin: Fact sheet 195, Japanese air raids on Darwin and northern Australia, 1942–43* at www.naa.gov.au/collection/fact-sheets

Simkin, John, Stretcher Bearers, Spartacus – Educational.com, at www.spartacus-educational.com/FWWstretcher.htm

United States Holocaust Memorial Museum, *World War II in the Pacific*, at www.ushmm.org

United States Holocaust Memorial Museum, *1941: Key dates*, at www.ushmm.org

Broken Hill, a gentle German and two world wars

SILVER LIES,
GOLDEN TRUTHS

CHRISTINE ELLIS

SILVER LIES, GOLDEN TRUTHS

Broken Hill, a gentle German and two world wars

Christine Ellis

Reinhold (Jack) Schuster was an illegal German immigrant. A trained soldier in the German Armeekorps, he sat out both world wars in the Australian outback of Broken Hill. Jack's story debunks the myth that salutes the mining town as the birthplace of solidarity – by exposing divisiveness, prejudice and powerlessness.

The only enemy attack to take place on Australian soil during World War I occurred in Broken Hill, and Jack was there to witness the mob violence that followed. He watched unionists stone the troop trains heading off to war and learned of brutality against his countrymen in the Torrens Island internment camp.

Christine Ellis's grandfather came to life through stories told by her mother – some of which defied belief. Christine's research confirmed them. *Silver Lies, Golden Truths* is Jack Schuster's story. It tells of the love between a father and his young daughter, of idyllic family times, and the cruel cost of working in the mines.

Praise for *Silver Lies, Golden Truths*:

'This book gives a gripping account of what life was like in a mining town in the first half of the twentieth century, with the added bonus of seeing the two world wars through the eyes of an enemy alien living in Australia at that time.' – Ian Harmstorf, *Journal of the Historical Society of South Australia*

'Quietly powerful and consistently fascinating, this work is a fine addition to the untold Australian story.' – Stephen Davenport, *InDaily*

'A timely, heartbreaking re-imagining of war and peace in the Silver City.' – Peter Goers

'A poignant tale about an extraordinary man, interesting and captivating.' – Nic Klaassen, *Flinders Research Journal*

For more information visit wakefieldpress.com.au

Printed in Australia
AUOC01n1318011117
291080AU00002B/2/P